D0883024

Managing Diversity and Interdependence
An Organizational Study of Multidivisional Firms

Library
I.U.P.
Indiana, P.

Managing Diversity and Interdependence

An Organizational Study of Multidivisional Firms

Jay W. Lorsch
Professor of Organizational Behavior

Stephen A. Allen III
Assistant Professor of Business Administration

HARVARD UNIVERSITY
GRADUATE SCHOOL OF BUSINESS ADMINISTRATION
DIVISION OF RESEARCH

Boston 1973

Library
I.U.P.
Indiana, Pa.

658.1146 L895m
C.1

© COPYRIGHT 1973
BY THE PRESIDENT AND FELLOWS OF HARVARD COLLEGE

Second printing 1975

Library of Congress Catalog Card No. 72–97571
ISBN 0–87584–103–1

*Faculty research at the Harvard Business School is undertaken with the
expectation of publication. In such publication the Faculty members
responsible for the research project are also responsible for statements
of facts, opinions, and conclusions expressed. Neither the Harvard
Business School, its Faculty as a whole, nor the President and Fellows
of Harvard College reach conclusions or make recommendations as
results of Faculty research.*

Printed in the United States of America

Acknowledgments

Nearly five years have passed since we began work on the pilot study of this research project. During that time a number of individuals and organizations have contributed in a variety of ways to the completion of this study. In the following paragraphs we wish to acknowledge our debt of gratitude to a few of the more significant contributors.

First of all, we wish to thank the more than four hundred managers in the six firms, each of whom gave as much as four hours from a busy schedule. These men occupied the top four levels in their organizations, and their contribution of time represents a very tangible investment in the set of ideas we have attempted to develop and test in this research. Equally important was their openness and high level of interest which made the field work both a fruitful and a highly stimulating experience.

We are also indebted to two Directors of the Division of Research, first Lawrence E. Fouraker and subsequently Richard E. Walton, for providing financial support through allocation of funds from the contributions of The Associates of the Harvard Business School which make Faculty research projects in various areas of business administration possible.

Two Research Associates who aided us with the field work were John J. Gabarro and Neil C. Milward. Mr. Gabarro, who now is an Assistant Professor at the Harvard Business School, also helped with the statistical analysis and provided critical comments on the early drafts of the manuscript.

Professor Paul R. Lawrence of the Harvard Business School also provided comments on early drafts of the manuscript as well as offering ideas on the design of the study.

Over the duration of this study four secretaries have contributed in countless ways to its completion. We are most appreciative to Cathy Tendler, Susan Christiansen, Judith Shanker, and Ann Walter.

We are grateful to Ruth Norton of the Division of Research for skillfully converting the authors' manuscript into a published book.

We wish also to thank Dean Lawrence E. Fouraker and Senior Associate Dean George F. F. Lombard for their support and particularly for arranging our schedules to provide the time necessary to execute this study.

Although we are grateful to these and many other people who helped bring this study to completion, we assume full responsibility for its findings and conclusions.

JAY W. LORSCH
STEPHEN A. ALLEN III

Soldiers Field
Boston, Massachusetts

January 1973

Table of Contents

List of Tables

List of Figures and Exhibits

Managing Diversity and Interdependence
An Organizational Study of Multidivisional Firms

I

Introduction

"THE language of organization," wrote Alfred P. Sloan, "has always suffered from some want of words to express the true facts and circumstances of human interaction. One usually asserts one aspect or another of it at different times, such as the absolute independence of the part, and again the need of coordinating, and again the concept of the whole with the guiding center." [1] In the early 1920s, when Sloan was grappling with the issues of managing a multidivisional organization consisting of semi-autonomous operating units and a separate corporate headquarters, they were a problem for only a few large enterprises such as General Motors, Du Pont, and Standard Oil. Today they represent a crucial top management issue for the multiproduct, multinational enterprises and many of the large public institutions which have come to play a prominent role in our society.

The important position which multidivisional industrial firms have assumed in the U.S. economy can be gauged from several pieces of evidence. Chandler[2] notes in his historical study of the relationship between corporate strategy and organizational structure that expansion into new market areas —both through internal development and mergers—led many companies to adopt multidivisional organizations during the post-World War II period. This movement gained further impetus as increasing numbers of companies began to make extensive use of conglomerate mergers in the late 1950s and throughout the 1960s.[3] Thus, if one examines the most recent attempt to classify the Fortune 500 firms by product line, one finds that about 60% of them sell products in more than five 3-digit standard industrial categories (Table I-1). In an examination of the relationship between strategy and structure in these firms, Wrigley[4] found that 86% of them had divisionalized organizations. This evidence takes on even greater significance when one considers that in 1969 these 500 largest firms accounted for 64% of the nation's industrial sales and 74% of its industrial profits.

TABLE I-1

460 of the "Fortune 500" Largest Firms Classified by Number of 3-Digit Standard Industrial Categories in Which Products Were Reported, 1965 [a]

Number of 3-Digit SICs	Number of Firms	Cumulative % of Firms	Selected Examples[b]
1–5	183	39.8%	Coca-Cola (4)
			IBM (5)
6–10	126	67.2	Procter & Gamble (7)
			ALCOA (10)
11–15	94	87.6	International Paper (11)
			General Foods (14)
16–20	25	93.0	Indian Head Mills (17)
			Dow Chemical (18)
21–25	18	96.9	ITT (22)
			Du Pont (23)
			TRW (24)
26–30	5	98.0	Union Carbide (26)
			AMF (27)
31–35	5	99.1	FMC (31)
			Borg-Warner (32)
36–40	1	99.3	General Motors (36)
			Litton (38)
41–45	2	99.8	Westinghouse (41)
			General Electric (42)
46–50	1	100.0	Textron (49)
Total	460	100.0%	

[a] 1965 is the most recent year for which such classifications are available.
[b] Numbers in parentheses indicate number of 3-digit SICs for each of the firms.
SOURCES: *Fortune Plant and Product Directory*, 1966. Chɑrles H. Berry, "Corporate Growth and Diversification," mimeo., Princeton University, 1969.

Although several recent studies by historians, economists, and students of business policy[5] have provided some important insights into the internal functioning of multidivisional firms, we are still a long way from having a knowledge base and a set of concepts of sufficient power to unravel the complexities and aid the effective management of part-whole relationships in these firms. While behavioral scientists and organizational theorists have developed considerable knowledge about man's behavior in purposive organizations, this group of authors has devoted virtually no explicit attention to multidivisional organizations. These researchers have employed psychology, social psychology, and sociology to study operating units in these large organizations, but they have not concerned themselves with the firm as a whole made up of diverse but interrelated parts.

This book represents an attempt to apply insights and tools developed by the behavioral sciences to the practical issues of managing corporate-divisional and interdivisional relationships in multidivisional business enterprises. More specifically, we have employed comparative field survey techniques to examine corporate headquarters and divisional top management groups in six multidivisional firms. Four of these enterprises were highly diversified (or conglomerate) firms which had embarked on diversification strategies during the middle and late 1950s. The other two firms were vertically integrated paper companies which both offered a line of products through several operating divisions and had important technological linkages among their divisions. Our basic objective is to develop and test a conceptual scheme which can identify important aspects of management perception and behavior within each organization and link these internal factors to economic performance and the ability of the firm to relate to the requirements of its environment.

The broader purpose of this study is to contribute to the development of a theory of organization which can be useful both to practicing managers and to students of organization. Such a dual focus may seem contradictory unless we are precise about our use of the term "theory." In using this term we adhere strictly to the dictionary definition: "a plan or scheme existing in the mind only but based on principles verifiable by experiment or observation." [6] We do not mean a statement about how things ought, ideally, to be, but rather an abstract model or language for mentally organizing the complexities of life in contemporary organizations. A theory, in this sense, can be a powerful tool for managers concerned with improving their organizations and adapting them to changing environmental conditions. In a similar vein, we feel that theory itself is best advanced when it is derived from careful observation of how things seem to operate in the real world.

In the remainder of this chapter we shall consider some of the management issues posed by multidivisional organizations, examine the usefulness of prior organizational research for understanding such problems, and outline the approach we shall use in this study.

The Management Issues

In considering the management problems which are common to most multidivisional organizations, it is important to hold in mind that this broad form of organization has been adopted to serve a wide range of corporate strategies. In their search for continued growth and stability of earnings and efficient use of capital, large industrial firms have moved into new product and/or market areas in several ways. Some have expanded geographically, offering existing products in previously untapped national or international market areas. Others have adopted strategies of vertical integration, moving into the manufacture of raw materials for existing products or moving into products which are closer to the ultimate consumer. Still others have focused on product diversification by acquiring or developing products which bear little market and/or technological relationship to their traditional product lines. Obviously many large firms have pursued a combination of these three broad strategies.

While a great many companies have adopted the multidivisional organization structure as a means of managing the complexity of their multi-market or multiproduct operations, this organizational form presents executives with a unique and difficult set of issues in managing on-going relationships between the corporate headquarters and its divisions and among the divisions. One needn't look very far for evidence of the importance and tenacity of these issues. Chandler[7] has chronicled the painstaking study and redesign of organizational schemes in several early multidivisional firms as they sought to effectively manage their diverse and widespread operations. More recently the business press has cited numerous cases of the newer multimarket firms faced with precipitous and often unexpected declines in the earnings of the businesses they had acquired.[8] Similarly, data from three independent studies suggest that the overall failure rate among recent mergers has approached 25%.[9]

Three common issues faced by the executives who manage multidivisional firms are (1) how to constitute the major operating units, or divisions, so that they can most effectively engage their particular industrial environments; (2) how to achieve the necessary coordination between these divisions and the corporate headquarters around the key issues of business planning, budgeting, and the allocation of the firm's resources; and (3) how to achieve interdivisional coordination around required or potential operating relationships (e.g., joint marketing and research efforts or major customer-supplier relationships). In dealing with these issues managers must come to grips with a number of difficult questions. These include:

- How much autonomy should a division have? How do you balance this autonomy with the need to maintain control over corporate earnings and funds flows?
- What activities should be centered at the corporate headquarters, and in what major areas should the corporation set policy?
- What sort of budgeting and reporting requirements should be developed for the divisions, and how do these systems and the way they are administered affect managers' perceptions and decision making?
- What sort of reward system will help insure that division managers' goals and interests will be consistent with those of the total corporation?

- How do you manage relationships with problematic divisions? How do you intervene in a constructive way but without making it even more difficult for the division to solve its problems?
- How do you allocate a pool of funds to the projects with the greatest promise and still maintain imaginative risk taking on the part of all division managers?
- How do you balance the demands for yearly profits with the need for long-term development of the business, both from the standpoint of individual divisions and the corporate whole?
- How do you simultaneously signal division managers to focus on their own particular industries and to establish worthwhile and effective relationships with sister divisions?

This list of questions is intended to be illustrative rather than exhaustive; it could undoubtedly be extended for several pages. The point is that these issues are both complex and rather abstract; and what both managers and students of management need is a mental map which can at once capture the crucial aspects of these issues, help make some sense of them, and point toward appropriate means of coping with them.

Centralization versus Decentralization

More often than not the sorts of questions outlined above have been pigeonholed under the convenient rubric of centralization versus decentralization. We feel that addressing these questions as a problem of centralization versus decentralization rapidly places one—whether he be an executive or a researcher—in a conceptual strait jacket. There are two reasons for this. First, the notion of decentralization is difficult, if not impossible, to operationalize. Second, even if it could be linked to concrete events, it focuses on only a small portion of the factors which seem to affect how executives make decisions in multidivisional organizations.

We can see the difficulties of linking this concept to the world of practical affairs by considering a fairly typical definition of centralization provided by Simon:

> An administrative organization is centralized to the extent that decisions are made at relatively high levels in the organization; decentralized to the extent that discretion and authority to make important decisions are delegated by top management to lower levels of executive authority.[10]

While this is probably one of the more succinct definitions available, it leaves many questions unanswered. What, for example, is meant by "high" and "lower" levels of authority? What sorts of decisions are involved? Since information relevant to various decisions may come from several different locations and/or levels in the organization, is this definition at all descriptive of how decisions are actually reached?

Those researchers who have devoted the greatest effort to unraveling the problems of centralization and decentralization—namely, the classical organization theorists[11] and the bureaucratic sociologists[12]—have focused mainly on the issues of formal structure and the delegation of authority. Furthermore, their major concern has been to derive universal principles regarding these issues. While formal structure and delegation of authority are certainly important, an overconcern with them has tended to obscure some equally important factors, such as the perceptual, informational, and interpersonal issues which underly interunit relationships in organizations. Also, the search for universal principles denies—either implicitly or explicitly—the importance of the differing environmental and economic issues facing various organizations.

A Systems Approach

The conceptual approach which we have developed differs from these past attempts to understand part-whole relationships in two important ways. It attempts to identify and produce systematic knowledge about interrelationships among the particular environmental requirements faced by a firm, how it is organized, its internal patterns of management behavior, and its record of economic performance. Also, in line with a developing trend in contemporary organizational theory, it assumes that the internal functioning of an organization can be understood only in relation to the requirements of the environment in which it seeks to operate.

Our conceptual approach also draws heavily on the insights provided by the developing field of general systems theory.[13] As suggested above, we find it useful to view the multidivisional firm as

a complex adaptive system that seeks to survive and grow by coping with changing external conditions and by dealing with its own recurring internal conflicts and performance deviations.

This systems view suggests that to understand the workings of headquarters and divisional management units it is necesary to map the basic patterns of their *interrelatedness* with one another and with particular segments of the firm's total environment.

This systems approach also has important implications for how we shall present and explain our findings. Despite the fact that we have employed a point-in-time comparative analysis, we feel it is useful to view the findings not simply as a set of one-time correlations but as a "snapshot" of dynamic, emerging behavior patterns in the firm. Indeed, we feel it is essential for managers and students of organization to move away from the traditional view of an organization as a set of position descriptions and formally defined relationships and to adopt the cybernetic view of organization as *the set of states and processes which emerge from the dynamic interrelationships of the parts of a system with one another and with the system's environment.*

Effective management of these organizational states and processes requires an explicit mental map that can take into account the complex interactions among them. As Forrester notes:

> Complex systems have many important behavior characteristics that we must understand if we expect to design systems with better behavior. Complex systems: (1) are counterintuitive; (2) are remarkably insensitive to changes in many system parameters; (3) stubbornly resist policy changes; (4) contain influential pressure points, often in unexpected places, from which forces will radiate to alter system balance; (5) counteract and compensate for externally applied corrective efforts by reducing the corresponding internally generated action (the corrective program is largely absorbed in replacing lost internal action); (6) often react to a policy change in the long run in a way opposite to how they react in the short run; (7) tend toward low performance.[14]

Because multidivisional organizations exhibit many of these general system properties, we feel that it is essential to have a conceptual scheme which can help account for why such behavior occurs.

To develop a systemic map of the multidivisional firm we must define what properties of the environment are related to management behavior within the organization and how the interrelationship of these environmental and internal factors may be related to the firm's performance. A useful way to begin this task is to consider some of the basic issues which arise in the on-going relationships between a corporate headquarters unit and its divisions.

Corporate-Divisional Relationships

Perhaps the most distinctive features of the multidivisional organization are the division of responsibilities between a separate corporate headquarters unit and several divisions and the simultaneous need to link these organizational units via formal and informal information systems to insure coordinated action by the total firm. What we want to understand are the on-going processes of planning, control, and resource allocation which are enacted between a corporate headquarters unit and its divisions and through the contacts between these units and various parts of the firm's total environment.

Figure I-1 is a generalized rendering of the territory we shall be exploring. It summarizes some of the major aspects of the corporate planning and resource allocation process in terms of the pieces of information required by the headquarters unit along with their sources. Typically, each division in a multidivisional organization draws together and transmits to the headquarters unit an annual budget and a long-range plan at some point prior to the beginning of the corporation's fiscal year. These plans and budgets are based on the division's assessment of sales expectations, costs, capacity requirements, and the like, which are derived from knowledge about and anticipated decisions with regard to its particular industrial environment. Essentially, the planning and budgeting system translates the division's expectations into financial figures which reflect the profit it will contribute and the funds it will require to finance its operations. Throughout the year each division also transmits formal requests for funds to the headquarters for all major capital and expense items.

One of the major tasks of the corporate headquarters is economic: the allocation of scarce resources among competing ends. This task involves determining for any given year what the probable size of the pool of funds available to the firm will be and then distributing this pool among three major competing uses in such a way that it best serves the overall goals of the corporation. The major uses which often place competing demands on available funds are (1) financial obligations to outside groups (e.g., the various classes of investors and commercial banks), (2) potential mergers or joint ventures which the firm may wish to undertake, and (3) the funds required for re-investment in existing divisions.

The task of the corporate headquarters extends far beyond simply allocating funds, however. In most cases it takes action—either directly or indirectly—to gain control over the funds flowing into the enterprise and how they are to be used. In controlling uses of funds the headquarters is constantly evaluating the reasonableness of the assumptions underlying a division's plans and weighing its related funding requests against other potential uses—in other divisions, for mergers, and for meeting external obligations and/or expectations. The headquarters' attempts to gain control over sources of funds extend both to its dealings with external suppliers of funds and to its efforts to insure a stable and growing base of funds from internal operations. Underneath the internal flow of funds there is usually a good deal of bargaining between the headquarters and each division concerning how much profit the division will contribute in any one year and a continuing

FIGURE I-1

**Major Elements of the Resource Allocation and Planning Processes
for a Single Division**

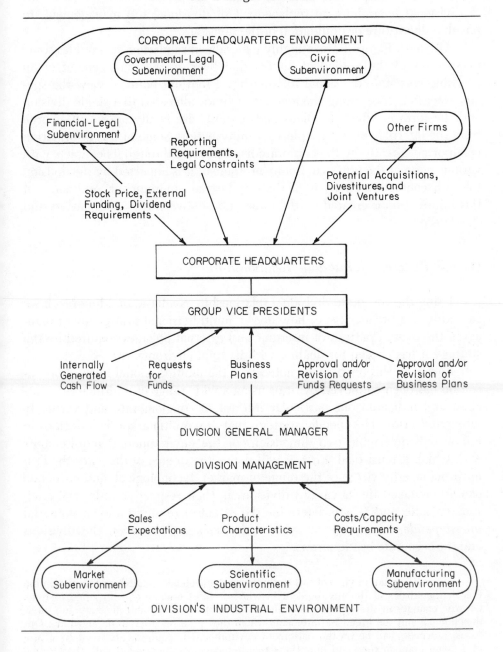

follow-up to insure that this profit contribution is in fact forthcoming. Continued failure of a division to meet its agreed-upon plans and budgets can jeopardize the corporate whole and usually invites some form of corrective effort by the headquarters. Such efforts may range from direct interventions in divisional operations, to replacement of divisional top management, to possible divestiture or liquidation of the division.

Although Figure I-1 is a highly generalized rendering, it provides some perspective of the myriad of factors that bear on the management of an on-going corporate-divisional relationship. From our point of view the specific decisions concerning the amount of funds allocated to a single division and the form in which its plans and requests are finally approved emerge from the interplay of several pieces of information. Some of this information is imported directly by the corporate headquarters through its contacts with various parts of the firm's environment, some of it is imported by the division through contacts with its immediate industrial environment, and some of this information is created by the interaction between the headquarters and the division.

Overall Patterns of Interunit Relationships

Using the corporate-divisional relationship as a basic building block we can address a broader issue: how does a multidivisional firm go about managing the overall pattern of interunit and external linkages required by the strategy it has chosen for dealing with its total environment?

Earlier in this chapter we noted that the multidivisional form of organization has been employed by firms using a wide range of multimarket strategies and indicated our particular interest in conglomerate and vertically integrated firms. The specific strategy that any multimarket firm decides to follow will determine two dimensions of the environmental requirements with which it must deal. First, it will define the degree of *diversity* the firm must manage by virtue of the range of market, technological, and economic conditions faced by its various divisions in their respective industrial environments. Second, it will determine the extent of required and/or potential *interdependence* among the various divisions and between the divisions and the corporate headquarters.*

---

* From the point of view of this study the strategic choices made by a firm determine the characteristics of the environment in which it must operate over a period of time. Clearly, changes in strategy can alter the patterns of environmental diversity and interdependence and the broad requirements which they pose for internal organization. Our focus, however, will be on the pattern of environmental requirements faced by a firm at a given point in time and how these requirements are interrelated with the internal functioning of its organization and its economic performance.

The work of Thompson[15] is particularly useful in mapping the patterns of interdependence with which various multidivisional firms may be faced. This author suggests that the following types of interdependence are commonly found in complex organizations:

(1) *Pooled interdependence,* where major operating units may have virtually no contact with one another but where each unit renders a discrete contribution to the whole organization and in turn is supported by the whole. Under these conditions the units operate independently of one another; but failure of any one unit may jeopardize the whole and, thus, the other parts of the organization.

(2) *Sequential interdependence,* where the output of one major unit is the input for another unit. Here the interdependence is *direct* but somewhat *asymmetrical.* That is to say, the supplier unit must perform its task properly before the recipient can act; and unless the recipient acts, the supplier cannot solve its output problem.

(3) *Reciprocal interdependence,* where the outputs of each unit represent inputs for the other units. In this case each unit presents direct contingencies for every other unit.

Thompson also makes the point that the difficulty and costs encountered in achieving coordination differ under these three patterns of interdependence. He states:

In the order introduced [pooled, sequential, reciprocal] the three types of interdependence are increasingly difficult to coordinate because they contain increasing degrees of contingency. With pooled interdependence, action in each position can proceed without regard to action in other positions so long as the overall organization remains viable. With sequential interdependence, however, each position in the set must be readjusted if any one of them acts improperly or fails to meet expectations. There is always an element of potential contingency with sequential interdependence. With reciprocal interdependence, contingency is not merely potential, for the actions of each position in the set must be adjusted to the actions of one or more others in the set.

Because the three types of interdependence are, in the order indicated, more difficult to coordinate, we shall say that they are more costly to coordinate, noting that measurement of such costs is far from perfect.[16]

In its purest form the conglomerate closely approximates Thompson's notion of pooled interdependence. Similarly, the vertically integrated firm corresponds to the concept of sequential interdependence; and the large, single-industry company is characterized by reciprocal interdependence among functional units. The simple diagrams in Figure I-2 clearly indicate

FIGURE I-2

Schematic Representation of Three Prototypical
Patterns of Diversity and Interdependence

I. THE CONGLOMERATE
   Degree of Product-Market Diversity: High
   Basic Interdependence: Pooled

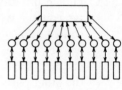

II. VERTICALLY INTEGRATED FIRM
    Degree of Product-Market Diversity: Moderate
    Basic Interdependence: Sequential

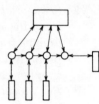

III. LARGE SINGLE-PRODUCT FIRM (OR DIVISION
     IN A MULTIDIVISIONAL FIRM)
     Degree of Product-Market Diversity: Low
     Basic Interdependence: Reciprocal

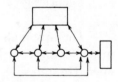

LEGEND: ▭   = corporate headquarters unit.
           O   = major operating units (i.e., product division or functional department).
           →   = direction of interdependence.
           ▯   = product-market environment.

why pooled interdependence is less costly to coordinate than either the sequential or reciprocal types. In a pure conglomerate there is frequently little reason for significant amounts of communication or joint decision making among the divisions. At the same time, the corporate headquarters can deal with each of the divisions individually. By way of contrast, in a vertically integrated or single-industry firm the headquarters cannot deal with its major operating units on a one-to-one basis because they are interdependent with one another.

Interdependence, however, is only one of several factors which can affect the relative difficulty of achieving coordination among major operating units in a firm. The number and diversity of divisions are also important factors. As Figure I-1 suggests, the conglomerate is faced with the task of managing a large number of separate divisions (ITT, for example, contains some 200 divisions). The vertically integrated firm usually consists of fewer major operating units (e.g., a paper company with woodlands, pulp and primary mills, and several different converting divisions). Similarly, the single-industry firm may have either three or four major functional units (e.g., R&D, engineering, manufacturing, and marketing). Not only does the conglomerate have a larger number of major divisions, but each of these divisions may be dealing with a distinctly different product-market environment.

Talking about idealized patterns of diversity and interdependence, such as "pure conglomerates" or "typical vertically integrated firms," is merely a convenient means for beginning to understand the particular patterns of environmental requirements actually faced by multidivisional firms. Most multidivisional firms undoubtedly lie somewhere between the extremes represented by these two idealized examples. For instance, many of the so-called conglomerates have made a number of product extension mergers which offer the possibility of establishing linkages among some divisions. Similarly, a large chemical company, such as Union Carbide, has considerable product-market diversity, extensive joint production and distribution facilities, as well as some divisions which are self-contained and have only a pooled interdependence with the corporate whole.[17] The question we shall be asking about each of the firms we have investigated is, "What is the particular pattern of environmental diversity and interdependence that this organization is trying to manage?"

Behavioral Science Concepts

Having developed an approach for thinking about the environmental requirements faced by a multidivisional firm, we need to determine what aspects of organization and management behavior may have a significant impact on the firm's ability to deal effectively with these requirements for diversity and interdependence. While the behavioral sciences have devoted little attention to multidivisional firms, there is a growing body of knowledge which points to some of the important organizational and behavioral factors which underlie relationships among the parts of an organization and between the organization and its environment. The behavioral science findings which we have found most pertinent to this study suggest several general statements about these part-whole relationships.

Several recent studies have focused on how different environmental conditions require different internal patterns of organization, information exchange, and decision making.[18] For example, Burns and Stalker[19] report that firms in the highly dynamic electronics industry seemed to be more effective when they had what was termed an "organic" pattern of organization, with lower emphasis on formal structure and widespread interaction of members around decisions. In the more stable textile machinery industry, these same researchers found that the more effective firms tended to have what they termed "mechanistic" patterns of organization, with heavier use of formal practices and stricter adherence to hierarchical position in decision making and information exchange.

A number of researchers have also been concerned with the impact of division of labor and specialization on the behavior of an organization's members. The findings of studies in this area converge on the idea that specialization in organizations leads to differences in goals and perceptions of members of specialized organizational units and that these differences create problems in achieving coordination among the units.[20] Another generalization suggested by this research is that differing types of specialization—e.g., by product, function, territory, or time—along with differences in the degree of interdependence among specialized units require different coordinative devices and entail different costs of coordination.[21] Most of these researchers also indicate that because of the existence of both specialization and the need for coordination interunit conflict is indigenous to all complex organizations. A number of behavioral scientists have been concerned with identifying patterns of behavior which prove particularly effective in managing this conflict.[22]

Building on much of this research, Lawrence and Lorsch[23] conducted a study of the problems of managing interdepartmental relationships in large, single-product organizations and developed a systematic set of concepts for understanding these issues. Since we shall be using many of the same concepts in this study, it is useful to outline the basic approach and findings of the Lawrence and Lorsch study.

As we consider this earlier work, it is important to hold in mind that while Lawrence and Lorsch used these concepts to understand the lateral relationships among functional units in ten single-product organizations in three different industries, we shall be using them to understand corporate-divisional and interdivisional relationships in multiproduct organizations.

The Lawrence and Lorsch study had three basic goals. First, it was aimed at developing a set of concepts which were capable of tracing the behavioral impact of formal organizational practices used by a firm. Second, it was concerned with how these organizational practices and their behavioral consequences differed in distinctly different industry settings—specifically, in the plastics, food, and container industries. Finally, the authors were interested in the degree to which an organization's ability to develop behavioral patterns which seemed to fit with the requirements posed by its environment were associated with relatively higher long-run performance.

One of the basic concepts used in the study was *differentiation*, which was defined as *the differences in behavior, cognitive and emotional orienta-tions, and ways of organizing work which develop among managers in dif-ferent organizational units as each of these units copes with its part of the organization's total environment.* Starting with a system's view of organiza-tions, the authors reasoned that the complexity of information exchange and decision-making processes required to deal effectively in a single-product industry would require specialization of work among separate sales, re-search, and production units. In effective organizations the managers in each of these units tended to focus their attention on a particular segment of the firm's total environment. For example, the sales unit was involved in gath-ering information from and making decisions about the market, while the research unit was concerned with information about the scientific part of the environment. As the members of each unit focused on a limited part of the environment, they tended to develop a particularly strong orientation toward the goals inherent in dealing with that environmental segment. For example, sales executives were concerned with such factors as competition, pricing, and customer relations, while production managers focused on plant efficiency, costs, and processing problems.

Managers in each functional unit also developed different time orienta-tions because the different environmental segments provided feedback about results at different intervals. Researchers received information about success or failure at infrequent intervals, perhaps a year or longer, and thus tended to be long-term oriented. Sales personnel, on the other hand, re-ceived information which enabled them to evaluate results on a monthly basis, and were oriented to shorter time frames.

Each unit's members also exhibited different interpersonal orientations. In some units members were more concerned with social relationships, get-ting along with others, while members of other units were more heavily concerned with task problems as they dealt with other people. Which of these interpersonal stances was predominant was related to the relative cer-tainty or uncertainty of the part of the environment with which a functional unit dealt. Where a unit's environment was highly certain (e.g., production) or highly uncertain (e.g., research), members tended to be more task-oriented in their interpersonal style. In units faced with a moderate degree of environmental uncertainty (e.g., sales) the members exhibited more so-cially oriented interpersonal stances.

The relative certainty or uncertainty of the environment was also found to be related to a fourth difference among functional units—the degree to which those units relied on formal practices. Units which dealt with rela-tively uncertain parts of the environment tended to use less formalized approaches to organizing their activities. Thus a research laboratory, which was solving problems stemming from the uncertain information in its part of the environment, had broad spans of control, few levels in the hierarchy, and few formal rules and procedures. With an uncertain task, the idea of programming decisions and activities through a highly formalized structure made little sense. In contrast, in a production unit with a much more certain task, a more formalized structure was found to be necessary. With a predictable task, the routine decision making which could be established through a more formalized structure produced effective results.

The overall pattern of these differences in goal, time, and interpersonal orientations and in formality of practices is what is meant by differentiation. While this general pattern of differentiation was found in all firms studied, there were important differences in the degree of differentiation which characterized firms in the three different industries and in the degree of differentiation achieved by higher performers in each industry. The researchers found that the degree of differentiation required in a particular firm depended on the diversity of the parts of its industry environment. For example, organizations in the plastics industry were faced with environmental sectors which were very heterogeneous, ranging from a scientific part of the environment with high uncertainty, long-term feedback and scientific goals to a production sector which was quite certain, providing almost immediate feedback and requiring manufacturing goals. Since the parts of the environment were so diverse, the various units needed quite different orientations and structures. In the container industry, however, the parts of the environment were not so heterogeneous; each of the sectors was characterized by relative certainty and more immediate feedback about results. Consequently the functional units in the effective container organization did not need to be so highly differentiated. The researchers also found that within each industry the higher performing firms had achieved a closer fit between their degree of differentiation and the degree of diversity of the environment than their less effective counterparts. The authors argued, therefore, that when a functional unit was able to develop an appropriate degree of differentiation from its sister units, its members seemed to be able to obtain and reach decisions on information from its environmental sector more effectively.

The second major concept with which Lawrence and Lorsch were concerned was the state of integration which existed among functional departments in each organization. *Integration was defined as the quality of collaboration which exists among departments required to achieve unity of effort by the environment.* The authors argued that as organizations divide up the work of dealing with environmental information, not all decisions can be made with the information available to any one unit. In other words, the environment presents a firm with the need for managing interdependence among its basic units. It was found that the more effective firms in each industry were both achieving a degree of differentiation which met their environmental requirements and also achieving a higher quality of integration. In these successful organizations the functional departments which were required to be interdependent were able to collaborate effectively and reach joint decisions.

Achieving a high quality of integration was not without its problems, however. For each of the functional units in all of the firms studied differentiation and integration were inversely related. The more differentiated any two interdependent units were, the more difficulty they encountered in achieving integration. These findings left the authors with the task of explaining how the more effective organizations achieved both differentiation and integration in spite of the basic antagonism between these variables.

This apparent paradox was explained by two other sets of variables. The first set of factors was the devices built into the formal organization to facilitate achieving integration (integrative devices). These devices include interunit committees and teams, special coordinating units and/or positions, and measurement and review practices intended to encourage integration. Although Lawrence and Lorsch did not find important variations among these integrative devices within any one industry, they did find that the number and elaborateness of such devices, and the amount of managerial time and effort devoted to achieving integration, did vary among organizations in the three industries studied.[24] These variations were related to both the degree of differentiation required in the various industries and the pattern of interdependence required among functional units. Where the required differentiation was higher and the pattern of interdependence more complex, more elaborate integrative devices were found. This finding, which fits closely with the theories of Thompson[25] and March and Simon,[26] suggests that as the required information flows among functional departments become more complex, the management hierarchy becomes inadequate to deal with the work load and additional integrative mechanisms must be established.

The second set of variables which Lawrence and Lorsch used to explain how organizations simultaneously achieved appropriate differentiation and integration was the behavior of managers in resolving interdepartmental conflicts. These variables were particularly important in explaining the differences among firms in the same industry. The authors reasoned that the presence of both differentiation and interdependence among functional units would inevitably lead to conflicts which would have to be successfully managed if effective integration was to be achieved. Thus, the degree to which managers were effective in resolving conflicts could have important consequences for the organization's ability to achieve both appropriate differentiation and integration. The conflict management variables which were found to be related to appropriate differentiation and integration included the extent to which managers took a problem-solving or "confronting" approach to the resolution of conflict; the emphasis which managers felt was placed on superordinate goals as a basis for evaluation and reward; the extent to which persons in integrating positions had orientations which were balanced among those of the units they were expected to link; and the congruence between the availability of the information to make decisions and the distribution of influence within the organization.

We have made extensive use of the Lawrence and Lorsch concepts and methodology for several reasons. First is our prior experience with this approach. Second, we feel that the concepts of differentiation and integration offer a useful and highly efficient means of exploring the management issues posed by the patterns of environmental diversity and interdependence with which multidivisional firms are faced. Third, by extending the use of these concepts from single-product organizations to multidivisional firms we open the possibility of using a single conceptual map to understand the functioning of multiple levels of a complex organization.

The Detailed Conceptual Scheme

Figure I-3 shows the major concepts and sets of concepts with which we shall be concerned. The first set of factors—the strategic decisions and mental set of top management—have been taken into account in two ways. First, we selected for investigation only firms with a historical and continued commitment to strategies of either diversification or vertical integration. We see management's choice of and continued commitment to these strategies as shaping the nature of the environment in which each firm operates for some period of time. Second, through interviews we have identified top managements' assumptions about organizing, controlling, and coordinating their firms, and we shall examine how these assumptions seem to affect the organizational choices they have actually made.

The next group of factors are the environmental requirements facing the corporate headquarters and its divisions. In order to understand the character and diversity of a firm's environment we shall begin by examining the broad pattern of corporate-divisional relationships in each firm. First, we shall determine what sorts of direct contacts the corporate headquarters has with groups outside the firm's organizational and/or legal boundaries. Next, along lines suggested by the earlier work of Lawrence and Lorsch, we shall examine the *uncertainty, time span of feedback,* and *dominant competitive issues* faced by each sample division in dealing with its particular industrial environment. With these pieces of data in hand, we shall then

FIGURE I-3

Major Factors Affecting Interunit Relationships

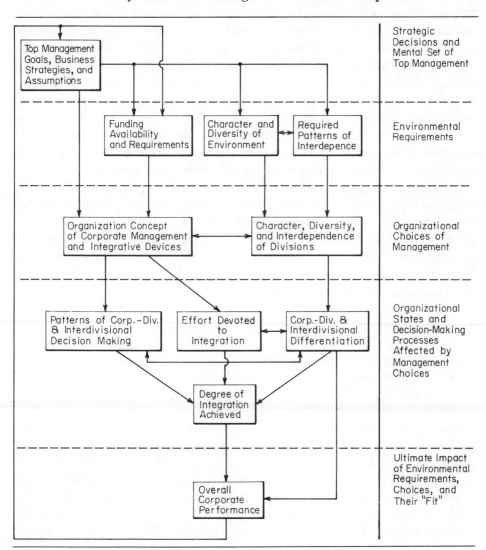

consider (1) the *diversity* of requirements posed by the corporation's total environment, (2) the patterns of *interdependence* required by this environment, and (3) the *patterns of sources and uses of funds* which the firm has encountered in dealing with this environment.

The next group of factors are what we have termed the *organizational choices* of top management. We shall consider these organizational choices both at the corporate-wide and division levels. More specifically, we shall first be concerned with how the divisions have been formally organized. Do the divisions contain all of the specialized facilities and management positions necessary to deal with their particular industries, or are some of these activities carried out by the corporate headquarters? What sorts of organizational devices and/or executive positions have been established for managing any requirements for interdivisional collaboration? Turning to the corporate headquarters unit, we shall be concerned with (a) the *organizational concept* top management has developed for thinking about how it will maintain control over divisional activities and (b) the *integrative devices*—e.g., executive roles, control and reward systems, and committees—corporate management uses to implement its organizational concepts.

Lying at the core of our conceptual scheme is a third set of factors: *organizational states and decision-making processes. Differentiation is the degree to which major organizational units (i.e., headquarters and divisions) differ from one another in overall goals, formality of management practices, and the cognitive and emotional orientations shared by their members.* More specifically, we shall be concerned with differences among major organizational units in terms of five factors:

(1) Broad goal orientations of managers in each unit.*
(2) Overall goal set of each unit.**
(3) Formality of structure of each unit.
(4) Time orientations of managers in each unit.
(5) Interpersonal orientations of managers in each unit.

Taken together, these five items provide a shorthand way of capturing important differences in the mental sets which organizational units use for dealing both with their segment of the firm's overall environment and with one another. These five factors are certainly not the only dimensions along which major organizational units may differ from one another; other items might include attitudes toward risk[27] and level of aspiration. We have focused on this particular set of differences because they seemed appropriate

---

* Item (1) measures the goal orientations of individual managers in terms of major content areas; e.g., financial, marketing, manufacturing, and engineering.

** Item (2), on the other hand, measures managers' perceptions of the overall goals of their organizational unit. This second measure is aimed at determining the relative importance of specific goal items which are common to the unit as a whole; e.g., return on investment, profit growth, inventory control, product diversification, and rate of new product introduction. While these two measures undoubtedly overlap, both were employed because we felt that differences in goals would be particularly important in corporate-divisional and interdivisional relationships.

for this top management setting and because known methods were available for measuring them.

The second organizational state we shall examine is *integration, which we define as the degree of collaboration and mutual understanding actually achieved among the various organizational units*. To measure this organizational state we simply asked managers in each organizational unit to rate the quality of collaboration and mutual understanding which they felt existed between their unit and other major units with which it was interdependent.

With measures of these two organizational states in hand, we can make several important comparisons between environmental requirements and organizational states in each firm. Has the firm achieved patterns of interunit differentiation which seem to be consistent with the patterns of environmental diversity it faces? Has it achieved high levels of integration among those organizational units which are interdependent with one another? Does the antagonistic relationship which Lawerence and Lorsch found between differentiation and integration also hold for interunit relationships in multidivisional organizations? Is long-term economic performance associated with achieving appropriate patterns of differentiation and integration?

Having determined the extent to which each firm has developed patterns of differentiation and integration which seem to fit the requirements posed by its total environment, we shall then attempt to identify what aspects of its interunit decision-making processes seem to facilitate or impede its ability to achieve this organization-environment fit. First, we shall consider *integrative effort*, which we define as *the amount of their working time managers devote to interunit relationships*. Our basic concern will be to determine what impact differing amounts of integrative effort seem to have on achieving appropriate patterns of differentiation and integration in a particular environment. As Figure I-3 suggests, we are hypothesizing that the integrative devices employed by a firm will have a significant impact on the amount of effort its managers devote to achieving integration. By unraveling the complex interplay between differentiation, integration, and integrative effort we shall be developing one means for testing whether a firm's organizational devices do, in fact, help it develop organizational states and processes which fit the requirements posed by its environment.

A second set of factors we shall be using to understand how a firm achieves appropriate patterns of differentiation and integration is what we have termed *patterns of interunit decision making*. By this we mean *several indicators of how managers in interdependent organizational units exchange information, resolve conflicts, and make joint decisions*. Specifically, we shall examine:

(1) Perceptions of the overall quality of information flowing between head-quarters and divisions and among divisions.

(2) Perceptions of the rapidity with which these units respond to one another's requests.

(3) Division managers' perceptions of the corporate-wide performance evaluation system.

(4) The degree to which integrating departments and positions are intermediate in orientations between the organizational units they are expected to link.

(5) The patterns of influence that varying organizational units and levels exert over policies which are followed by the operating divisions.

(6) The degree to which confrontation, or problem-solving, behavior seems to be employed in reaching joint decisions and resolving conflicts.

Finally, we shall attempt to link these concepts to *economic performance* in two ways. First, we wish to consider the degree to which achieving a closer fit between organizational states and processes and environmental requirements is associated with higher long-term economic performance. Second, we shall examine the ways in which performance at the corporate and divisional levels seems to impact on organizational states and processes.

One way to draw together the various parts of our conceptual scheme is to view Figure I-3 as a broad set of hypotheses aimed at explaining how organizational choices and organizational states seem to develop over time. This diagram suggests that organizational choices can usefully be viewed as being made and continually elaborated on the basis of the environmental requirements faced by the firm as these requirements are filtered through the mental sets of the firm's top management. It also suggests that organizational choices are related to overall performance through their impact on the organizational states and decision-making processes which operate within the firm. Finally, the process through which organizational choices and organizational states and processes emerge may be viewed as dynamic in the sense that overall performance feeds back upon the availability of financial resources and upon top management goals, assumptions, and strategies.

Considering our conceptual approach in this way highlights its predominant assumption. It is a contingency approach. Basically, we shall be arguing that there is no single best way to organize, no guiding universal principles. Instead we shall take the position that the internal characteristics and organizational devices which will be effective are contingent on the particular pattern of requirements posed by the firm's environment. The task of this study, as we see it, is to begin to identify what sorts of organizational states and processes seem to fit the particular patterns of environmental diversity and interdependence and related economic requirements faced by each of our research sites.

Design of the Study

Selection of Companies

To test and further develop the conceptual scheme outlined above we have designed a comparative study of six multidivisional firms, four conglomerates and two vertically integrated paper companies. In selecting the four conglomerate firms we attempted to control for several factors. First, we decided to avoid the highly acquisitive, or "go-go," conglomerate[28] and to focus on firms whose continued performance seemed to depend as much on the management of existing divisions as upon their merger activities. Put another way, we chose firms which had had several years of experience in managing diverse interunit relationships. Second, we selected firms which were roughly the same size—between $300 and $600 million in annual sales. Third, we selected firms which had a number of similarities in their corporate goals and in the broad product-market areas in which they had decided to operate. More specifically, all four of the conglomerates were as interested in return on investment as in sheer earnings growth; and each of them was heavily involved in the areas of producer durables, consumer durables, and defense.

While each of the conglomerates was broadly similar with respect to size, major product-market areas, and basic goals, they had quite different records of long-term economic performance. Although each of them could be considered a successful corporation, two of the firms were selected because they had maintained relatively high records of growth and return on investment over a ten-year period. The other two conglomerates were chosen for study because they had more modest records of economic performance.

Because of their size and complexity—each firm had at least ten operating divisions—it was not feasible to study all interunit relationships in each of the conglomerates. We decided instead to make a comprehensive study of the corporate headquarters and four divisions in each of the firms. The divisions to be studied were selected according to two criteria. First, we selected two high-performing and two low-performing divisions in each firm.* Second, we attempted to select the four divisions in each firm so that

---

* Initial identification of high- and low-performing divisions in each firm was based on informal discussions with corporate headquarters executives. During our investiga-

they would be broadly representative of the range of product-market environments in which the firm was involved.

Table I-2 shows some of the major characteristics of the divisions which were studied. Clearly, they represent a very heterogeneous set of businesses. Although none of the divisions in the various companies was a major competitor, our selection criteria did build in considerable overlap in terms of broad product-market areas; e.g., defense, automotive parts and transportation equipment, and consumer durables. This overlap reflects the broad similarity which characterized the overall operations of the four corporations. Although the divisions ranged in size from annual sales of from $12.5 million to $100 million, the typical division had 1967 sales of approximately $45 million. It also should be noted that, with the exception of Divisions 1:II and 4:II, all of the divisions had been part of their parent corporation for five or more years.

The two vertically integrated companies and the divisional samples within these firms were selected in a different manner. In this setting we were interested in studying organizations which had had significant and long-established linkages among major operating divisions. We selected two companies whose earnings were dependent mainly on the technology of paper making and which had required technological linkages among divisions beginning with timber holdings and moving forward to paper mills and finally to converting operations. While we had originally intended to select two companies with quite different levels of long-term economic performance, we found that the range of variation among large vertically integrated paper firms was so narrow as to make this impractical. We were able, however, to find two such companies which had moderately different performance records. Thus, although we still have been able to explore the relationships between organizational characteristics and economic performance in this setting, we will not see such dramatic differences as those which characterized the four conglomerates.

Again, because of the size and complexity of these firms, it was not feasible to study all of their interunit relationships. We decided to focus our attention on the relationships among the headquarters, paper mill operations, and two different converting divisions—corrugated containers and flexible packaging. In both firms these operating units were involved in the manufacture and sale of a roughly identical set of products. In some, but not all, geographic areas the two firms were direct competitors.

---

tions we sought to validate these informal assessments by using questionnaire items to obtain both corporate and divisional managers' perceptions of a division's performance. This approach was used because in most of the firms divisional profitability data were considered highly confidential.

Library
I.U.P.
Indiana, Pa.

658.1146 L895m
C. 1

TABLE I-2

Broad Characteristics of Divisional Sample in Four Conglomerate Firms

Division[a]	Performance Relative to Corporate Expectation[b]	Major Products	Sales[c] (in millions)	Date of Acquisition[d]
1:I	High	Defense, aerospace, aviation systems and components	$77.6	1962
1:II	High	Automotive parts	50.3	1966
1:III	Low	Heating and air conditioning equipment	13.0	OB
1:IV	Low	Consumer electrical appliances	20.6	1957
2:I	High	Defense, aerospace, aviation components	$12.5	1959
2:II	High	Automotive parts	42.5	OB
2:III	Low	Industrial and apparel fibers and yarns	42.1	1961
2:IV	Low	Air conditioning equipment	12.8	1959
3:I	High	Machinery for extractive industries	$16.0	1953
3:II	High	Industrial and transportation equipment and components	56.0	OB
3:III	Low	Industrial controls, special equipment and components	36.4	OB
3:IV	Low	Construction and mining equipment	100.0	1953
4:I	High	Equipment for gas, oil, chemical, and transportation industries	$35.0	1957
4:II	High	Defense, aerospace, aviation systems and components	90.0	1964
4:III	Low	Equipment, supplies, and services for leisure markets	80.0	OB
4:IV	Low	Consumer durables—nonelectrical	30.0	1963

[a] Arabic numbers designate the firm, while roman numerals indicate the divisions within each firm.

[b] Based on discussions with corporate headquarters executives.

[c] For 1967 calendar year.

[d] OB indicates "original business"; i.e., division was not acquired by parent corporation.

Data Collection

Data were collected in the six companies in three ways:

(1) Through examination of documents made available by company management; e.g., organization charts, performance data, written goal statements, planning and budgetary documents, capital project requests, and
procedure manuals.
(2) Through semistructured interviews.
(3) Through questionnaires.

The basic formats for interviews and questionnaires are shown in Appendix B. Questionnaires were completed by all key headquarters and group
executives and by general managers of each sample division, their immediate subordinates, and a selected group of managers at the next organiza-

TABLE I-3

Number of Interviews and Questionnaires Completed in Six Firms

	Corporate Headquarters[a]	*I*	*II*	*III*	*IV*	*Total*
FIRM 1						
Interviews	8	7	7	4	6	32
Long questionnaires	10	10	9	7	10	46
Short questionnaires	0	13	12	10	7	32
FIRM 2						
Interviews	12	4	4	7	4	31
Questionnaires	15	6	8	12	12	53
FIRM 3						
Interviews	8	6	7	7	7	35
Questionnaires	14	9	11	14	11	59
FIRM 4						
Interviews	15	7	10	8	6	46
Long questionnaires	15	11	11	9	8	54
Short questionnaires	0	15	17	23	12	67
FIRM 5						
Interviews	10	7	8	6	—	31
Questionnaires	20	30	28	24	—	102
FIRM 6						
Interviews	15	9	6	6	—	36
Questionnaires	20	21	24	20	—	85

The column header *Divisions* spans columns *I*, *II*, *III*, and *IV*.

[a] Includes group executives.

tional level. The basic criterion for choosing divisional respondents was the general manager's indication that these executives played an important role in (a) interunit relationships and/or (b) the formulation of the division's product-market strategy. In two of the conglomerates a larger sample of managers was employed to get a clearer understanding of the importance of achieving a fit between the divisions' internal characteristics and the demands of their environments. Table I-3 shows the number of interviews and questionnaires obtained in each firm.

Outline of the Book

Chapters II through V are devoted to presenting and discussing our findings in the four conglomerates. In Chapter II we consider the relationship between environmental diversity and corporate-divisional differentiation and explore the impact of corporate-divisional relationships on the ability of the firm to achieve a fit with its environment. Chapter III deals with the issues of achieving effective corporate-divisional integration. In Chapter IV we explore the characteristics of corporate-divisional decision-making processes which are associated with achieving appropriate differentiation and integration. Chapter V summarizes the various strands of our analysis and explores their implications for managing corporate-divisional relations in the conglomerate setting.

Chapter VI compares the experiences of two vertically integrated paper companies in managing corporate-divisional and interdivisional relationships. In Chapter VII we systematically compare the environmental requirements, organizational choices, and organizational states which characterized the more effective conglomerate and vertically integrated firms.

Chapter VIII combines the findings of this study with those of others who have utilized a contingency approach to understanding organizations. In this chapter we develop an interrelated set of propositions which represents our view of the current state of knowledge about the functioning of complex, multiunit, multilevel organizations. Finally, in Chapter IX we return to the implications of this study for practicing managers in multiunit organizations. This way of dividing the task of summarizing our results and discussing their implications is intended to help readers with different interests concentrate on the areas which may be of most use to them. Chapter VIII should be of more interest to the theoretically or research-oriented reader, while Chapter IX should be more interesting to the practicing manager.

II

Diversity and Differentiation

THIS chapter examines the relationship between environmental diversity and corporate-divisional differentiation in the four conglomerate firms. It has the dual purpose of providing an overview of the basic characteristics of each firm and of exploring the degree to which its corporate and divisional units have developed orientations and practices which seem to fit the diverse requirements posed by the firm's environment. As we proceed with this description and analysis we shall be concerned with four questions: How do corporate headquarters and divisional units differ from one another in their goals, orientations, and management practices? How does this differentiation seem to arise? Is the degree of fit between environmental requirements and organizational states achieved by a division and a firm associated with its relative economic performance? What role, if any, does corporate-divisional differentiation play in achieving an effective organization-environment fit?

As noted in Chapter I, the four conglomerates were similar with respect to size, broad product-market areas, and basic goals. These firms differed, however, in terms of economic performance and the total number of specific product-market environments in which they operated. Before launching into the body of our data, we wish to describe in more detail the history, structure, and performance of these firms.

Background Information on Each Firm

Firm 1 had its inception with the acquisition of a small consumer durables company in the early 1950s. From this base management set out to build a broadly based, multimarket company with balanced participation in government, industrial, and consumer segments of the economy. Top management had three major goals in its diversification program: to increase earnings per share more than 10% annually, to balance involvement in stable and dynamic industries, and to pursue an aggressive acquisition program as a strong adjunct to orderly internal growth. At the time of the study Firm 1 consisted of 34 divisions clustered into five major group organizations. No group accounted for more than 30% of corporate sales.

In the late 1950s Firm 2 embarked on a diversification program that transformed it from a relatively small, two-product company into a major corporation with 17 separate operating units. At the inception of its diversification program Firm 2 was selling nearly all of its output to approximately a dozen customers in a highly fluctuating and competitive market. At the same time, it was vulnerable to both product obsolescence and backward integration by its customers. By 1968, 25 firms had been acquired in areas such as capital goods, defense, and consumer durables and nondurables. No major industry category accounted for more than 30% of corporate sales. Firm 2's management described its acquisition program as one of related diversification aimed at three broad objectives: independence from a captive industry, stability of cash flow, and additional growth. The corporation was seeking orderly growth through a moderate rate of acquisition of companies that already had considerable management talent and which could make a distinct contribution to its diversification objectives. At the time of our study Firm 2 was operating with a partial group organization for its 17 divisions. Four divisions with similar technologies and markets reported to one group vice president, while a second group vice president presided over eight rather diverse divisions. The other five divisions reported directly to the president.

Firm 3 had begun diversifying several years before Firm 2. Like Firm 2, it had originally been a relatively small company with two divisions selling a range of products to one industry. Its diversification objectives were also much the same: increased growth, stability of cash flow, and independence from the cycles and limitations of a single industry. By 1968, Firm 3 registered sales of between $300 and $400 million and consisted of nine divisions and a number of foreign subsidiaries. Unlike Firm 2, Firm 3 had confined its diversification mainly to the area of producer durables. Within this broad category, however, its divisions manufactured 35 basic product lines that were sold in seven major market areas. Also, one major acquisition along with internal development by its divisions provided Firm 3 with a limited entry into the defense and aerospace area. No major market area accounted for more than 30% of corporate sales. At the time of our study, three divisions which represented the original businesses reported to the president. The position of group vice president had been created in 1967 to oversee four producer durables divisions which employed somewhat similar technologies but which had quite dissimilar products and markets. Two newly acquired businesses and all foreign subsidiaries reported to the chairman.

In the late 1940s Firm 4 was a small producer of two lines of highly specialized capital goods. During the next fifteen years some 40 firms were acquired in the areas of defense, capital goods, consumer durables, and nondurables. As of 1968 Firm 4 had 21 product divisions in six major operating groups. Firm 4's management cited the following goals for its diversification program: to achieve a balanced participation in government, industrial, and consumer markets; to achieve earnings growth; and to achieve sufficient size to support a sophisticated technical base. During its early years Firm 4 had followed a strategy of nonrelated diversification; however, more recently management efforts had focused on stimulating internal growth and on a smaller number of acquisitions related to existing businesses.

While, as this description suggests, these firms were similar in many ways, they had turned in quite different performance records. Firms 1 and 2 had outstripped Firms 3 and 4 in sales and profit growth and on return on capital, over both the most recent five years and the most recent ten years (Table II-1). Even though Firm 3 had shown considerable improvement over the most recent five years, this improvement was a good deal less than that registered by Firms 1 and 2. On the basis of the statistics reported in

TABLE II-1

Comparative Performance Statistics for Four Conglomerate Firms

	Firm 1	Firm 2	Firm 3	Firm 4
SALES GROWTH (COMPOUNDED)				
Most recent 5 years[a]	27%	19%	11%	0%
Most recent 10 years[b]	21	15	4	9
PROFIT GROWTH (COMPOUNDED)				
Most recent 5 years[a]	28%	24%	8.5%	(decrease)
Most recent 10 years[b]	23	14	0	11%
RETURN ON CAPITAL[c]				
Five-year average	8.6%	8.9%	6.3%	5.0%
Ten-year average	9.4	7.7	6.0	7.1
PERFORMANCE RATING	Higher	Higher	Lower	Lower

[a] Average of 1960–62 v. 1967.
[b] Average of 1955–57 v. 1967.
[c] Profit after taxes ÷ (total assets − current liabilities).

Table II-1 we felt justified in rating the first pair of firms as higher performers and the second as lower performers.*

Having briefly examined the broad characteristics and performance of the four firms, we now turn to a description of their corporate headquarters and the setting in which these organizational units operated.

Corporate Environments and Headquarters Organization

Corporate Environments

As noted in Chapter I, we expected that the headquarters units and product divisions in highly diversified companies would direct their efforts to different segments of the firm's total environment. We reasoned that while the divisions would be mainly concerned with profitably developing, manufacturing, and selling products within their own industries, the cor-

---

* This comparison is based on publicly reported results for the four firms with certain adjustments where differences in financial reporting policies would have had a material impact on the figures. A number of performance indices might have been employed to assess relative performance. We chose sales and profit growth and average return on capital because, taken together, they provide a broad picture of top managements' ability to (1) achieve sustained progress over time (2) consistent with the efficient use of the capital employed by the enterprise. We chose both five-year and ten-year comparison periods because of the specific way we were viewing economic performance. That is, we were hypothesizing that performance was at once an outcome of effective organizational practices and an input to the process of developing these practices. Thus, in assessing performance as an outcome we felt that both five-year and ten-year trends were necessary. In considering performance as a system input (as we shall in Chapter III) the five-year trend would have been sufficient. For a discussion of the use of comparative ratios based on publicly reported figures the interested reader may refer to Graham, Dodd, et al., *Security Analysis*, pp. 24–35, 85–97, 239–249, and Anthony, *Management Accounting*, pp. 293–313.

It is important to question the degree to which these performance differences reflect on-going operations versus the impact of differences in merger activity. While we cannot provide a definitive answer to this question, we were able to determine the sales added by all major acquisitions made by these firms between 1963 and 1967 and use this figure to adjust their sales growth rates downward. That is, we reduced their 1967 reported sales by a figure obtained by cumulating the reported sales of acquired companies or units during their last full year of independent operation. The resulting figures are as follows:

Firm	Number of Acquisitions	Annual Sales Growth Over Most Recent Five Years As Reported in Table II-1	Adjusted for Effect of Acquisitions
1	10	27%	13%
2	3	19	12
3	3	11	8
4	5	0	(decrease)

porate headquarters would focus attention on securing external funding, acquiring other firms, allocating resources among the divisions, and meeting the requirements faced by the corporation as a legal entity.

As a point of departure, let's simply examine the relevant dimensions of the corporate headquarters environment. Corporate managers in each firm were asked how they divided their working time among contacts and work required by contacts with a number of groups lying outside the legal and/or organizational boundaries of their company. The relationships with the financial community, potential merger candidates, and legal or governmental bodies accounted for a major proportion of the external contacts of corporate executives in the four firms (Table II-2). Less than one-fifth of

TABLE II-2

Relevant Dimensions of the Corporate Headquarters' Environment: Percentage of Members' Time Devoted to Various Environmental Sectors[a]

Financial subenvironment	24.9%
Potential acquisitions, divestitures, and joint ventures	15.7
Legal-governmental subenvironment	17.5
Divisional environments (trade associations, customers, and suppliers of divisions)	17.0
Other (community relations, professional associations, and consultants)	24.9
Total	100.0%

[a] Mean ratings by corporate managers in the four conglomerate firms. Numbers are the proportion of time devoted to all external groups attributable to specific environmental sectors. See Appendix B for questionnaire items used to secure this information.

their external activities involved direct contacts with groups in their divisions' environments. From this we can conclude that, by and large, corporate executives were concerned with a segment of the firm's environment which was quite distinct from the environments of the various divisions.

Of course, direct contacts with external groups represent only one part of the corporate headquarters' activities. This unit also has an *indirect* impact on how the divisions deal with their segment of the total environment through its ability to allocate resources and its attempts to control divisional profit contributions. Taken together, the external demands of groups such as stockholders, banks, and investment houses and the internal requirements of planning, control, and resource allocation form the basic set of issues with which the headquarters must deal.

Some of the specific problems faced by the headquarters in each of the four research sites can be understood by examining their respective financial positions. Five statistics were used to indicate (1) the availability of external financing and (2) the character of internal funds requirements for each corporation. In terms of external financing, the median price-earnings multiple of each firm's common stock during the most recent year indicates how costly it would be to secure funds from this and related sources (e.g., convertible securities). An estimate of available debt capacity indicates how many dollars might be secured through this medium. These two measures provide a rough picture of the munificence of each firm's financial environment; i.e., the degree to which outside sources would be willing to finance potential mergers or internal requirements.

Three statistics provide us with a gauge of the internal funds requirements faced by each corporation.[1] First, the ratio of net cash flow after dividends to gross plant and equipment is used as an indicator of resources generated relative to capital stock. Assuming roughly similar asset life cycles, we would expect that the higher this ratio, the greater the internally generated funds available to meet investment needs. Second, the ratio of cash flow after dividends to capital expenditures yields a picture of the actual supply/demand relationship for investment funds. The lower this ratio, the greater the demand for funds and the more critical the matter of financing expenditures. Finally, year-to-year variations in cash flow give us a rough indication of the risks associated with committing funds to projects. Hence, the standard deviation around a regression line describing historical cash generation is one measure of the uncertainty faced by corporate management in financial planning. Taken together these three measures allow us to gauge the difficulties and uncertainties faced by the headquarters management units in each firm.

Looking first at the availability of external financing, the common stock of the four firms sold at roughly similar price-earnings multiples (Table II-3). These multiples were slightly below the median registered by the Dow-Jones Industrials during 1968, and corporate managers in the four firms noted that they did not consider them as highly favorable conditions under which to issue common stock or other securities tied to the price of common stock. At the same time, however, Firms 1 and 2 had considerably more unused debt capacity than Firms 3 and 4.

Turning to internal funds requirements, Firm 2 faced somewhat more demanding and uncertain conditions than the other three companies. First of all, Firm 2 tended to generate less cash relative to its fixed assets. Although the four firms were remarkably similar in the relationship between net cash flow and annual capital expenditures, Firm 2 was also spending a somewhat greater proportion of its cash flow on capital projects. Finally, Firm 2 had experienced greater variations in its annual cash flow than the other firms. At the same time, however, Firm 2 had more debt capacity with which to work.

TABLE II-3

Measures of Financial Position for Four Conglomerate Firms

Firm	Median P/E of Common Stock[a]	Available Debt Capacity[b] (in millions)	NCF/GFA[c]	NCF/CE[c]	Std. Dev. NCF[c] / x̄ NCF
1	15X	$20.3	.274	1.61	.148
2	13X	27.4	.096	1.52	.206
3	16X	1.4	.155	1.58	.114
4	14X	14.5	.115	1.61	.125

Key: NCF—Net cash flow after dividends
     GFA—Gross fixed assets
     CE —Capital expenditures

[a] Computed on basis of median market value during most recent calendar year.
[b] Based on managers' estimates of maximum debt-equity ratio minus existing debt during most current year.
[c] Ratios are five-year averages, and the standard deviation of NCF is based on a five-year, least squares regression line.

While the particular funds flow problems encountered by the four firms were somewhat different, it does not appear that these differences made financial planning appreciably more difficult for any of the companies. Indeed, the differences often seemed to cancel one another. For instance, Firm 2 faced considerably more uncertainty relative to the availability of internally generated funds; but at the same time its larger debt capacity provided some flexibility in dealing with this issue. Similarly, Firm 1 faced moderate variations in cash flow, but it was the least capital intensive and also had a fairly large unused debt capacity. Firms 3 and 4 had less debt capacity; however, their patterns of internal funds flow were also more certain. Thus, the data suggest that, while each was encountering somewhat different areas of uncertainty, the four headquarters units did not differ markedly in the overall uncertainty and difficulty associated with their financial planning activities. Now let us turn to the organizational patterns that each of the headquarters units had developed to cope with these requirements.

Headquarters Units

The organizational arrangements and managerial orientations which characterized corporate headquarters units were measured in terms of five attributes, which the previous work of Lawrence and Lorsch suggested were important.[2] These attributes were formality of organizational practices of the headquarters unit, time, interpersonal and goal orientations of corporate level managers, and the overall goal set of the headquarters unit.

In light of the broad similarity in corporate environments and funding requirements reported above, we would expect these organizational patterns also to be similar. The data indicate that the headquarters units of the four firms were indeed quite similar (Table II-4). There were no significant

TABLE II-4

Basic Characteristics of Headquarters Units in Four Conglomerate Firms[a]

	Firm 1	Firm 2	Firm 3	Firm 4
Formality of structure	17.0	14.0	17.0	20.0
Interpersonal orientations[b]	92.0	92.3	93.2	97.1
Time orientations[b]	3.2	3.1	3.0	3.2
Goal orientations:				
Financial[c]	1.56	1.29	1.35	1.74
Marketing[d]	2.23	1.99	1.83	2.29
Manufacturing[b]	2.30	2.24	2.35	2.22
R&D/Engineering[b]	2.37	2.51	2.64	2.31

[a] Higher scores indicate more formality of structure, more socially oriented interpersonal styles, longer time horizons, and *less* emphasis on various goal items. See Appendix B for questionnaire items used to secure this information.

[b] Differences among four firms are not statistically significant.

[c] Differences among Firms 1, 2, and 3 are not significant. Difference between Firm 4 and other firms is significant at .01 level (analysis of variance).

[d] Difference between Firms 1 and 4 and Firms 2 and 3 is significant at .01 level (analysis of variance).

differences among the firms in time and in interpersonal orientations. While there were some differences in goal orientations, these were not marked differences. Financial goals were given the heaviest emphasis by corporate managers in each of the firms. This emphasis was consistent with the prominent role which contact with the financial community and merger candidates played in corporate activities. Also, financial language provided a common means of communicating with diverse product divisions.[3] The other goal areas tended to receive much less emphasis; and in most cases the relative emphasis placed on marketing, manufacturing, and R&D goals was not terribly different. It is noteworthy, however, that Firms 2 and 3 did underscore marketing goals somewhat more. By and large, however, the goal orientations of the four firms were quite similar. This conclusion is further supported by our measures of overall corporate goal sets for the four firms.

Corporate executives were asked to rank 21 specific goal items in terms of their relative importance as guidelines for corporate decision making (Table II-5). The four firms were quite similar to one another with respect

TABLE II-5

Overall Goal Sets of Corporate Headquarters Units in Four Conglomerate Firms[a]

	Firm 1	Firm 2	Firm 3	Firm 4
OVERALL FINANCIAL GOALS				
Return on investment	1	1	1	3
% growth-profits	2	2	4	2
% growth-sales	4.5	5	7	5
Profit margin on sales	4.5	6.5	6	11
Absolute level of profits	9.5	4	8	1
Desired profit mix among product lines	16	19	17	13.5
Sales volume	9.5	6.5	5	4
OVERALL PRODUCT-MARKET GOALS				
Product diversification into related areas	6.5	14	10	10
Rate of new product introduction	8	16.5	12	7.5
Product diversification into unrelated areas	19	20	20	19.5
Geographic expansion of product sales	21	21	21	21
MAJOR OPERATING GOALS				
Market share	14	13	9	12
Customer relations	16	16.5	16	18
Product improvement	13	10.5	11	9
Cost reduction	11	3	3	6
Inventory control	12	8	2	7.5
Level of fixed costs	18	9	13	13.5
Plant expansion	20	18	19	19.5
OTHER GOALS				
Development and motivation of personnel	3	12	14	16
Corporate image	6.5	10.5	15	15
Maintenance of unique corporate skills	16	15	18	17

[a] Ranking of 21 goal items by corporate headquarters executives. Lower number indicates more important goal item. Differences in ratings of top five goals for the four firms are not statistically significant (Kruskal-Wallis one-way analysis of variance). For a more comprehensive listing of these goal items and how they were analyzed, see Appendix B.

to the ratings of these items in their overall goal sets (Kruskal-Wallis one-way analysis of variance for top five goal items showed no significant difference among the firms). These ratings were also consistent with the patterns of goal emphasis reported in Table II-4. Financial goals relating to sales, profits, ROI, and costs were seen as most important. A cluster of secondary goals included both financial and nonfinancial items; e.g., profit margin, inventory control, product innovation, diversification, and public image.*

The data in Table II-5 also provide support for our contention in Chapter I that these firms were not the highly acquisitive type of conglomerate. For one thing, they were just as interested in return on investment as in rate of earnings growth. Also, their broad product-market goals focused most heavily on related product diversification and new product development; each of the firms rated unrelated diversification as a relatively unimportant goal.

There was a difference among the firms in the formality of structure which characterized their corporate headquarters units (Table II-4). Firm 2 had a less formal structure, while Firm 4 exhibited higher formality. Our interviews with corporate executives suggested that both these differences in formality of structure and the emphasis placed on marketing goals in Firms 2 and 3 were related mainly to differing management assumptions rather than differences in the corporate environments (the issue of management assumptions about organization and their importance will be taken up in Chapter III). At this point in our analysis, however, we can conclude that the organizational patterns of these headquarters units were similar in most respects, and that they had been developed to deal with the longer term, *financial* requirements posed by the total environment.

While the corporate headquarters units in each firm had similar organizational arrangements and managerial orientations, we shall see that each of these units differed in a number of ways from its various divisions. In order to understand these differences between corporate and divisional units and why they arose, let us now turn to the environmental requirements faced by the divisions and their relationship to divisional organizational patterns.

Divisional Environments and Organizations

In order to gauge the range of markets and technologies of the divisions in our four research sites and the different requirements posed by their diverse industrial environments, a sample of four divisions in each firm was

---

* It may appear to the reader that these goal rankings differ somewhat from the major goals cited in our description of the firms at the beginning of this chapter. The source of this difference is that the goals cited earlier were used to describe the historic objectives of each firm's diversification program, whereas the ranking in Table II-5 represents managers' perceptions of the current goals of the total enterprise.

selected for intensive study. As noted in Chapter I, these divisions were selected so as to be representative of both the product-market diversity and range of divisional performance faced by each firm. Because a detailed description of all 16 divisional environments would be unnecessarily repetitive, we shall focus on the divisional sample at Firm 1 to get a feel for just how diverse the divisional environments were. The four divisions studied in this corporation accounted for 34% of its sales. They range from a large, highly profitable defense and aerospace facility to a lower performing operation which made durable goods sold in leisure markets.

Diverse Industrial Environments at Firm 1

DEFENSE (1:I)

Division 1:I was a large, highly profitable unit which developed and manufactured precision instrument systems and components used in the defense and aerospace industry. Most of its products were built to order on the basis of government contracts or contracts with other defense manufacturers. The single most important selling point for Division 1:I's products was their performance characteristics and reliability. Price was the next most important consideration. Division 1:I operated a single manufacturing facility which also housed its development laboratories, contract negotiation, and field engineering functions. At any one time this facility was working on between 300 and 500 active contracts; and in an average month it produced 250 different kinds of products, ranging from large, complex systems to tiny half-inch-square microcircuit modules.

Division management noted that advanced product development was a major competitive issue in its business. Approximately 40% of Division 1:I's sales consisted of products that were either new or represented fundamental modifications of items offered five years ago. Over the years Division 1:I had established a reputation for superior product performance and reliability that gave it a strong market position. At the same time, management had been able to maintain tight controls over costs, permitting the division to achieve reasonable earnings in a market which was increasingly dominated by fixed-price contracts.

Of the four divisions that were studied in Firm 1, this division faced the most dynamic and uncertain environment. Much of Division 1:I's product development capability depended on its ability to import and apply information from a rapidly developing body of scientific knowledge well ahead of its competitors. Customer requirements were complex, diverse, and also tended to change a good bit from year to year. At the same time, the uncertainties surrounding the patterns which defense spending might take made longer range market forecasting extremely difficult. Since the division's products were made to order, there was also considerable uncertainty surrounding the manufacturing function.

At the same time, the systems nature of Division 1:I's business required a high order of integration among all functions. Engineering and marketing had to work closely together both to anticipate and influence customer specifications and to develop bids for major contracts. Engineering and manufacturing had to be in constant contact regarding the design and actual fabrication of products as well as to insure that they could be properly installed at the customers' sites.

AUTOMOTIVE PARTS (1:II)

The environmental requirements faced by Division 1:II contrasted sharply with those of Division 1:I. This division was a large, five-plant operation which manufactured and sold a line of standardized (component) products to approximately a dozen automobile and truck manufacturers. Division 1:II's manufacturing operations were characterized by a high volume of output produced mainly through medium-and-large-batch technologies. Although this division held long-term contracts with its customers, the customers' volume requirements tended to fluctuate a good deal during any given year. Although Division 1:II was the largest independent producer of its line of products, there was intense competition for customer contracts; and profit margins were very slim. Major selling points in this industry were price and delivery.

Division management stated that the critical issues for 1:II were cost reduction and meeting customers' delivery requirements. The division spent only about 1% of its annual sales on product development, which was aimed mainly at product redesign for cost savings. Indeed, most engineering effort was focused on cost reduction through improved materials flow and new methods of manufacturing.

Compared with Division 1:I, Division 1:II faced rather stable environmental conditions. Most product changes were devised by the customer, and they were fairly infrequent. The marketing environment, although very competitive, was quite certain as to the basis of competition. During recent years Division 1:II's performance had been equal to or slightly above the mean performance of its competitors.

HEATING AND AIR CONDITIONING EQUIPMENT (1:III)

The third division in our sample manufactured a specialized line of heating and air conditioning equipment for commercial and residential use. Products were sold by a 40-man field organization to a large number of small independent distributors. Division 1:III was a relatively small unit which had been the original core of Firm 1 in the early 1950s. The market for its products was declining at a rate of 5% to 10% a year, and profits were under considerable pressure.

Merchandising was seen by division management as the critical element of success in its business. The technology involved in manufacturing was well-known and highly stable. Engineering efforts were devoted to devising more attractive coverings for existing equipment and developing simple products to be marketed through existing channels.

A new general manager had been brought in in 1967. He described his strategy as one of holding the line in existing products and forming an organization that could develop new products to be sold in different market segments from those in which Division 1:III had traditionally operated. At the time of this study his program was at a very early stage.

Compared with other divisions at Firm 1, Division 1:III faced very stable environmental conditions. Manufacturing and engineering were highly certain. Market conditions for existing products were moderately certain, being affected mainly by declining consumption rather than significant competitive activity.

Consumer Electrical Appliances (1:IV)

The final division in our sample at Firm 1 presented a yet different range of environmental issues. Division 1:IV manufactured a line of electrical appliances sold in consumer markets. Although Division 1:IV was a medium-sized division within Firm 1, it was a relatively small factor in a market dominated by eight large firms. While Division 1:IV's market was growing at a moderate rate, it was also characterized by enormous overcapacity and severe price competition. Additional competitive pressure was exerted on Division 1:IV's existing lines by a new line of products which this division as yet did not offer. Thus, Division 1:IV had experienced significant profit declines in recent years.

The main selling points for Division 1:IV's products were attractive design, price, and promotion and merchandising programs. The products were distributed to retailers through a wide range of channels, including direct sales, factory branches, independent wholesalers, and manufacturers' representatives. Marketing and distribution were the critical elements of success. However, product design and low manufacturing costs played an important secondary role.

A new general manager with extensive experience in consumer durables had recently been brought in. His approach was to achieve wider and more selective market penetration through product redesign, lower prices, and improved distribution. Considerable emphasis was placed on lower manufacturing and inventory costs, particularly through importing major subassemblies from Europe and Japan. This general manager noted that one critical problem faced by Division 1:IV was achieving a reasonable profit margin in an industry in which large competitors had significantly lower manufacturing costs. Work was also under way to introduce a new line which would be competitive with similar products already offered by major competitors.

As the foregoing discussion suggests, Division 1:IV was faced with considerable market uncertainty. At the same time, product redesign and new product development created moderate uncertainty for the engineering function. On the other hand, basic manufacturing methods were fairly stable and well known.

These brief profiles indicate that the four product divisions studied at Firm 1 faced very diverse environmental requirements. Although each of the four conglomerates in our study differed somewhat in their *degree* of diversity, the differing environmental demands faced by Firm 1's divisions are quite typical of what was found in the other firms.* These divisional profiles were based on interview data and company records; however, questionnaire data were also collected which permit us to quantitatively describe the environmental demands faced by the divisions in each firm.

The major subenvironments (i.e., Scientific-Engineering, Manufacturing, and Market) of each division were measured in terms of three major variables. First, division managers were asked to rate the amount of change which was occurring in each subenvironment. Second, these executives were asked to indicate how long it tended to take to learn how successful their efforts had been in each subenvironment. Taken together, these two measures—rate of change and time span of feedback—provide a rough measure of the uncertainty associated with each major segment of a division's industrial environment. Finally, a measure of the dominant segments of each division's environment was obtained by asking its managers to rate the degree to which efforts in each subenvironment contributed to the overall ability of the division to compete in its industry. By quantifying basic environmental requirements in this way we were able to summarize the unique issues faced by each division as well as making interdivisional and interfirm comparisons.

In order to get a clearer picture of what these measures involved let us return to the four divisions which were studied at Firm 1. Our measures

---

* The interested reader can find similar profiles and quantitative descriptions of the sample divisions at Firms 2, 3, and 4 in Appendix A.

TABLE II-6

Basic Environmental Requirements Faced by Four Divisions at Firm 1

Divisions	Environmental Requirements[a]		
	Rate of Change[b]	Time Span of Environmental Feedback[c]	Relative Importance of Subenvironment[d]
DEFENSE (1:I)			
Scientific-Engineering	5.9	4.6	1.2
Manufacturing	4.9	4.0	2.6
Market	5.1	3.5	2.2
AUTOMOTIVE PARTS (1:II)			
Scientific-Engineering	5.4	3.9	2.1
Manufacturing	3.8	3.1	1.2
Market	4.2	2.1	2.3
HEATING AND AIR CONDITIONING EQUIPMENT (1:III)			
Scientific-Engineering	3.1	3.9	2.0
Manufacturing	3.1	3.1	2.7
Market	4.4	2.7	1.3
CONSUMER ELECTRICAL APPLIANCES (1:IV)			
Scientific-Engineering	4.0	3.7	2.5
Manufacturing	3.6	2.7	2.3
Market	5.3	2.8	1.2

[a] Higher scores indicate a greater rate of environmental change, a longer time span of feedback, and less importance attributed to a subenvironment.

[b] Differences among divisions by subenvironment are significant at the following levels: Scientific (.01), Manufacturing (.10), Market (.05) (analysis of variance).

[c] Differences among divisions by subenvironment are significant at the following levels: Scientific (not significant), Manufacturing (.10), Market (.05) (analysis of variance).

[d] Differences among divisions by subenvironment are all significant at .01 level (analysis of variance).

(Table II-6) closely parallel the more qualitative profiles presented above. For example, relative to other divisions Division 1:I faced a high rate of environmental change and fairly long time spans of feedback in all parts of its environment. At the same time, the Scientific-Engineering part of the environment was seen as the most critical. In contrast, Division 1:III faced relatively certain conditions in most parts of its environment and placed major emphasis on its market subenvironment. Thus, these data provide further evidence of the environmental diversity which characterized Firm 1. Similar measures were used in the other three firms, and later in this chapter we will compare the diversity of these firms' divisional environments. First, however, it is important to consider the extent to which the 16 divisions we have studied in the four firms had developed distinctly different organizational patterns to cope with their particular industry environments.

Divisional Organizations

As noted in Chapter I, we expected the demands posed by different industry environments to lead to considerable differences in organizational arrangements and management orientations among divisions. The organizational patterns in each division were measured in the same way that we measured the organizational patterns of the headquarters units. The 16 divisions in the four research sites differed widely in formality of organizational practices and in interpersonal, time, and goal orientations of divisional executives (Table II-7). We also found wide differences among the overall goal

TABLE II-7

Differing Characteristics of Divisional Units:
Range of Differences Among 16 Divisions in Four Conglomerate Firms[a]

Formality of structure		17 – 24
Interpersonal orientations		84.2–102.2
Time orientations		2.3– 3.0
Goal orientations:		
Financial	1.68–2.29	
Marketing	1.67–2.31	
Manufacturing	1.86–2.45	
R&D/Engineering	1.78–2.56	

[a] Numbers are the highest and lowest scores on each attribute across the 16 divisions which were intensively studied. Higher scores indicate more formality of structure, more socially oriented interpersonal styles, longer time horizons, and *less* emphasis on various goal items.

sets of the 16 divisions (differences in ratings of the top five goals of these divisions were significant at the .001 level, Kruskal-Wallis one-way analysis of variance). Table II-8 illustrates the sorts of differences we found in the overall goals of divisions. These differences among divisions in goals, orientations, and practices occurred within each firm as well as across firms.

An important implication of these data is that as a division develops

TABLE II-8

Comparison of Overall Goal Sets[a] of Two Divisions in Firm 1

	Division 1:II Automotive Parts	Division 1:IV Consumer Electrical Appliances
OVERALL FINANCIAL GOALS		
Return on investment	1	11
% growth-profits	2	12
% growth-sales	4	3
Profit margin on sales	3	2
Absolute level of profits	5	10
Desired profit mix among product lines	17	5
Sales volume	6	1
OVERALL PRODUCT-MARKET GOALS		
Product diversification into related areas	12.5	14.5
Rate of new product introduction	9	18
Product diversification into unrelated areas	20	19
Geographic expansion of product sales	21	17
MAJOR OPERATING GOALS		
Market share	12.5	9
Customer relations	8	13
Product improvement	10	4
Cost reduction	7	6
Inventory control	15.5	7
Level of fixed costs	19	14.5
Plant expansion	18	20
OTHER GOALS		
Development and motivation of personnel	15.5	16
Divisional image	12.5	8
Maintenance of unique divisional skills	12.5	21

[a] Ranking of 21 goal items by executives in each division. Lower number indicates more important goal item.

organizational arrangements aimed at coping with the demands of its particular industry environment, these organizational arrangements and management orientations will very often be quite different from those of its sister divisions or its corporate headquarters unit. Stated another way, environmental diversity will tend to create interunit differentiation. This broad statement tells us little, however, about the *degree* to which each division and each firm had achieved a fit between its organizational patterns and the requirements of its environment. To explore this question we must take a slightly different look at the relationship between organizational patterns and environmental requirements.

The Issues of Organization-Environment Fit

Previous research by Lawrence and Lorsch[4] indicated that high performing, single-industry companies tended to achieve a higher degree of organization-environment fit than their less effective counterparts. The questions we wish to pursue are whether and in what ways organization-environment fit is associated with divisional and corporate-wide economic performance in these conglomerate firms.

Fit at the Divisional Level

To determine the degree of fit between a division and its industry environment we used the same approach as Lawrence and Lorsch.[5] Because this technique entailed collecting data on management orientations and organizational arrangements by major functional department (i.e., R&D/engineering, sales, and manufacturing) several levels down in each division, we decided to focus our efforts on two of the conglomerates. Firms 1 and 4 were selected for this additional data collection because they were roughly comparable in environmental diversity and also because they differed widely in overall corporate performance. Based on norms established from questionnaire results, comparisons were made between required and actual organizational patterns for each functional department in each division.*

Table II-9 reports the number of positive comparisons which we found between the attributes required by the environment and those actually present. Our basic finding was that the low performing divisions in Firm 4 had significantly fewer positive comparisons than the high performing divisions in either firm. Environmental fit for low performing divisions in Firm 1, however, was not significantly different from the fit achieved by high performing divisions in either firm. Although differences between the low performing pairs of divisions in the two firms were not statistically significant (.20 level), they were in the predicted direction.

These data indicate that Firm 1 was achieving a somewhat better organization-environment fit than Firm 4; and this better fit is associated with higher corporate performance. It should also be noted, however, that the major difference between the two firms was the lower fit achieved by low performing divisions at Firm 4. Why was Firm 4 experiencing this lack of fit in its low performing divisions? Was it simply that division manage-

---

* See Appendix B for a description of these norms and how comparisons were made between environmental requirements and organizational states.

TABLE II-9

Fit Between Environmental Requirements and Organizational Patterns in Two Conglomerate Firms: Number of Positive Comparisons[a]

Division	Divisional Performance[b]	Firm 1[c]	Firm 4[c]
I	Higher	10	9
II	Higher	7	7
III	Lower	6	4
IV	Lower	7	3

[a] Positive comparisons represent the number of attributes (structure, interpersonal, time, and goal orientations) for R&D/Engineering, Sales, and Production departments in each division which were consistent with the requirements of their respective subenvironments. Highest possible score for each division was 12 positive comparisons.

[b] Based on subjective ratings by corporate and divisional managers of sales, profit, and return on investment results over most recent five years. Differences in ratings between higher performing pairs of divisions and lower performing pairs at both firms are significant at .001 level (analysis of variance).

[c] Differences between low performing pair in Firm 4 and high performing pairs in Firms 1 and 4 are significant at .05 level (chi-square test). Other differences among high and low performing pairs are not significant.

ment was unaware of or unwilling to confront the realities of its environment? Was there anything about the interface between the corporate headquarters and the divisions at Firm 4 which contributed to this lower environmental fit? In order to pose at least partial answers to these questions we must return to the topic of environmental diversity and its relationship to corporate-divisional differentiation.

Diversity, Differentiation, and Corporate Performance

So far we have been primarily concerned with how corporate headquarters and divisional units develop organizational patterns to deal with the particular segment of the firm's overall environment with which they are concerned. In other words, we have focused on the mechanisms through which individual organizational units interface with their part of the firm's total environment. One important issue we have not yet explicitly addressed is the degree to which the firms in our sample were able to achieve a level of corporate-divisional differentiation which was consistent with the overall environmental conditions which they faced. Before turning to the evidence on this question, let us first review what we mean by corporate-divisional differentiation and why it is an important consideration.

We have argued that due to their differing organizational roles and environmental contacts, headquarters and divisional units could develop very different cognitive orientations and ways of organizing work. In fact, we found a number of consistent differences between headquarters units and divisions in the four firms. These differences were as follows:

(1) *Formality of structure.* Corporate headquarters units were much less formal in their structure than were the divisions. In other words, they tended to depend less on formal rules, review results less frequently, have fewer formally stated goals, and have wider spans of control.

(2) *Orientations toward time.* The corporate offices tended to have longer time horizons than their divisions.

(3) *Goal orientations.* Although concern for financial goals was high among both corporate and divisional managers, there was a much heavier emphasis placed on them at the corporate level. There was considerable differentiation among headquarters and divisional units in terms of the emphasis managers placed on nonfinancial goals. In three of the firms corporate executives indicated that they emphasized financial, marketing, manufacturing, and engineering/research goals (in that order) in evaluating plans. Division managers, however, ranked these same goals in a manner that was consistent with the dominant strategic issues posed by their particular industries. For example, managers in a defense division ranked research goals as the most important criterion in their decisions, whereas executives in a producers' durables division ranked manufacturing goals as more important.

(4) *Overall goal sets.* Corporate headquarters units and divisions also differed as to the relative emphasis placed on 21 common goal items. For instance, return on investment, growth, cost reduction, related diversification, and public image figured importantly in the corporate headquarters' goal sets. While divisional managers were highly concerned about return on investment and growth, they also emphasized other goals such as market share, management development, customer relations, and plant expansion, which were consistent with their particular environmental requirements.

(5) *Interpersonal orientations.* There were moderate differences between headquarters and divisional units in terms of interpersonal orientations measured along a task versus social continuum. However, these differences were not consistently in one direction.

Taken together, these five dimensions of differences between headquarters and divisional units are what we mean by corporate-divisional differentiation.

If a conglomerate firm is to maintain both headquarters orientations consistent with its corporate environment and divisional orientations con-

sistent with these units' particular industrial environments, then by definition it must develop and nurture a considerable degree of corporate-
divisional differentiation. We reasoned that, given the broad similarities in
headquarters environments among our four research sites, the greater the
diversity of the environments faced by each firm's divisions, the greater the
degree of corporate-divisional differentiation the firm would be required to
develop in order to deal effectively with its total environment. This hypothesized relationship between environmental diversity and required corporate-
divisional differentiation is schematically represented in Figure II-1.

FIGURE II-1

The Requirement for Corporate-Divisional Differentiation

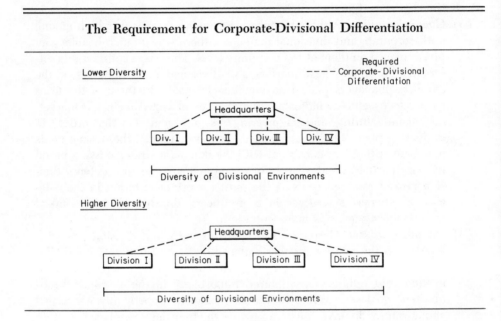

Two measures were devised to reflect the relative diversity of each firm.
First, on the basis of company records we counted the number of three-digit
Standard Industrial Categories* accounted for by the product lines of each
firm. Second, based on the questionnaire measures of environmental requirements discussed earlier in this chapter (i.e., rate of change, time span
of feedback, and relative emphasis) we constructed an index of environmental diversity for the four divisions which were intensively studied in
each firm. This index was designed in such a way as to reflect the degree
to which each major subenvironment of a division (i.e., market, scientific,
manufacturing) differed from the same subenvironments in its sister divi-

---

* Standard Industrial Categories have been established by the U.S. Bureau of the
Census for classifying all domestic establishments engaged in economic activities.

sions. Taken together these two measures provide a rough means of gauging the degree to which the four firms differed in their diversity. Corporate-divisional differentiation scores were computed on the basis of formality of structure; overall goal sets; and time, interpersonal, and goal orientations of managers. Average differentiation scores were obtained for each firm by summing the scores for the four corporate-divisional pairs and dividing by four.*

Turning first to the diversity scores, there was a close agreement between the number of SIC categories for each firm and our diversity index for the sample divisions (Table II-10). This suggests that our sampling pro-

TABLE II-10

Diversity, Differentiation, and Performance in Four Conglomerate Firms[a]

Firm	No. of SIC Categories	Firm Measures of Diversity Index of Environmental Diversity	Average Corporate-Divisional Differentiation[b]	Overall Corporate Performance
1	28 (4)	43 (4)	14.0	Higher
2	17 (2)	33 (2)	16.3	Higher
3	7 (1)	27 (1)	9.5	Lower
4	21 (3)	38 (3)	11.0	Lower

[a] Higher scores indicate greater diversity and greater differentiation. Numbers in parentheses are ranks. Corporate performance ratings are taken from Table II-1. (See Appendix B for a more detailed discussion of how these scores were computed.)
[b] For four sample divisions in each firm.

cedure was in fact representative of the overall diversity faced by each corporation. As our descriptions at the beginning of this chapter suggested, Firms 1 and 4 were more diverse than Firms 2 and 3. Firm 3 was the least diverse.

Now let us examine the degree to which each of the four firms were able to achieve a level of corporate-divisional differentiation consistent with their relative diversity. High performing Firms 1 and 2 had the highest levels of differentiation. Firm 1 seems to have achieved a level of differentiation which was broadly consistent with its environment's diversity. This conclusion is further supported by our previous finding that this company had achieved a better organization-environment fit at the division level than

---

* The procedures used to arrive at the index of environmental diversity and corporate-divisional differentiation scores are described in Appendix B.

Firm 4. Firm 2 appeared to have somewhat higher differentiation than its environment required; however, this condition did not appear to have an adverse effect on performance. Clearly, divisions at Firm 2 were not being pulled away from their environmental interface by too low a level of differentiation.

Both of the low performing corporations were characterized by lower differentiation. In the case of Firm 3 there is little evidence to support the conclusion that lower differentiation was creating problems for the company as a whole. This firm was the least diverse in our sample, and thus relatively low differentiation was consistent with its overall environmental conditions.

For Firm 4, however, there is considerable evidence that there were problems in achieving an appropriate level of differentiation. Although faced with fairly high diversity, this company exhibited rather low differentiation. We have already seen that Firm 4 was also encountering difficulties in achieving an adequate environmental-organization fit at the division level. It would appear, therefore, that Firm 4's organizational patterns tended to draw its divisions more toward the concerns of the corporate headquarters unit and away from the demands of their environments. Furthermore, this state of affairs was also related to lower corporate performance. Why this company was achieving differentiation which was lower than that required by its diversity is a very complex issue. However, we can begin to get a feel for the problem from the following comments of a high ranking divisional executive at Firm 4:

Corporate-divisional relationships all boil down to how much autonomy a business unit has. I feel that centralization and controls in this company are much too rigid. There should be more flexibility. Let me give you two examples.

For one thing, we have a bonus system which is based solely on profit relative to annual budget. This builds in tremendous conservatism in forecasting. Furthermore, managers are much more interested in how they are doing relative to a figure they established nearly a year before. In a rapidly changing business like ours that just isn't healthy. The whole thing creates a lot of gamesmanship at the division level—both when budgets are initially established and during the year when people are more worried about the paper system than what the business requires.

Capital budgeting raises the same issues when we're trying to decide whether to sell a project as an expansion or a cost reduction. On cost reduction the requirements are often so unrealistic you might as well not bother. When you really feel you need a project, you usually figure out a way to put the numbers in the boxes. . . . We have cash flow patterns that are very different from other divisions in this company, but corporate says, "Make your requests and budgets this way." And I know damned well that they don't see any difference between our business and a toy factory when they look at the figures.

By way of contrast, an executive at one of Firm 2's divisions which operated in the same broad industrial environment discussed corporate-divisional differentiation this way:

> We are very different from the other divisions at Firm 2. We operate in a very complex and changing market environment, and we have no standard product line as such. We're a custom shop and build most of our products to customer specifications. Thus, each year we're essentially making a different line of products. This is quite unlike the majority of divisions at Firm 2, which manufacture standardized products in considerable volume. The fact that we're so different from other divisions, however, has little effect on our relations with the corporate office. They pretty well know our overall capabilities. Over the years we've found that if we do our homework on a project and take it up to the corporate office, subject to their overall financial picture, we usually come home with their approval and support.

It would appear that Firm 4 was sacrificing differentiation to achieve tighter controls over its divisions. In essence divisions were finding it difficult to achieve a fit with the requirements of their environment because of headquarters procedures uniformly imposed upon them.

Our discussion of the relationship between diversity and corporate-divisional differentiation points to one of the major issues which conglomerate firms face in managing relationships between the company as a whole and its various parts: achieving a satisfactory organization-environment fit. The data suggest that there is a relationship between achieving a level of corporate-divisional differentiation which is consistent with environmental diversity and corporate performance. The appropriate level of differentiation allows the headquarters and divisions to deal effectively with their respective portions of the total environment.

At the same time, however, we might expect this differentiation to contribute to the problems of achieving integration around the issues of planning, budgeting, and resource allocation.* In other words, the greater the differences in viewpoints which corporate and divisional managers bring to a situation requiring a joint decision, the more difficult we would expect it to be for them to arrive at a mutually acceptable decision. Thus, while

---

* We expected to find the same basic antagonism between differentiation and integration that Lawrence and Lorsch reported in their earlier research, op cit., pp. 47–49.

managing differentiation may play a critical role in achieving effective divisional and corporate performance, it is only one side of the equation. The other side has to do with how diversified firms go about achieving integration and what approaches to this problem seem to be most effective. It is to this topic that we now turn our attention.

III

Achieving Effective Corporate-Divisional Relations

THIS and the next chapter compare and contrast the basic approaches which the four conglomerate firms used in managing corporate-divisional relationships. This chapter focuses on the basic patterns formed by these corporate-divisional relationships. In identifying these basic patterns we shall be concerned with three questions: To what degree was each firm able to nurture a level of corporate-divisional differentiation consistent with its environmental diversity and still achieve effective corporate-divisional integration around the issues of planning, budgeting, and resource allocation? In what ways were these organizational states interrelated with the broad economic risks posed by divisions and with corporate performance? What role did the organizational devices employed by the corporate headquarters seem to play in achieving appropriate patterns of differentiation and integration? In Chapter IV we shall identify several aspects of corporate-divisional decision-making processes which also seemed to facilitate the development of appropriate differentiation and integration.

Organizational Assumptions and Integrative Devices

We begin this discussion by examining the assumptions held by corporate officers in each firm about how corporate-divisional relations should be managed as well as the integrative devices employed to implement these assumptions about organization. By management's assumptions about organization we mean its views concerning (1) how the operating divisions should be constituted and (2) in what areas joint decision making between the headquarters and divisional management units should be required. Integrative devices are the formal structural and procedural mechanisms used to facilitate integration. Included in this definition are coordinating positions and committees, as well as planning, measurement, evaluation, and compensation systems.

Management Assumptions about Organization

The four firms differed very little with respect to how top managers thought about the scope of divisional activities. Divisions in each firm were self-contained in that they possessed all of the specialized facilities and personnel necessary to design, manufacture, and market their products. This self-containment also entailed very limited contacts among divisions. Although in certain instances men, materials, and ideas were transferred among divisions, these transfers were relatively unimportant to the overall operations of most divisions. While top management in the four firms expressed varying degrees of interest in stimulating interdivisional collaboration, they all agreed that it was first necessary to maintain a high degree of divisional self-containment so that these units were able to adapt successfully to the requirements of their specific industries and so that divisional management could be held responsible for profit performance. In line with these views about self-containment, each division possessed its own management group, headed by a general manager, which was responsible for the overall planning and control of the division.

Although the top management of these firms held similar views about how divisions should be constituted, they differed on the issue of how control over total profitability and funds flows should be maintained. To understand these differing views, let us look at each firm.

Firm 1's chairman described his company's approach to corporate-divisional relations as being aimed at maintaining an entrepreneurial atmosphere along with achieving effective financial control and stimulating improved planning and management development at the division level. In outlining Firm 1's concept of organization he stated:

> There are two key words as far as I'm concerned: "profit responsibility." We never tell a division that it is autonomous. Rather, we give them considerable latitude in operations and then hold them responsible for agreed-upon profit contributions to the corporation. I guess we're really talking about a sort of limited autonomy. We have only a 21-page procedure manual which details divisional reporting requirements and the things that they must secure corporate approval on—e.g., capital and major expense items, executive raises, legal matters—things of this sort. Of course, we want the division

people to take the initiative and come to us with their ideas, but we also recognize the necessity of maintaining controls in these areas.

Above and beyond financial controls we also impact on division operations in certain ways. Through the group vice presidents and our newly formed operations analysis staff we try to help them do a better job of planning and controlling operations. We underscore our concern by requiring a monthly operations report and by making forecasting accuracy one of the criteria in our bonus system. We also informally push the divisions to show improvement in their management development efforts.

While I've talked a lot about controls and approvals, let me emphasize that we're heavily committed to maintaining an entrepreneurial atmosphere in this company. Our whole philosophy revolves around where profit responsibility is placed—the divisional general manager. I don't want anyone in this organization to have any doubts that the general manager is boss. This is where the entrepreneurial atmosphere begins. For this reason we try to keep our corporate staff at a minimum, avoid setting down a lot of unnecessary policies and procedures, and focus our efforts on open and rapid communication among division general managers, group vice presidents, and members of the president's office here. Along this line we depend heavily on informal, face-to-face contacts.

As the foregoing suggests, Firm 1's management felt that the major area of joint decision making between the corporate office and its divisions should be restricted to financial planning—e.g., divisional profit contributions and approval of capital and major expense projects. At the same time, however, corporate officers also felt that they should take a limited but active interest in divisional operations and in management development.

Firm 2 was similar in many ways to Firm 1 in its concept of organization. Firm 2's management stressed the need for short lines of communication and rapid decision making between corporate and divisional levels. Similarly, its corporate staff was confined mainly to providing specialized services in industrial relations, legal matters, and the design of information systems plus auditing and interpreting the divisions' financial reports. However, Firm 2's top management focused almost entirely on financial planning and indicated less concern with directly monitoring divisional operations than did corporate executives at Firm 1. Firm 2's president described his company's assumptions about organization as follows:

In this company we lean toward complete decentralization. Every division has responsibility for its own growth and profitability. We want these divisions to think of themselves as separate companies. Within the constraints posed by our financial resources, we let the divisions move in the directions they want as long as they can produce a reasonable level of earnings. Of course, we want them to dream and move into exciting new areas; but the onus is on them and we're not going to force them.

When you're as diversified as we are, you must have substantial decentralization. With our dissimilar product lines, trying to quarterback decisions at the corporate level would be extremely hazardous. Not long ago, some people recommended that we establish staff functions at the corporate level in areas such as engineering, purchasing, and manufacturing. I think this misses a lot of things. First, our divisions are so diverse that I fail to see how these centralized functions could play a constructive role. Second, and perhaps more important, as you begin building a large corporate staff, you suddenly find that the division manager is no longer the sole determinant of his own profitability. So, then, how can you judge his performance?

Our philosophy of decentralization has been a major element in our acquisition program. On acquiring new firms we seldom make any major management changes for at least two years. We try to buy well-run operations, and we stick with the current management. We simply don't have the personnel for dissecting sick companies and producing dazzling turnarounds. Furthermore, we think that this kind of surgery gives an outside image of acting indiscriminately. I might add that we have had a history of earnings growth for all the major companies we have acquired.

All this talk about decentralization comes down to getting competent top level division managers and giving them plenty of room to maneuver. If they get into trouble, you try to go along with them for a while and help where you can. If you find it increasingly difficult to believe that they will produce what they promise, then perhaps it's time to get a new manager. If this doesn't work, then we'd consider disposing of the division.

Firm 3's approach to corporate-divisional relations provides a marked contrast to the emphasis in the first two companies on limited corporate involvement, divisional profit responsibility, and short lines of communication. Its corporate management stressed the need for fairly intense involvement in both financial and business planning. In addition to the staff functions found in Firms 1 and 2, Firm 3 also had corporate staff units for manufacturing and marketing. Firm 3's president outlined his company's approach in this way:

Our diversification program has resulted in three important corporate resources that we are committed to utilizing in the most effective way we can. First, we have a larger pool of funds, which allows individual divisions to take higher risks than they could take if they were separate companies. Second, our range of operations provides an opportunity for division managers to avoid re-inventing the wheel; the divisions can learn from one another's successes and mistakes. Finally, we encompass a wide enough area of opportunities to attract and hold highly competent people at the top levels of division management. We at the corporate level are committed to active leadership in employing these resources rather than simply following a holding company philosophy.

We use three major devices for delegating authority. First, in our business planning exercise we aim at achieving an in-depth understanding by the entire corporate management group of what our divisions plan to do. Even though our staff is fairly small, Firm 3's size allows us to get intimately involved in a division's plan. Second, our annual budgeting system focuses on financial measures and a statement of the major objectives to be achieved by each division during the year. We use this system to judge how well our division managers are doing, and it is tied directly to our incentive compensation system. Finally, we use a 3-month rolling forecast. Here, we're looking at the short range, and we want to make sure that the divisions reconcile their labor and material inputs with sales outputs. Taken together, these three devices allow us to secure an understanding of a commitment against objectives which in turn allows divisional autonomy.

Firm 3's concept of organization entailed a very different role for the corporate staff from that in the first two firms. One staff vice president characterized this role:

We don't just sit back as experts on call. This is an active staff which tends to search out and develop solutions to problems with divisional people. The chairman believes that the staff has clear responsibility. We are responsible for things that go sour in our particular functional areas. We are expected to know whether the right things are being done, and it's up to us to see that they get done. We often work on a project basis and are evaluated on our ability to complete these projects. Since we have no line authority over the divisions, we must depend on our ability to sell division managers on a course of action or in highly problematic cases we have recourse to the president.

Much like Firm 3, Firm 4 stressed the need for an intimate understanding of divisional operations. Rather than depending on functional staff units at the corporate level, however, Firm 4's corporate management saw the control system as the means to achieving the in-depth understanding which it felt was required. Firm 4's chairman outlined his approach as follows:

There are many pitfalls in managing conglomerates, and over the years I suspect we've fallen into many of them. At this point, however, we have a control-oriented system of management which permits both early warning about problems and a means of responding.

The biggest issue of all is to decide whether you are going to be an op-

erating or a holding company. Are you going to be decentralized or centralized? If you have too much centralization, you destroy the profit center
manager's creativity. But if you have too much decentralization, you're in
trouble before you know it. I feel that we have struck a definite balance between these two extremes.

Our control system is the guts of our approach—i.e., flexible budgeting.
We know every element of cost by divisions and by groups. It is the corporate staff's responsibility to get in and ask what we need to know, e.g.,
fixed costs in relation to margin, variable costs, profit mix, plans about pricing. The division manager, in turn, is evaluated against these elements. This
leads to questions about his authority, and these limits are worked out as a
result of the control system.

Controls are the eyes and ears of corporate management as well as aids
to the field. However, I've found that most corporate staff people are gen-
eralists, not specialists, and that it's difficult for them to work effectively with
people in the field. So we use the staff for gathering information, and then we
form special task forces of line managers to actually intervene in problem
areas. These task force members are borrowed from their current jobs in the
various divisions. They are paid extra salary for this "doctoring" role, and they
go out to the field as recognized specialists in their areas.

I insist that we are an operating company and that we must know as
much as we can humanly know about division operations. To accomplish this
end we also have operating management committees for each group, which
consist of corporate and group officers and which meet every two months.
In these meetings group and division people present their plans and results.
They have to explain every single discrepancy on the cost control charts.
Plus they must give "make good" reports on capital programs. If they don't
make good, we respond by putting more and more controls on their capital
decisions.

There was thus a marked contrast between the organizational assumptions of corporate executives in Firms 1 and 2 and those of corporate executives in Firms 3 and 4. In the first two firms corporate officers felt that they
should carefully limit their direct involvement in divisional operations. The
division was the profit center, and corporate management should depend
upon the budgetary systems, performance evaluation mechanisms, and
direct, personal contacts to maintain the necessary control. In Firms 3 and
4, however, corporate management leaned further in the direction of more
active and short-range corporate monitoring of and involvement in division
operations. These managers also assumed that the most effective way to
achieve this corporate involvement was through complex reporting procedures and an active corporate staff. With these contrasts in mind let us
examine the integrative devices corporate managers used to implement their
organizational assumptions.

Implementing Organizational Assumptions: Integrative Devices

At first glance, it appears that the types of integrative devices found at each of the firms were roughly similar (Table III-1). These broad similarities seem to have been dictated by the general requirements of achieving integration around issues of planning, control, and resource allocation in a diverse setting. Each firm placed considerable emphasis on four types of procedures: five-year plans, budgets, project approval mechanisms, and

TABLE III-1

Major Integrative Devices in Four Conglomerate Firms

	Firm 1	Firm 2	Firm 3	Firm 4
PAPER SYSTEMS				
Five-year planning system	X*	X	X*	X
Annual budgeting system	X*	X*	X*	X*
Quarterly budget forecast			X*	
Monthly budget review	X	X*	X*	X*
Monthly operating reports	X*			
Approval system for major capital and expense items	X*	X*	X*	X*
Cash management system	X	X	X*	X
Formal goal-setting system performance evaluation and incentive compensation system	X*	X*	X*	X*
Approval system for hiring, replacement, and salary changes of key division personnel	X*			
INTEGRATIVE POSITIONS				
Group vice presidents	X*	X*	X*	X*
Divisional "specialists" in corporate controller's office				X
COMMITTEES, TASK FORCES, AND FORMAL MEETINGS				
Annual meetings between corporate and division general managers	X	X		
Group management committees	X			X*
Technical evaluation board for capital projects				X*
Permanent cross-divisional committees			X	
Line management task forces				X*
Ad hoc cross-divisional meetings for functional managers	X	X		
DIRECT MANAGERIAL CONTACT	X*	X*	X*	X*

X—indicates presence of devices in each firm.
*—indicates those devices that managers believed played the most significant role in corporate-divisional relations.
SOURCE: Interview data and company records.

formal performance evaluations which were directly tied to incentive compensation. Direct managerial contact and group vice president positions also played a role in achieving integration; however, much of the face-to-face and telephone contact which these two approaches entailed focused on issues highlighted by the planning, budgeting, and project approval systems.

This broad pattern of integrative devices employed to achieve corporate-divisional integration contrasts sharply with the devices which Lawrence and Lorsch report were used to achieve integration among functional departments within a single business organization.[1] For example, they found that in addition to paper systems, direct contact, and the organizational hierarchy, organizations requiring high differentiation in the plastics and foods industries also employed more elaborate integrative mechanisms such as integrative departments and permanent cross-functional teams at three levels of management. It appears that the pooled interdependence which characterized corporate-divisional relations in conglomerate firms required less elaborate integrative devices than the more complex interdependence required in interdepartmental relations within a single-product business.[2] At the same time, the conglomerate firms in this study applied their integrative devices to the divisions on a one-to-one basis, while the integrative devices described by Lawrence and Lorsch were designed to facilitate each-to-every communications. This too seems consistent with the requirements of pooled interdependence. Thus, in general, the four conglomerate firms had developed integrative devices which were broadly consistent with the pooled interdependence which they sought to manage.

Nevertheless, a closer look at the integrative devices in these four firms indicates that they differed considerably in the *relative emphasis placed on particular devices* and *in the ways these devices were employed*. These differences were consistent with the different organizational assumptions held by each firm's top management. For example, corporate managers at Firms 1 and 2 placed major emphasis on fewer integrative devices than their counterparts at Firms 3 and 4 (Table III-1). This difference reflects the more elaborate formal planning and budgeting procedures at Firms 3 and 4. Corporate managers at Firms 1 and 2 stressed fairly informal corporate-divisional relations and the use of a bare minimum of formal systems. Managers at Firms 3 and 4, on the other hand, placed considerable stock in formal systems and their value in improving decision making.

Looking in more detail at the integrative devices employed by the four firms, we get a clearer picture of how the firms differed. Table III-2 summarizes three major aspects of each organization: (1) the size and broad structure of the headquarters unit, (2) the formal planning and control devices which were the primary sources of information for joint decision mak-

TABLE III-2

Formal Integrative Devices in Four Conglomerate Firms

	Firm 1	Firm 2	Firm 3	Firm 4
ORGANIZATIONAL STRUCTURE				
1. Total management and professional employees at corporate office	17	20	25	230
2. Number of major staff units	4	2	5	9
3. Number of group vice presidents	5	2	1	9
FORMAL PLANNING AND CONTROL DEVICES				
1. Number of major devices used by corporate management[a]	8	6	10	9
2. Character of review of divisional plans, requests, and results	informal, selective	informal, selective	formal, detailed	formal, detailed
3. Number of corporate executives involved in approval of plans and requests	7	6	11	14
MEASUREMENT AND REWARD SYSTEMS				
1. Criteria	overall sales, profit, ROI, accuracy to forecast, and working capital expense control	overall sales profit, ROI	sales and profit overall and by product line *plus* market share, rate of new product development, cost reduction, employee relations	overall profit, ROI
2. Time span of evaluation	annual and 3-year trend	annual and 3-year trend	annual	annual

[a] Derived from Table III-1.

SOURCE: Interview data and company records.

ing, and (3) the measurement and reward systems used by top management to evaluate and motivate division managers. These data clearly indicate that Firm 3's and Firm 4's assumptions about organization led to much more complex, formalized, and detailed integrative mechanisms than did those of Firms 1 and 2. In terms of headquarters staffing, for instance, Firm 4 had 230 management and professional employees, over half of whom were in the controller's office. The remainder worked in eight other functional areas —e.g., treasurer, planning and acquisitions, legal, research, and group services. By way of contrast, Firm 2 employed only 20 management personnel at the corporate level who worked in two broad areas—finance and administrative services. Although Firm 3 did not boast the large staff that Firm 4 did, its staff was organized into five specialized areas and became heavily involved on a formal basis in planning and budgeting.

Planning and control devices in Firms 1 and 2 tended to be less complex and more informally applied. At Firms 3 and 4, however, there were more complex devices which were formally applied and which involved considerably more corporate executives in approvals. By the same token, measurement and reward systems at Firms 3 and 4 focused on annual results relative to forecast. At Firms 1 and 2 these same devices focused on improvement over historical results relative to other divisions, and were applied both to yearly and longer-run results. Thus, measurements and rewards at Firms 3 and 4 tended to place more stringent and shorter term requirements on divisional managers.

Another way of understanding the differences among these firms is to compare how planning and budgeting was actually carried out in Firms 2 and 3.* Firm 3 placed a good deal more weight on five-year planning systems than Firm 2. It also employed a formal system for setting divisional objectives and focused a good deal of attention on quarterly budget revisions. Formally established divisional objectives provided the underlying assumptions for both plans and budgets at Firm 3, and these objectives were also directly linked to the incentive compensation which division top management received each year. Firm 2, however, had explicitly chosen to separate planning and budgeting from its performance appraisal and incentive compensation system and, also, to take a longer view. In this firm division management was judged on its historical improvement relative to other divisions on several financial indices.

The planning and budgeting process at Firm 3 also entailed a more detailed review by corporate managers and, as we have indicated, involved a larger group of executives. Each year division management at Firm 3 gave

---

* A similar contrast was present between Firms 1 and 4.

a full-day, formal presentation of both their five-year plans and annual budgets to corporate officers and key members of their corporate staff. Detailed written versions of plans and budgets containing financial figures plus a somewhat standardized set of supporting data were then transmitted to the corporate office for further scrutiny. The corporate staff reviewed and commented on specific aspects of these documents before they were sent on to the president and chairman. This process of review and approval involved a considerable amount of contact between all members of the headquarters unit and divisional managers one and two levels below the general manager.

In contrast, at Firm 2, division managements prepared five-year plans and annual budgets which were transmitted directly to the corporate office. While a standard set of accounting, funds flow, and backlog data was required of all divisions, other supporting data ranged from short two-page statements to elaborate fifty-page descriptions of divisional markets and programs depending on each general manager's particular style. These documents were reviewed by seven high-ranking corporate officers, and their final form was negotiated directly between each division general manager and the president and/or group vice presidents. Thus, we see that planning and budgeting procedures at Firm 2 were a good deal less complex and involved much less widespread contact between headquarters and divisional personnel.

At this point, let us summarize our analysis concerning organizational assumptions and integrative devices. By comparing corporate managements' assumptions about organizations, we have seen that the top management of Firms 3 and 4 felt a need for more integrative effort between the corporate headquarters and its divisions than did their counterparts in Firms 1 and 2. Corporate managers at Firms 3 and 4 believed there should be more intensive involvement by the corporate office in the planning, budgeting, and resource allocation process and that corporate involvement should also encompass a broader set of issues (i.e., it should go considerably beyond budgeting financial results and should often focus on specific policy and operating issues faced by the divisions). Our examination of integrative devices indicates that these organizational assumptions were more than mere theorizing about how to approach corporate-divisional relations. Indeed, each of the firms developed a set of integrative devices consistent with the organizational assumptions of its top management. Thus, Firms 3 and 4 had a set of integrative devices requiring more management effort in dealing with relations between corporate and divisional managements.

Having considered the basic approaches to managing corporate-divisional relations followed by each firm, the next step is to determine how well these approaches worked in practice. To what degree was each firm able to achieve both effective corporate-divisional integration and the necessary differentiation? What were the key factors associated with developing these organizational states?

Basic Patterns of Corporate-Divisional Relations

The first step in answering this question will be to examine the pattern of corporate-divisional relations which was achieved by each of the 16 corporate-divisional pairs in all four companies. This is necessary both because we need to develop an understanding of corporate-divisional relationships in general and because, as noted above, each corporate headquarters unit dealt with its divisions on a one-to-one basis. Thus, although each firm had developed a basic approach to achieving corporate-divisional integration, we expected that its management might apply this approach differently among divisions depending on four factors.

First, based on the earlier work of Lawrence and Lorsch, we expected that the higher the differentiation between the headquarters and a division the more difficult it would be to achieve integration.[3] In Chapter II we found that each of the four firms required considerable corporate-divisional differentiation in order to deal with environmental diversity; and the greater this diversity, the greater these differences in managerial orientations and ways of organizing work needed to be. We reasoned that this required differentiation between corporate and divisional management units would increase the difficulty of the integrative task.

A second factor that we also expected to affect the difficulty of the integrative task was the degree to which a division posed an economic risk for the corporation as a whole. In essence, corporate-divisional integration centers around achieving levels of total corporate performance that permit the firm to meet the expectations of its financial subenvironment plus managing the internal flow of funds among all divisions. The greater the extent to which any single division—either through declining profit performance or heavy and/or unexpected funding requirements—posed an economic risk for the corporation, the more problematic we would expect corporate-divisional integration to be for that unit. Higher economic risks could invite increased corporate review of and intervention in divisional activities; and this would tend to produce a greater potential for conflict.

While expecting that differentiation and the degree of economic risk to the corporate whole would be inversely related to the difficulties of achieving integration, we also expected that management might attempt to overcome these factors in two ways. For one thing, management could devote more or less time to achieving integration. Second, it could work to improve the quality of the decision-making processes between the head-quarters and the various divisions. In the following pages we shall focus on the relationships among integrative effort, differentiation, the economic risk to the corporation, and the quality of corporate-divisional integration which

TABLE III-3

Summary Measures of Corporate-Divisional Relationships in Four Conglomerate Firms[a]

Corporate-Divisional Relationships	Differentiation	Integration[b]	Effort Devoted to Integration	Divisional Performance[c]
1:I	13	4.11	38.5	Higher
1:II	11	4.84	95.4	Higher
1:III	14	4.40	39.0	Lower
1:IV	18	3.42	49.2	Lower
2:I	19	5.14	31.9	Higher
2:II	16	4.87	47.8	Higher
2:III	18	3.56	121.0	Lower
2:IV	12	3.75	65.3	Lower
3:I	13	4.94	127.5	Higher
3:II	9	4.33	134.7	Higher
3:III	8	4.89	140.0	Lower
3:IV	8	2.62	189.4	Lower
4:I	10	4.38	95.3	Higher
4:II	10	3.96	107.0	Higher
4:III	9	3.54	147.8	Lower
4:IV	15	2.59	107.0	Lower

[a] Higher scores indicate greater differentiation, more effective integration, and more effort devoted to achieving integration. Relationships among these measures are as follows:

Spearman's coefficient of rank correlation between divisional performance and integration for 16 corporate-divisional relationships is .62 (significant at .01 level). Coefficient of correlation between differentiation and integrative effort is −.70 (significant at .01 level). All other rank correlations for the 16 relationships are not significant.

Coefficient of correlation between differentiation and integration for 8 high performing divisions is .70 (significant at .05 level) and for 8 low performing divisions −.35 (not significant).

Coefficients of correlation between integration and integrative effort for Firms 2 and 3 are −1.0 and −.80, respectively ($p > .03$, combined tests of significance).

Coefficients of correlation between divisional performance and integrative effort for Firms 2 and 3 are −.80 and −1.0 respectively ($p > .03$, combined tests of significance).

[b] Difference between integration scores for high performing and low performing pairs of divisions are significant at .001 level (analysis of variance) in Firms 2, 3, and 4. Differences between these pairs in Firm 1 are significant at .05 level.

[c] Based on managers' ratings of performance. Differences between numeric scores for high and low performing pairs of divisions are significant at .001 level in each firm.

was actually achieved. The quality of the decision-making process will be discussed in Chapter IV.

Table III-3 summarizes the relationships that existed between the 16 corporate-divisional pairs in all four firms along four dimensions: *differentiation scores*, indicating the degree to which corporate and division managers diverge in their goals, working styles, and orientations; *integration scores*, which are based on corporate and division managers' ratings of the quality of collaboration actually achieved between the headquarters unit and the managers' respective divisions; *the amount of effort devoted to achieving integration*, which was determined by asking both corporate and division managers to rate the amount of their working time over the past year which had been devoted to particular corporate-divisional relationships; and *divisional performance ratings*,* which are subjective estimates by corporate and division managers of sales, profit, and return on investment results over the most recent five years.**

Differentiation, Integration, and Divisional Performance

As expected, there was a strong positive correlation between divisional performance and integration (.62, significant at the .01 level).† The higher a division's performance, the more effective the integration it tended to achieve with its headquarters unit. At the same time, however, there was no simple negative relationship between differentiation and integration across all 16 of the corporate-divisional pairs.

Since divisional performance was so closely tied to corporate-divisional integration and we were predicting that both differentiation and divisional performance would affect the difficulty of achieving integration, we reasoned that perhaps differentiation would have a different effect in high and low performing divisional situations. The data do support this conclusion. There was a strong positive correlation (.70, significant at the .05 level)

---

* To simplify our discussion we will focus on divisional performance as one indicator of degree of economic risk for the corporate whole. Later in our discussion we will introduce contingency for financial planning as the second aspect of economic risk for the corporation.

** Rankings based on these performance estimates coincided with rankings based on actual figures at Firm 2. Actual figures were not available for divisions at the other firms. A more complete description of methods used to collect and analyze data on differentiation, integration, integrative effort, and divisional performance may be found in Appendix B.

† It should be stressed that in this discussion and those in subsequent chapters we are not implying any direction of causality from a single set of correlational data. Rather inferences about causation are drawn from interview data, our total understanding of the situation in these firms, and the total pattern of correlations.

between differentiation and integration for the eight high performing divisions in the four companies. The higher performing the division, the more we found both high differentiation and high integration. The low performing divisions presented a very different picture. A negative, but not significant ($-.35$), correlation was found between differentiation and integration in the eight low performing corporate-divisional pairs. Even though this relationship was not significant, a closer look at the data suggests that differentiation is negatively related to the problems of achieving integration in low performing situations. Looking at the two low performing divisions in each firm (Divisions III and IV) we find that, in three of the four firms, the more highly differentiated of the two low performers has lower integration. (In the other firm [3] both pairs had the *same* level of differentiation.) One reason that the correlation coefficient does not strongly reflect this negative relationship is that Firms 1 and 2 tended to have much higher corporate-divisional differentiation among all pairs than Firms 3 and 4, and these systematic interfirm differences obscured the underlying relationship. Thus, in the low performing corporate-divisional pairs the more differentiation the poorer the integration, while in the high performing pairs there was a tendency to achieve both high differentiation and high integration.

One conclusion we can draw from this contrast between high and low performing pairs is that each corporate-divisional pair is to a certain extent an independent subsystem within its larger organizational system. Given the pooled interdependence which characterized these conglomerate firms, each division is dealt with on a one-to-one basis by the headquarters unit and therefore each corporate-divisional pair develops certain unique characteristics, even though it is also influenced by the firm's general approach to corporate-divisional relationships. However, we are still left with the problem of determining why this contrast occurs. At least three related explanations seem possible. First, high divisional performance may reduce the complexity of the integrative task, making it easier to achieve both differentiation and integration. Since divisional performance is high relative to other divisions in the same firm, corporate management may allow a relatively free rein for the division so that it can maintain the necessary differentiation while still obtaining effective integration. A second explanation may be that corporate and division managers actually devote more time and effort to achieving integration in the high performing pairs and as a result they achieve high integration in spite of the high differentiation present. The third explanation is that the managers in high performing pairs could actually be doing a more effective job of managing the decision processes between the two units, so they can more effectively exchange information and resolve conflicts and thus achieve both differentiation and integration. Obviously, this third possibility may operate concurrently with either of the other two. Before we consider it, we have to test whether either of the first two possibilities explains why the higher performing pairs achieved higher differentiation and integration. Was it a result of the favorable performance records of these higher performing divisions or because management devoted more integrative effort to these pairs?

Factors Affecting Integrative Effort

From Table III-3 we can very quickly see that more integrative effort is not necessarily associated with more effective integration. In fact, in Firms 2 and 3 there was a significant negative correlation between integrative effort and integration; the more effort, the lower the integration. These data plus interview data suggest that the managers in these two firms were simply devoting effort to those situations where divisional performance, and hence integration, was a problem. Since our data were collected at only one point in time, we have no means of determining whether this increased effort would ultimately pay off in improved integration and performance. Nevertheless, our evidence does not provide any support for the explanation that more integrative effort tends to lead to both high differentiation and integration in the higher performing situations. Rather, the data for two of the firms would suggest that the alternative explanation might be true. It appears that because high performance reduces the economic risk the division poses for the corporation, there is less difficulty in achieving integration; therefore, management devotes less effort to the relationship. The data on the relationship between integrative effort and the differentiation offer even stronger support for this explanation. There is a strong negative correlation ($-.70$, significant at .01 level) between integrative effort and differentiation for the 16 pairs. That is, the *more* differentiated the pair, the *less* the integrative effort that was being devoted to it. One explanation for this finding is that low integrative effort may provide a division the autonomy needed to achieve the differentiation necessary to operate in its particular environment. This interpretation of our findings fits closely with what we learned from interviews with high ranking corporate and divisional managers. One division general manager at Firm 3 summarized this view as follows:

A high profit contribution gives you a considerable "go to hell factor" in dealing with the headquarters people. But when you're losing, it's a whole new ball game. In fact, I'd say that the amount of supervision that a division receives is directly proportional to the trouble it's in. If you're meeting most of your objectives, and don't surprise corporate management too much, you're in fine shape. If you start missing budgets or request large amounts of capital, then you've got to spend more time explaining your situation. When things get really bad, they send the staff in to make a study, whether you've invited them or not. All this is as it should be. We division managers are always great proponents of "splendid independence." But when a person is in trouble, he often loses his objectivity; and he needs somebody else to ask the right questions.

This manager is also making another important point—"the squeaky wheel gets the most oil." If you have problems, devote effort to them. This view was underscored by the president of Firm 3:

Involvement on the part of the headquarters unit depends on who is having the biggest problems. We try to concentrate our shots rather than spreading our efforts equally among the nine divisions. We try to set priorities in allocating headquarters' attention. Thus, we tend to get involved in those divisions where we think our efforts will have the greatest impact on ROI. This means that high performing divisions run fairly independently.

These comments further support the notion that higher performing pairs achieve both high differentiation and high integration, because there are fewer problems in the relationship and corporate management does not become so heavily involved in divisional affairs. Another way to test whether the data support this explanation is to examine the relationship between integrative effort and divisional performance. If the explanation was true, we would expect a negative relationship between these two variables. Such a relationship did exist at a significant level ($p > .03$) in two of the firms and the relationship was in the same direction in the other firms (Table III-3). These data plus those on the relationship between integration and integrative effort and between differentiation and integrative effort point so strongly in the direction of this explanation that we wish to explore it further.

Interviews with managers suggested that another factor which should be taken into account in understanding integrative effort was the degree of contingency which a division posed for corporate financial planning. For example, one high-ranking officer at one of Firm 1's smaller, low performing divisions noted:

Our relations with the corporate office have changed quite a bit over the years. We used to be viewed as more important in the past because Firm 1 was much smaller and we were a larger percentage of the total operation. Today, despite our performance problems, we're not big enough to hurt their earnings picture. At one time two of the executive vice presidents used to come out here quite frequently to meet with us, and I used to send them copies of all my major reports. This doesn't happen as much anymore. In many ways I feel they're much less interested in us and the problems we're trying to solve now.

Thus, we reasoned that the economic risk which a division posed for the corporate whole was a function of both its relative performance and the degree of contingency it posed for financial planning. Taken together, we felt that these two factors might enable us to better understand differences in the relative effort devoted to achieving integration among the 16 pairs and thus shed more light on how the high performers achieved differentiation and integration. In order to gauge the degree of contingency posed for financial planning, three aspects of the financial positions of product divisions in each firm were examined: first, relative size (the larger the division, the greater the impact shifts in its earnings could have on financial planning); second, funding requirements (the greater the level of capital funds requested and received by a division, the greater the contingency it would pose); and finally, forecasted versus actual earnings (to the degree that a division's actual earnings fell below forecast, it would present problems for financial planning). Table III-4 ranks divisions at each firm in terms of size in sales, amount of capital required, and downside deviations from earnings forecasts. While these measures obviously overlap, total rankings provide a rough indication of the contingency posed for corporate financial planning by each division. It is noteworthy that these total rankings differ a good bit from divisional performance rankings (in each firm Division I is the highest performer, Division IV the lowest).

Table III-5 shows the relationship between integrative effort and both contingency for financial planning and divisional performance. In Firms 3 and 4 there was a strong correlation between the contingency for financial planning posed by a division and integrative effort. Divisions which posed higher contingencies were characterized by greater integrative effort. This same correlation did not hold in Firms 1 and 2. However, by computing a multiple correlation coefficient, we were able to analyze the combined effect of divisional performance and contingency for financial planning on the effort devoted to achieving integration. The data indicate that in three out of four firms knowing these two factors would allow one to accurately predict the relative amount of effort devoted to integration (Table III-5). Only in the case of Firm 1 did these basic relationships not hold. We have no way of determining precisely why Firm 1 deviated from the basic patterns we found in the other three research sites. One explanation might be that there were other important factors affecting integrative effort which our measures did not pick up. For example, the division in Firm 1 which was character-

TABLE III-4

Contingency for Financial Planning Posed by Divisions in Each Conglomerate Firm[a]

Division	Level of Sales[b]	Level of Capital Requirements[c]	Downside Deviations from Earnings Forecasts[d]	Rank Total[e]
1:I	4	3	2	9 (4)
1:II	3	4	1	8 (3)
1:III	1	2	3	6 (1)
1:IV	2	1	4	7 (2)
2:I	2	2	1	5 (1)
2:II	4	3	3	10 (4)
2:III	3	4	2	9 (3)
2:IV	1	1	4	6 (2)
3:I	1	1	1	3 (1)
3:II	3	3	2	8 (3)
3:III	2	2	3	7 (2)
3:IV	4	4	4	12 (4)
4:I	2	2	1	5 (1)
4:II	3	3	3	9 (3)
4:III	4	4	2	10 (4)
4:IV	1	1	4	6 (2)

[a] All numbers are rank orders within each firm; higher numbers indicate higher sales, capital requirements, earnings deviations, and contingency. All rankings are based on company accounting records. Because of the confidential nature of much of these data, however, rankings were established by interviewing corporate controllers and thus interfirm comparisons could not be made.

[b] 1967 sales.

[c] Average of actual capital expenditures for most recent five years plus forecasts of requirements for three years in the future.

[d] Model deviation during most recent five years.

[e] Ranking of total in parentheses.

ized by the highest integrative effort had been acquired only two years previous to the study. It is possible that stable relationships between this unit and the corporate office were still in the process of being established. Nevertheless, our basic findings do suggest that the greater the economic risk to the corporation posed by contingency for financial planning and divisional performance, the more integrative effort management devotes to a relationship. Since we have already seen that effort was negatively correlated with differentiation, we can now understand more clearly how higher performing divisions tended to achieve higher differentiation. The ability of these

TABLE III-5

Factors Related to Integrative Effort in Four Conglomerate Firms[a]

	Firm 1	Firm 2	Firm 3	Firm 4
CORRELATION BETWEEN INTEGRATIVE EFFORT AND:				
Contingency for financial planning	−.20	.40	.80[b]	.95[b]
Divisional performance	−.40	−.80[c]	−1.0[c]	−.32
Multiple correlation among factors[d]	.41	.80	1.0	.97

[a] Numbers are Spearman rank difference correlation coefficients for four sample divisions in each firm.

[b] Correlations found at Firms 3 and 4 are significant at .05 level (combined tests of significance).

[c] Correlations at Firms 2 and 3 are significant at .03 level (combined tests of significance).

[d] Where integrative effort is treated as dependent variable and contingency for financial planning and divisional performance as independent variables.

higher performing divisions to achieve higher integration despite higher differentiation also seemed to be connected with the lower economic risk they posed for the corporation.

Corporate-Divisional Relations in Operation

Having considered the correlations among differentiation, integration, integrative effort, and the economic risk which a division poses for the corporation, we are now in a position to hypothesize how corporate-divisional relationships generally seemed to operate in the four conglomerates. Figure III-1 summarizes the basic patterns of corporate-divisional relationships which we have discussed in the preceding pages and relates these findings to our conclusions in Chapter II regarding organization-environment fit. The signs of the relationships (i.e., positive or negative) are simply based on the correlations already reported. Assumptions regarding the direction of causation among the variables are based on our interviews with corporate and divisional executives. The pattern which emerges from these findings suggests what might be termed a "cyclical" explanation of corporate-divisional relationships.

In essence, Figure III-1 describes a set of mutual causal relationships, some of which counteract one another and some of which feed back upon themselves.[4] The counteracting relationships among differentiation, integration, and integrative effort provide one explanation of how high performing divisions tend to achieve both high differentiation and high integration.

FIGURE III-1

Basic Pattern of Corporate-Divisional Relationships

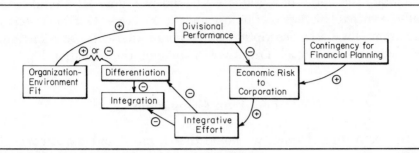

LEGEND: Arrow indicates hypothesized direction of influence.
Plus (+) indicates positive relationship.
Minus (−) indicates negative relationship.
Plus or minus (+ or −) and wavy line indicate contingent relationship.

That is to say, higher divisional performance poses a lower economic risk for the corporation, which leads to a decrease in the effort which managers devote to that corporate-divisional relationship. A decrease in integrative effort seems to permit higher differentiation but also tends to be associated with higher integration. Although higher differentiation creates problems for achieving integration, these problems appear to be counteracted by the positive effect that lower integrative effort has on integration. This same counteracting effect would seem to explain why applying more integrative effort to low performing divisions does not necessarily result in higher integration even though it does tend to reduce differentiation.

The other important aspect of Figure III-1 is the feedback loop from Divisional Performance to Economic Risk, Integrative Effort, Differentiation, Fit, and back to Divisional Performance. Let's trace through these relationships for a low performing division. Lower performance creates a greater risk, leading to higher integrative effort and to lower differentiation. At this point in the loop we encounter a contingent relationship which is supported by our findings in Chapter II. *If* lower corporate-divisional differentiation leads to a higher fit between the division and its particular environment, this in turn leads to higher divisional performance and the cycle will tend to come to rest. If, however, lower corporate-divisional differentiation leads to a lower fit, nothing but more problems seem to result. In other words, if lower differentiation leads to lower fit, lower performance results, which then leads to more integrative effort. Thus, the feedback loop can continue to amplify the very pressures which make it increasingly more difficult for the division to cope with its performance problems.

At this point in our discussion we have considered only the bare essentials necessary to understand corporate-divisional relationships in general. In the remainder of this chapter and in Chapters IV and V we shall continue to elaborate the initial description contained in Figure III-1 until we have a full-blown explanation of this organizational issue. Our next step is to move from this basic description of corporate-divisional relations and to assess how successful each firm was in managing these relationships.

Four-Firm Comparison

Earlier in this chapter, we noted that Firms 3 and 4 had concepts of organization and integrative devices which entailed more detailed reviews and greater involvement in divisional operations than those found in Firms 1 and 2. For this reason we expected that, by and large, managers in Firms 3 and 4 would devote considerably more effort to achieving integration. Table III-6 indicates that corporate and division managers in Firms 3 and 4 did in fact devote more time to integration. In all of the firms, division man-

TABLE III-6

Effort Devoted to Achieving Integration by Corporate and Division Managers in Four Conglomerate Firms[a]

	Firm 1				Firm 2		
	Corp. Mgt.	Div. Mgt.	Total		Corp. Mgt.	Div. Mgt.	Total
Division							
I	19.5	19.0	38.5		12.4	19.5	31.9
II	29.4	66.0	95.4		27.8	20.0	47.8
III	18.0	21.0	39.0		25.0	96.0	121.0
IV	14.2	35.0	49.2		25.3	40.0	65.3
Total	81.1	141.0	222.1		90.5	175.5	266.0

	Firm 3				Firm 4		
	Corp. Mgt.	Div. Mgt.	Total		Corp. Mgt.	Div. Mgt.	Total
Division							
I	38.5	89.0	127.5		20.3	75.0	95.3
II	52.7	82.0	134.7		34.0	73.0	107.0
III	70.0	70.0	140.0		32.8	115.0	147.8
IV	104.4	85.0	189.4		72.0	35.0	107.0
Total	265.6	326.0	591.6		159.1	298.0	457.1

[a] Numbers are a summation of all managers' time devoted to corporate-divisional relationships during the most recent year. Higher scores indicate greater integrative effort.

agers devoted more time to achieving integration than their corporate counterparts; however, we see a tendency toward higher integrative effort on the
part of division managers at Firms 3 and 4. It is also noteworthy that corporate managers in each of the four firms allocated their time among divisions in very different ways. In Firms 1 and 2 corporate managers tended in
most cases to devote the same level of effort to each division.* In Firms 3
and 4, however, corporate managers tended to devote somewhat more effort
to low performing divisions.

The time allocations of corporate and division managers in each firm
appear to be consistent with the organization concepts and integrative devices reported earlier. Firms 1 and 2 had an approach which dictated fairly
low corporate-divisional involvement with all divisions, although in Firm 2
low performing divisions were evidently required to spend a good deal more
time supporting their plans and requests. By way of contrast, the organization concepts and integrative devices of Firms 3 and 4 required all divisions
to devote a fairly high level of effort to supplying information about their
plans and operations. At the same time, the corporate management in these
two firms devoted more effort to reviewing divisional plans and budgets and
even conducting their own studies of divisional operations. How did all this
affect the overall functioning of the four firms?

From Chapter II we know that Firms 1 and 4 were characterized by
somewhat higher environmental diversity than Firm 2 and considerably
more diversity than Firm 3. High performing Firms 1 and 2 and low performing Firm 3 seemed to have achieved a degree of corporate-divisional
differentiation which was consistent with the diversity of their total environments, but low performing Firm 4 had achieved less differentiation than its
environment required. The measure of differentiation at that stage of our
analysis was the average differentiation of the four corporate-divisional pairs
studied in each firm. We now want to introduce an estimated measure of
total firm differentiation which takes account of not only the average corporate-divisional differentiation, but also the number of divisions in each
firm. This seems necessary, because the amount of integrative effort which
is appropriate in a given organization could be affected not only by the
average degree of differentiation in corporate-divisional pairs, but also by
the number of such corporate-divisional pairs in each firm. On the assumption, which is supported by the data in Chapter II, that our sample divisions
are representative of the diversity in each firm's total environment we have

---

* There are two exceptions to this statement. Division 2:I, a low contingency, high
performing division, received minimal attention. Also, Division 1:II, a newly acquired,
high contingency division with a relatively high record of performance, received somewhat more attention.

computed total differentiation scores by multiplying the average corporate-divisional differentiation found in the sample divisions in each firm by the total number of divisions in that firm. The overall integration scores used are the mean ratings by corporate managers of *all* major divisions weighted by the divisions' ranks in total sales. Scores for overall integrative effort are the mean percentages of time during the past year devoted to corporate-divisional relations by the corporate office only.*

The data point to the conclusion that Firms 1 and 2 had developed organizational systems that were functioning more effectively than those developed by Firms 3 and 4 (Table III-7). Despite the fact that Firms 1

TABLE III-7

Diversity, Organizational States, and Corporate Performance in Four Conglomerate Firms

Firm	Environ- mental Diversity	Average Differ- entiation Scores	Number of Divisions	Estimate of Overall Differ- entiation[a]	Overall Integra- tion[b]	Overall Effort Devoted to Integration[c]	Corporate Perform- ance
1	Higher	14.0	34	476	4.86	26.5	Higher
2	Lower	16.3	17	272	4.23	27.7	Higher
3	Lower	9.5	9	86	3.77	33.9	Lower
4	Higher	11.0	21	231	3.88	30.7	Lower

[a] Higher scores indicate higher total differentiation. Numbers are average differentiation scores multiplied by total number of divisions in each firm.

[b] Higher scores indicate more effective integration. Numbers are mean ratings by corporate managers for all major divisions, weighted to reflect the size of the respective divisions.

[c] Numbers are the mean percentages of time during the last year devoted to corporate-divisional relations by the headquarters unit. Higher numbers indicate more time devoted to achieving integration.

and 2 had obtained higher corporate-divisional differentiation, they were also achieving higher overall integration. These two firms, consistent with their managers' assumptions about corporate-divisional relationships, were also devoting less effort to achieving integration.** These patterns in Firms 1 and 2 were associated with a higher record of performance.

---

* See Appendix B for a more complete description of how these scores were computed.

** Overall integrative effort scores in Figure III-7 are for the corporate unit only and probably understate the overall differences among firms. From Figure III-6 we know that both corporate and division managers in Firms 1 and 2 tended to devote considerably less effort to integration than their counterparts at Firms 3 and 4.

Although both Firms 1 and 2 were functioning more effectively on several counts, it should be noted that the broad relationship between corporate performance and organizational states formed a somewhat different pattern in each firm. Firm 1 seems to have achieved an excellent balance between the need for control and the need for divisional autonomy. Not only was it achieving high integration in the face of considerable differentiation, but it also had a degree of corporate-divisional differentiation which fit the diversity of its environment. Firm 2 was perhaps more differentiated than its environment required, but it was also achieving effective integration in the face of high differentiation. This pattern is consistent with Firm 2's concept of "leaning toward complete decentralization," discussed early in this chapter. It appears that Firm 2 was still able to achieve effective control over earnings and funds flows even though it permitted a high level of divisional autonomy.

By way of contrast, Firm 3 was devoting considerable effort to integration but achieving much lower integration than either Firm 1 or Firm 2. Firm 3's integrative effort did not, however, seem to be adversely affecting its divisions' fit with their environments. Indeed, Firm 3 had a level of total corporate-divisional differentiation which was broadly consistent with its somewhat lower degree of environmental diversity. Firm 4, on the other hand, seemed to be encountering problems both in achieving corporate-divisional integration and in managing the interfaces with its environments. This company had a level of corporate-divisional differentiation which was considerably lower than its diversity would suggest was needed. Despite the relatively high effort which Firm 4 devoted to integration, it was also achieving lower integration than Firms 1 and 2; and it also appears that this company's integrative efforts were having adverse effects on environmental fit.

This discussion of overall organizational states in each firm lends further support to our cyclical explanation of corporate-divisional relationships. Indeed, it would appear at first glance that the particular states which characterized each firm were merely a cumulation of the states achieved by its individual corporate-divisional pairs. At the same time, however, it seems that two broader factors—overall corporate performance and the organizational assumptions and integrative devices of the total corporate system—exert an influence in their own right. Figure III-2 points to the role that these corporate-wide factors seemed to play in each firm. First, this diagram suggests that top management's assumptions and choice of integrative devices tend to have an impact on integrative effort which is more or less independent of the economic risk posed by a particular division. Thus, in Firms 1 and 2, which had less elaborate integrative devices, we found lower integrative effort and both higher differentiation and integration for all divisions. Just the opposite seemed to be occurring in Firms 3 and 4.

FIGURE III-2

Pattern of Corporate-Divisional Relationships within the Context of the Total Firm

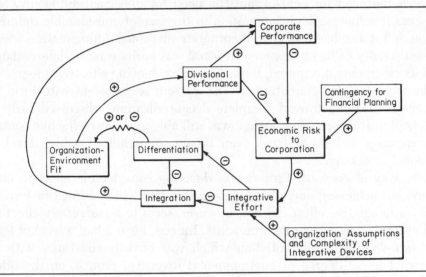

LEGEND: Arrow indicates hypothesized direction of influence.
Plus (+) indicates positive relationship.
Minus (−) indicates negative relationship.
Plus or minus (+ or −) and wavy line indicate contingent relationship.

Figure III-2 also points to the *interrelationship* between organizational states and corporate performance. A combination of sufficient differentiation to permit divisions to achieve a fit with their industry environments and sufficient corporate-divisional integration to permit the firm to manage the planning, budgeting, and resource allocation process was associated with higher corporate performance in Firms 1 and 2.

On the other hand, the lower corporate performance of Firms 3 and 4 seemed to create unique pressures in its own right. That is, it raised the economic risk that any of the divisions posed for the corporate whole, thus leading to yet higher levels of integrative effort, lower differentiation, and lower integration. This feedback effect represents an important elaboration of our argument because it suggests that lower corporate performance is not simply an effect of the patterns we are describing. It can also be one of the causes of these patterns.

This explanation does not point to an abdication of corporate control in favor of divisional autonomy. Neither does it suggest that lower corporate performance must of necessity lead to a self-defeating cycle. The important issue is to achieve a balance between the autonomy required by the divisions and the control required by the corporate whole. The allocation of integrative effort in a manner consistent with achieving appropriate corporate-divisional differentiation, high integration, and the necessary organization-environment fit at the division level contributes to achieving this balance. But we must also consider how executives manage decision making between the headquarters unit and the divisions. This is the topic of the next chapter.

IV

Managing Corporate-Divisional Decision Making

IN THIS chapter we focus on the role that each firm's decision-making processes seemed to play in its ability to achieve appropriate patterns of differentiation and integration. By decision-making processes we mean the recurrent patterns formed by the ways corporate and division managers exchange information, resolve conflicts, and make joint decisions. As we begin to identify salient characteristics of each firm's decision-making processes, we shall be concerned with several questions. Did the high performing firms and divisions tend to develop more effective decision-making processes? What impact did each firm's organizational assumptions and integrative devices seem to have on corporate-divisional decision-making patterns? How did all of these factors contribute to achieving appropriate corporate-divisional differentiation and integration in light of the particular environmental requirements faced by each firm?

Before launching into a discussion of the findings it is necessary to review the setting in which corporate-divisional decision making was taking place and to outline the set of indicators we have chosen to capture important aspects of the decision-making process.

Decision-Making Processes in the Four Conglomerates

As we have seen in previous chapters, corporate-divisional relationships in the four conglomerates were characterized by pooled interdependence. More specifically, the product divisions were relatively self-contained; joint decision making was required between individual divisions and the corporate headquarters; and this decision making focused mainly on the issues of planning, control over profit contribution, and allocation of resources.

The key decision makers in the planning, control, and allocation processes in each firm were members of the headquarters unit (corporate officers and their staff), the group vice presidents, and the division general managers. Although managers at lower levels in the divisions were the ultimate source of information about the requirements of their divisions' industrial environments, it was the top three echelons in each firm which faced the task of reconciling divisional plans and requests with corporate-wide goals and financial capabilities. In other words, it was their task to insure that adequate information was brought together about both corporate and divisional goals and requirements, that conflicts which arose between these goals and requirements were somehow resolved, and that final decisions around plans and budgets were reached in a timely fashion.

In Chapter III we identified three factors which could increase the difficulty of the integrative task faced by these managers. A division could pose a higher economic risk for its corporation through low performance and/or a high contingency for financial planning. Low corporate performance could contribute to perceptions of high economic risk in its own right. Finally, higher differentiation between a division and the corporate headquarters could raise the potential for conflict, particularly if it existed in a corporate-divisional relationship which was also viewed as posing a high economic risk for the corporation. There were two other factors which we have not specifically addressed in this study but which clearly affected the difficulty of the integrative task in these conglomerate firms. One was the wide geographic separation of the headquarters and divisional units; the other was the general tendency of divisional management units to seek a high degree of autonomy, or discretion.[1] Since each of these five factors as well as a combination of them can contribute to misunderstandings and outright conflicts which, in turn, can impair the quality of a firm's planning, budgeting, and resource allocation decisions, there is a clear need for maintaining a high *quality of information flows* and devising *effective means of managing conflicts* between the headquarters and divisional units.

This discussion of corporate-divisional decision-making processes implies a view of management decision making in large organizations which we wish to state explicitly before we proceed. We view managerial decision making as a social process in which conflicting viewpoints and information about market, technical, and economic issues are brought together and discussed until a decision is reached. While many popular writers seem to assume that top management reaches decisions while sitting at a large desk in splendid isolation or simply through the use of formal decision techniques, the data which follow clearly suggest that decision making at the upper levels of a large firm is a complex process of exchanging information and resolving conflicts.

Determinants of Effective Decision Making

In discussing the factors which contribute to effective decision making, we shall first examine two aspects of information flows between divisions and headquarters—managers' perceptions of the quality of information flows in both directions and the rapidity with which the corporate headquarters responds to divisional requests. The higher the quality of information flows and the more rapid the corporate response to divisional requests, the more effective we would expect the decision-making process to be.

We shall also examine certain factors which contribute to effective conflict management. Lawrence and Lorsch[2] found that such factors as the orientations of persons in integrating roles, the distribution of influence over decisions requiring joint action, and the mode of behavior used to resolve conflicts, were important determinants of whether a single business organization was effectively resolving interdepartmental conflict. Certain of these factors, e.g., the mode of behavior used to resolve conflict and the intermediate orientation of persons in integrating positions, were important regardless of environmental requirements. But others, most notably the distribution of influence, both hierarchically and laterally, varied depending upon environmental requirements. While we used these findings as the basis for our examination of conflict management in conglomerate firms, we reasoned that the ways in which they would operate might be somewhat different in this setting.

In the remainder of this chapter we shall present data collected about seven partial determinants of effective decision making (1) by comparing the extent to which each of the four firms met each determinant and (2) by determining the correlation of each factor and all seven factors with effective integration for the 16 corporate-divisional relationships which were intensively studied.

Although for purposes of discussion each of the seven determinants will be presented separately, we are not so much concerned with how well a particular corporate-divisional relationship or a firm met any particular determinant as we are with the extent to which each firm met the entire set of determinants. As we shall see, it is the total pattern of these factors which seemed to be connected with how well the corporate-divisional decision process was managed.

Quality of Information Exchange

The first of the factors is the quality of information or communication between the corporate headquarters and its divisions. As has been suggested, if conflicts are to be resolved and sound decisions reached, a prime requisite is that information about both divisional and corporate needs be considered.

We were initially predicting that the quality of information in both directions from the corporate headquarters to the divisions and vice versa would be related to effective decision making and ultimately integration. In fact, we did find a significant (.01) correlation between the rank order of the integration scores for the 16 corporate-divisional pairs and the rank order of both the quality of upward information and the quality of downward information. However, when the data are arranged on a total firm basis, it is the quality of downward communication which seems to be the more critical determinant of effective decision making (Table IV-1). The two high performing firms were obtaining significantly more effective downward information flows than the lower performing firms. In terms of upward communication Firm 3 was achieving significantly more effective communication than the two high performing firms. Our interview data, however, did not indicate any particular problems in the upward communication of information in the other three firms. The situation seemed to be that Firm 3 was obtaining an unusually high quality of upward flow of information because of its complex control and reporting procedures (which we have described in Chapter III). These more complex integrative devices were highly effective in channeling information upward in Firm 3, but apparently did little in either Firm 3 or Firm 4 to foster a flow of information from corporate headquarters to the divisions. Thus a lack of downward information flow was certainly a problem in these low performing firms. For example, a division executive in Firm 3 noted:

> Capital allocation procedures here are not satisfactory. You submit a project and they [the corporate office] cut it or whatever they feel like. I don't think their approach is very effective, and it's not very well thought through. The corporate people really take a rather short-term view of things. There are no longer-term commitments so that we know what we can do.
> . . . Don't get me wrong, we've ultimately gotten approval on almost everything we've needed. But it simply takes too long; they want to go over every nit-picking detail with us. One of the problems is that I haven't any idea what the corporate goals are. I'd really like to know. Frankly, it looks to me as though very little planning takes place at the corporate level.

TABLE IV-1

**Overall Quality of Information Received by Corporate and Divisional
Management Units in Four Conglomerate Firms[a]**

| Division | Quality and Quantity of Information Received | |
	Upward Flow (from Division)[b]	Downward Flow (from Corporate)[c]
1:I	3.0	2.9
1:II	2.8	2.8
1:III	1.9	2.8
1:IV	2.1	2.1
2:I	3.0	3.5
2:II	2.5	3.2
2:III	2.1	2.4
2:IV	1.4	2.7
3:I	3.1	3.0
3:II	3.1	2.4
3:III	3.0	2.3
3:IV	2.5	2.2
4:I	2.9	2.9
4:II	2.1	1.9
4:III	2.5	2.8
4:IV	1.6	1.6

[a] Higher numbers indicate higher quality of information. Upward flows are mean ratings by corporate managers of quality of information received from each division; downward flows are mean ratings by managers in each division.

[b] Difference between Firms 1 and 2 and Firm 3 is significant at .001 level (analysis of variance). Difference between Firms 1 and 2 and Firm 4 is not significant.

[c] Difference between Firms 1 and 2 and Firms 3 and 4 is significant at .05 level (analysis of variance).

In contrast, a division executive at Firm 2 spoke about the importance of sound downward communication in his firm:

The corporate people keep us well informed on interest rates, runs on funds, and the like. I simply don't ask for things that I'd be turned down on or that would be unnecessarily delayed. It's sort of a "court-martial" theory of capital budgeting; few people come to trial in the army unless they are guilty. Similarly, few projects come up for approval in this company unless they stand a good chance of acceptance.

These data suggest that Firms 1 and 2 seemed to be maintaining flows of information which were more consistent with the requirements for effective decision making than were Firms 3 and 4. Their organizational approaches, with less reliance on complex and formal procedures, seemed to foster a higher quality information flow downward, but also presented no problems with regard to the upward flow of information.

Rapidity of Corporate Response to Divisional Requests

A second factor related to effective decision making in these firms is the rapidity with which the corporate headquarters responded to divisional requests for funds or assistance. The more rapidly the corporate headquarters reacted to such requests, the more quickly information was transmitted and the more rapidly the decision process could proceed. This factor correlated significantly with integration ($p > .01$) for the 16 pairs of relationships. It also discriminated between the high performing firms and the less effective ones (Table IV-2). These data suggest that the more complex

TABLE IV-2

Rapidity of Corporate Headquarters in Responding to
Divisional Requests in Four Conglomerate Firms[a]

Division	Rating
1:I	3.3
1:II	3.0
1:III	2.9
1:IV	2.6
2:I	3.3
2:II	3.5
2:III	2.2
2:IV	2.8
3:I	2.7
3:II	2.3
3:III	2.8
3:IV	2.3
4:I	2.7
4:II	2.3
4:III	2.9
4:IV	1.8

[a] Higher numbers indicate greater rapidity in responding to requests. Scores are mean ratings by managers in each division. Difference between Firms 1 and 2 and Firms 3 and 4 is significant at .01 level (analysis of variance).

integrative mechanisms in Firms 3 and 4 did not help corporate management in these firms respond more rapidly to divisional requests. From the viewpoint of division managers the emphasis on direct contact and less complex integrative devices in Firms 1 and 2 seemed to lead to more rapid responses from the headquarters. As one of the division managers in Firm 2 put it:

> This corporation has a practical line operator's viewpoint. There is a small staff and we [general managers] have a direct line to the president and group vice president. If I feel the staff is sitting on things, I'll go around them and top management will accept this approach. This may not be the textbook approach to lines of command, but it allows us to move fast when we need to.

We can also speculate that the corporate managers in these higher performing firms were getting selective data which helped them to identify problem situations as they arose, whereas managers in Firms 3 and 4 may actually have been inundated by the information provided by their more complex integrative devices.

So far the two factors discussed pertain broadly to the flow of information between the headquarters and divisional units. But, even if the information flows are sound, the executives who are expected to reach decisions will be faced with conflicts which must be constructively managed. We now turn to the factors which pertain more directly to the management of conflict.

Perceived Characteristics of Corporate Performance Evaluation Scheme

The first of these factors is the perceptions executives had of the reward scheme utilized in their firm. As noted in Chapter III, while each corporate-divisional relationship takes on certain unique characteristics, such factors as corporate rewards are common to all divisions. The way executives perceive these rewards can have an important impact on their behavior in resolving conflict, causing them to give balanced attention to corporate and divisional requirements, or directing their attention entirely to one set of needs or the other. Similarly, such perceptions can focus attention on short-term versus long-term issues. In this way, these rewards can affect the orientations of managers in both corporate and divisional units. If the effect of these rewards is to pull division managers away from their particular environments, on the one hand, or to increase the level of conflict between them and corporate executives, on the other, it complicates the problems of conflict management. These reward schemes help to define the rules by which the game of conflict management is played, and it is important that they direct attention to the actual requirements of each division and that they help to develop consensus between divisional and corporate executives about what constitutes satisfactory performance for each division.

Two variables were used to measure managers' perceptions of the reward system used in each firm:

(1) *The extent of agreement between corporate and divisional executives about the relative emphasis placed on particular reward criteria*—This provided a measure of the extent to which corporate and divisional executives had common expectations about what sorts of divisional results would be rewarded. To the degree that these expectations diverge, we would expect the reward system to produce continuing conflicts between headquarters and divisional units.

(2) *The balance between short-run and long-run performance criteria as perceived by division managers*—This was interpreted as a measure of the extent to which division managers felt encouraged to focus on the time frame appropriate to their particular environment. Since divisions were diverse in their required time orientations, a balance in these two considerations would suggest that divisional executives would feel rewarded for focusing on the time perspective relevant to their division's problems. If division managers felt they were evaluated in this way, the evaluation system would at least not increase the level of conflict between corporate and divisional units.

The data from the four firms indicate that high performing Firm 2 met these requirements to a greater extent than the other firms, while high performing Firm 1 met them to a moderate extent (Table IV-3).* While all four firms had high agreement between corporate and divisional executives regarding the emphasis placed on particular performance criteria, the low performing firms had not achieved as much of a balance between long-run and short-run criteria. In the low performing firms divisional executives apparently felt more short-term pressures from the evaluation system and this often created tension between the performance criteria established by corporate management and longer-term demands in some divisional environments. The perceived emphasis on short-term criteria in these low performing firms is not surprising, since the integrative devices in these firms did in

---

* Since these data represent a comparison of the four firms as total systems, it was not possible to develop a correlation for the 16 corporate-divisional pairs.

TABLE IV-3

Perceived Characteristics of Corporate Performance Evaluation Systems in Four Conglomerate Firms[a]

Characteristic	Firm 1	Firm 2	Firm 3	Firm 4
(1) Agreement between corporate and divisional executives concerning relative emphasis placed on criteria (Kendall coefficient of concordance)[b]	.78	1.04	.75	.86
(2) Balance between long-run and short-run performance criteria (raw difference score)	1.91	.95	2.79	2.53

[a] Higher scores indicate higher agreement *but* less long-run/short-run balance. See Appendix B for a discussion of how these statistics were computed.

[b] Coefficients of concordance for Firms 1, 3, and 4 are significant at the .01 level. Coefficient for Firm 2 is significant at the .001 level.

fact emphasize shorter-term performance. This provides additional evidence of how the selection of integrative devices can impact on the decision-making process.

Intermediate Position of General Managers and Group Vice Presidents

The next factor which we felt might be a determinant of how effectively conflict was managed was the orientations of division general managers and the group vice presidents. Lawrence and Lorsch had found that persons in integrating roles who were effective in resolving conflict tended to have time, goal, and interpersonal orientations which were intermediate between those of the units they were trying to integrate.[3] We reasoned that persons acting as integrators at the corporate-divisional interface would also be more effective if they had developed time, goal, and interpersonal orientations which were intermediate between those of headquarters and divisional units which they sought to link.

The two positions in all four firms which had formal responsibility for linking corporate and divisional concerns were the division general managers and the group vice presidents, where such positions had been established. In comparing the four firms, we found that in three of the four firms these executives did tend to have intermediate orientations in at least two of the three orientations measured (time, goal, and interpersonal [Table IV-4]). Only in Firm 4 were such balanced orientations not present to a considerable extent. What appeared to happen as a result was that managers

TABLE IV-4

Balanced Orientations of Integrating Positions in Four Conglomerate Firms[a]

Firm	No. of integrating positions which were intermediate on 2 or more dimensions
1	5 out of 8
2	4 out of 6
3	5 out of 6
4	2 out of 7

[a] Since each firm differed in the number of executives who occupied integrating positions, scores indicate the number of executives who had achieved intermediate position relative to the total number of integrating positions. See Appendix B for a description of how intermediate orientations were determined.

in these integrating roles encountered difficulties in resolving conflicts among themselves and with other corporate and divisional executives. Because they did not share in many of the orientations of members of one or the other units, they tended to have only part of the information involved in any decision, and thus often did not fully comprehend the issues as the other party saw them. Also, they were often seen as allied with one unit or the other; and thus their involvement in the decision-making process was viewed with some mistrust.

It appears that this problem was closely tied to the selection of integrative devices at Firm 4 and particularly the reward scheme. A corporate executive discussed this problem:

One of the problems with our incentive scheme is that it gives no incentive for group and division executives to look to and prepare for the future. There's a tendency to forego expenditures which should be made this year, so they'll look good. . . . You would think divsion general managers would be more long-term oriented because they are looking ahead to vice president or headquarters jobs. But the general manager is solely compensated on his division's annual results. This makes him provincial.

By way of contrast, a group executive at Firm 1 who scored as intermediate in all three orientations described his role as

. . . conducting continuing discussions with headquarters and division managers concerning how to plan our business so as to make the most effective use of our overall resources. The divisions often tend to be more risk prone than the corporate office. They have an anxiety to get going and often want to run before their thesis is really demonstrated. My job centers around insuring that we select alternatives which are both consistent with our organization and skills and will produce a satisfactory return. It comes down to achieving a balance between the short run and the long run, and I assure you there is no simple formula for this.

In committing capital to specific projects we work from the top down and the bottom up. The divisions are developing their requirements and we are determining what we can and should spend. I work from both sides with the divisions and try to help them in the interface.

While lack of intermediate orientations seemed to cause difficulties in Firm 4, it was not a problem in the other firms. However, the importance of balanced orientations for group vice presidents and especially general managers is reinforced by the next conflict management factor we examined —influence over divisional policies attributed to the various managerial levels.

Distribution of Influence over Divisional Policies

We reasoned that an important determinant of whether conflicts were effectively resolved would be the extent to which divisional general managers and group vice presidents had relatively high influence over divisional policies. The general manager, especially if he had an intermediate orientation, would be in the best position to contribute to decisions which shaped divisional policies so that they met the environmental issues facing the division as well as overall corporate requirements. He would have available and would understand information both about divisional environmental conditions and about the corporate environment.

In three of the four firms the division general manager did have the highest level of influence over divisional policies (Figure IV-1). Firm 4 was the only exception. In this firm the division general managers had significantly less influence than their counterparts in the other firms and significantly less influence than their group vice presidents. Coupled with the lack of balanced orientation at these levels, this, as we shall see shortly, reduced the division unit's voice in corporate-divisional decisions.

In the other three firms the second most important level in influencing divisional policy was the group vice president. This is also consistent with our initial prediction. Since these group executives were expected to link their division with the corporate headquarters, they had a great deal of

FIGURE IV-1

Influence Over Divisional Policies Attributed to Four Major Organizational Levels in Four Conglomerate Firms[a]

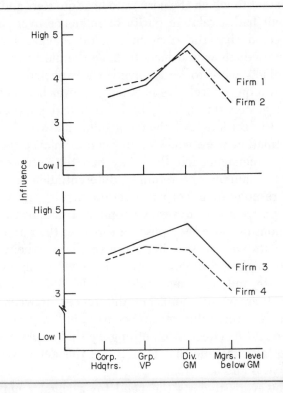

[a] Scores represent overall mean for four divisions in each firm, based on ratings by corporate and division managers for each of the divisions. Differences among levels in each firm are significant at .01 level (analysis of variance). Difference between general managers' influence in Firm 4 versus general managers' influence in other firms is significant at .001 level. See Appendix B for questionnaire items and how scores were computed.

relevant information about corporate requirements. By having an important voice in the decisions which made up divisional policy, they could make certain that corporate information was also taken into account. These data also reinforce the importance of these group executives having an intermediate orientation if conflict management is to be accomplished effectively. For example, if they had a higher concern with divisional affairs, they could become so active in divisional matters that they would not only fail to communicate corporate positions, but would also reduce the influence of division general managers.

Corporate-Divisional Influence Balance

Another factor expected to be important in affecting conflict management was the extent to which the corporate headquarters and each divisional management unit had a relative parity of influence over division policies. While we expected that the division general managers and group vice presidents as individuals would have to have the most influence over these decisions if conflicts were to be resolved, we expected also that effective resolution would require a relative balance of power between the two units. As we have suggested throughout, both units had important information inputs to make to decisions. A balance of influence would assure that both sources of information were considered. Such a balance would also insure that the division managers felt that they had the autonomy required for their divisions to maintain the required differentiation from the corporate unit, while still responding to corporate requirements. This would encourage them to work constructively to resolve conflict situations rather than ignoring these situations because they posed a threat to their autonomy.

From the data we can see that these predictions held in three of the four firms. In the high performing Firm 2, there was no significant difference between corporate and divisional units (Table IV-5). In low performing Firms 3 and 4 there were significant differences between corporate and divisional power and these differences occurred in low performing divisions. Why this was so and its effect is something we shall explore fully in the next chapter but we can conclude that Firm 2 met this determinant to a greater extent than Firms 3 and 4.

Firm 1, however, suggests the need for a slight complication in our argument. This high performing organization had significant differences in power in two of the corporate-divisional pairs investigated. However, it is important to note that both of these differences were in the direction of more power for divisions. This suggests that erring in this direction may be less costly than erring in the direction of overcontrol by the corporation. This is especially so if, as in the case of Firm 1, other means are present to assure effective corporate-divisional integration.

In any case, the situation at Firm 1 is the major reason that the correlation among the 16 pairs between integration and balance of influence was not highly significant ($p > .10$). But in spite of this complication the data as a whole seem to support the notion that a rough balance of influence between corporate and divisional units is important to the effective resolution of conflict. However, if management is going to err in one direction or the other, these data would suggest that it may be better to err on the side of divisional autonomy, rather than corporate control.

TABLE IV-5

Influence over Divisional Policies Attributed to Corporate and Divisional Management Systems in Four Conglomerate Firms[a]

Division	Corporate Management	Divisional Management	Difference[b]
1:I	3.40	4.35	+.95[d]
1:II	3.84	3.95	+.11[c]
1:III	3.79	4.29	+.50[c]
1:IV	3.05	4.20	+1.15[d]
2:I	4.17	4.25	+.08[c]
2:II	4.38	4.18	−.20[c]
2:III	4.23	4.17	−.06[c]
2:IV	3.29	3.71	+.42[c]
3:I	3.94	3.72	−.22[c]
3:II	4.09	4.32	+.23[c]
3:III	3.93	4.32	+.39[e]
3:IV	4.15	3.55	−.60[d]
4:I	3.95	3.45	−.50[c]
4:II	4.14	4.0	−.14[c]
4:III	4.39	3.55	−.84[e]
4:IV	3.43	3.37	−.06[c]

[a] Numbers are mean ratings by divisional managers; higher scores indicate higher perceived influence. Corporate management scores include group vice presidents; divisional management scores are division general managers and executives one level below general managers. See Appendix B for detailed description of how scores were computed.

[b] Plus (+) indicates more divisional influence; minus (−) indicates more corporate influence.

[c] Differences between corporate and divisional management systems are not statistically significant.

[d] Differences are significant at .01 level (two-tailed t test).

[e] Differences are significant at .02 level.

Both this factor and the prior one of general manager and group vice president influence suggest two important conclusions. First, they seem to contradict the traditional views of power in an organization, which indicate that power increases as one moves up the hierarchy. Rather they suggest that the influence distribution in an organization is a function of several factors, including management's assumptions about organization, the formal integrative mechanisms, and the information about environmental requirements available to various levels. Closely related to this is the second point. Since information about different parts of the environment is available to both corporate and division managers, both need to have influence over decisions. If there is an adequate balance in the decision-making process between divisional autonomy and corporate control, the firm will be able to achieve the differentiation and integration necessary to deal with diverse pieces of information from its complex environment.

Modes of Resolving Conflict

This brings us to the final factor related to how conflict is managed—the actual behavioral mode managers use to resolve conflict. A number of different ways that organization members can utilize to handle conflict have been suggsted by various researchers concerned with the topic of organizational conflict.[4] We have focused on three modes of resolving conflict previously measured by Lawrence and Lorsch—confrontation, forcing, and smoothing.[5]

Based on these earlier findings, we anticipated that confrontation would be the most effective means of resolving conflict. By *confrontation* we mean an approach to the resolution of conflict which emphasizes problem-solving and exploration of issues and perceptions of issues until a satisfactory solution is reached. In the corporate-divisional setting, such an approach involves an open exchange of information from both headquarters and divisions until all the facts are out on the table. Then the managers together must make an assessment, based on this information, as to the best course of action. Given the differences in viewpoints of the two groups, this means a working through of these viewpoints until a solution is found. Such an approach requires persistence and patience on the part of the participants. It also requires that the persons involved, particularly on the corporate side, do not arbitrarily use the power of their positions to bring about a decision. Too much corporate influence can destroy the balance between control and autonomy and can lead to reliance on one of the other two modes of resolving conflict.

For example, *forcing behavior* can be defined as the use of power, whether derived from position, knowledge, or coalition, by one party to influence the other to accept a decision that is satisfactory from only one point of view. If conflict is resolved in this manner, it obviously means that important pieces of information may be given too little weight or at worst be totally ignored. But at least forcing behavior means the conflict issues are being engaged.

This is in contrast to the *smoothing* mode of behavior. As the label implies, this involves smoothing over the conflict. The managers involved in the conflict implicitly agree not to disagree in the hope that perhaps the source of the conflict will disappear. However, the sources of conflicts at the corporate-divisional interface are usually real and enduring. Conflicts do not just disappear. They must be worked through, and for this reason smoothing is seldom an effective approach to conflict management.

The data collected in the four firms supported our prediction that the confrontation of conflict would be associated with effective decision making and integration. There was a significant correlation within the 16 pairs between the confrontation of conflict and effective integration ($p > .02$). Furthermore, among the four firms there was a clear pattern of more confronting in the higher performing firms with Firms 1 and 2 doing significantly more confronting of conflict than Firms 3 and 4 (Table IV-6).

TABLE IV-6

Modes of Conflict Resolution in Four Conglomerate Firms[a]

Division	Confrontation[b]	Factor Forcing[c]	Smoothing[d]
1:I	11.5	5.5	7.2
1:II	11.7	6.3	8.8
1:III	12.6	5.0	5.4
1:IV	10.0	8.4	8.2
2:I	12.0	6.3	7.7
2:II	11.8	6.3	7.3
2:III	12.3	7.1	7.6
2:IV	9.7	6.3	5.5
3:I	11.2	6.5	6.3
3:II	10.4	7.3	7.3
3:III	10.3	5.9	8.0
3:IV	10.1	8.0	6.8
4:I	10.4	8.2	7.3
4:II	9.3	9.3	6.6
4:III	10.2	8.4	7.7
4:IV	9.0	9.3	6.7

[a] Scores are based on responses of division managers; higher scores indicate more typical behavior. See Appendix B for a detailed description of questionnaire items used and means of computing scores.

[b] Differences between Firms 1 and 2 and Firms 3 and 4 are significant at the .05 level (analysis of variance).

[c] Differences between Firms 1 and 2 and Firms 3 and 4 are significant at the .01 level.

[d] Differences between Firms 1 and 2 and Firms 3 and 4 are not statistically significant.

While confronting was more typical in the high performing firms, it is also important to note that managers in the low performing firms were doing significantly more forcing than those in the high performers (Table IV-6). Forcing was especially prevalent in Firm 4. This fact, taken together with the influence imbalance in favor of corporate headquarters and the lower influence of divisional general managers in this firm, begins to suggest another of the ways these variables may interact. As the corporate headquarters exerts more influence over decisions, division managers may feel that more conflicts are resolved through forcing behavior on the part of corporate managers. This pattern of behavior is consistent with the management assumptions and integrative mechanisms used by Firm 4. Such controlling behavior on the part of corporate managers seems to be an important factor in explaining why Firm 4 was not able to achieve appropriate patterns of differentiation and integration.

A more systematic summary of patterns of effective decision making in the four conglomerates can be developed by examining how the several determinants correlate with one another and with higher integration.

The Pattern of Effective Decision Making

Looking first at a summary of the correlation data for the 16 corporate-divisional relationships (Table IV-7), there is a strong relationship between

TABLE IV-7

Integration and the Determinants of Effective Decision Making in the 16 Corporate-Divisional Pairs

Overall Multiple Correlation = .8946
Overall Multiple Correlation Squared = .8003

Variable	Correlation with Integration[a]	Level of Significance of Correlations	Unique Variance[b]
General manager influence	.734	.01	.0512
Influence balance	.411	.10	.0810
Confrontation	.561	.02	.0002
Quality information—up	.638	.01	.0595
Quality information—down	.708	.01	.0005
Rapidity	.695	.01	.0156
		Cumulative unique variance	.2080
		Multiple correlation squared	.8003
		Less: Cumulative unique variance	.208
	Accounted for by interaction among variables		.5923

[a] Simple correlation between integration and each variable (Spearman coefficient of rank correlations).

[b] Unique variance measures the individual contribution of each factor to the multiple correlation, as determined by a stepwise regression.

these factors and integration. As previously discussed in presenting the data about each determinant, all but influence balance were individually significantly correlated with higher integration. More important, however, is the multiple correlation which is significant at the .01 level. This high multiple correlation coefficient points to the necessity of understanding the collective impact of the seven aspects of decision making. It would appear that developing effective corporate-divisional relations was related to the total pattern of decision-making and conflict resolution variables, as opposed to the presence or absence of any single variable.[6]

These findings offer one explanation of why the more highly differentiated high performing corporate-divisional pairs achieved higher integration with less effort. They did it through more effective decision-making practices. This is not to gainsay the point made in Chapter III that high divisional performance may reduce the integrative task, making it easier to get both differentiation and integration. It simply suggests that in the corporate-divisional pairs with higher integration there was also apt to be a more effective decision-making pattern. Thus, these pairs were able to overcome the antagonistic relationship between differentiation and integration. In the low performing pairs the decision-making practices tended to be less effective. This, coupled with the effects of low performance, made it more difficult to get appropriate differentiation and effective integration in spite of the greater integrative effort.

A comparison of the overall pattern of determinants of effective decision making by firm provides further evidence of their role in achieving *both* appropriate differentiation and integration (Table IV-8). The high performing firms (1 and 2) met these determinants of effective decision making to a greater extent than the less effective firms. Firm 2 met these determinants almost perfectly while Firm 1 clearly met these factors to a greater extent than Firms 3 and 4. Thus, these factors help to explain how Firms 1 and 2 achieved both higher differentiation and higher integration with less managerial effort. The managers in these firms were able to resolve conflicts and reach joint decisions more effectively. These executives managed the joint decision process in such a way that there was room for both divisional autonomy and the coordinated planning and allocation of resources required at the corporate level.

If a firm is to achieve the differentiation and integration required by its total environment with the least management effort, whatever else its top level managers manage, they must manage corporate-divisional decision making effectively. This requires integrative devices which facilitate two-way flows of communication and which encourage managers to handle conflict so that a balance between corporate control and divisional autonomy is reached. Thus, we can now see more clearly why the more complicated

TABLE IV-8

The Determinants of Effective Decision Making:
An Overview of the Four Conglomerate Firms[a]

Factor	Firm 1	Firm 2	Firm 3	Firm 4
1. Quality of communications	H	H	L	L
2. Rapidity in responding to divisional requests	H	H	L	L
3. Performance evaluation system	H	H	L	L
4. Intermediate position of general manager and group vice president	H	H	H	L
5. High influence of general manager and group vice president	H	H	H	L
6. Balance between corporate and divisional influence	L	H	L	L
7. Modes of conflict resolution	H	H	L	L

[a] These comparative summaries are based on the degree to which the sample of four divisions in each firm met each determinant. H = High and L = Low degree.

and extensive integrative devices at Firms 3 and 4 created problems. They tended to emphasize corporate control at the expense of divisional autonomy and differentiation. The integrative devices in Firms 1 and 2 were designed to more adequately encourage the necessary balance in the decision-making process. But we must also recognize that achieving this balance between autonomy and control also requires that managers have the interpersonal skill necessary to understand communications across the gap created by different orientations, to confront conflict, and to avoid the raw use of positional power, so that conflicts can be resolved in terms of the relevant information available to corporate and division managers.

We have argued in this chapter that effective decision-making problems tend to facilitate appropriate differentiation and integration which in turn are related to higher long-term performance. In concluding, we should stress that we are not ignoring the way divisional and/or corporate performance may affect the level of conflict in these relationships and the decision-making process. However, from the point of view of practicing managers, it is important to describe how effective decision-making processes can improve corporate-divisional relationships. The fact that it may be harder to accomplish this in low performing situations does not make it any less important. It is this practical issue of how conglomerate firms can go about developing an overall approach for achieving appropriate differentiation and integration that we now wish to address.

V

Managerial Issues and Remedies:
A Summary

IN THE preceding chapters we have identified a number of factors which we feel are important in understanding corporate-divisional relationships in conglomerate firms. In spite of an effort to utilize only variables which seemed essential, we have actually discussed some 25 factors, which are interrelated in complex ways. It therefore seems wise to create a breathing spell for the reader in which we summarize our findings, more fully illustrate their interrelationships, and point to the major issues they raise for managers of conglomerate firms. At the same time, we shall introduce the next major phase of this study.

The Basic Findings

The diversification strategy which firms such as these four employ means that the organization must be divided into a number of operating divisions each of which deals with a particular market or product area. Such divisionalization is aimed at creating a scope of operations which a group of managers can handle efficiently. However, if divisions are to be effective in dealing with their individual portion of the total environment, they must develop internal organizational practices which are consistent with the nature of that environment. Similarly, division management personnel must develop goal, time, and interpersonal orientations which meet environmental requirements. This consistency between divisional organization and environment is important because it seems to permit division managers to effectively process information from the environment and to reach decisions.

We can also speculate that it is important because it meets the psychological needs of these executives for a degree of autonomy in their work.

While this fit between divisional organizations and environments is important for division performance, it also leads to differentiation between division managers and corporate managers. As we have seen, corporate managers deal with a part of the total corporate environment which is different from that of any division. In fact, it is largely financial in nature. Corporate executives develop longer term orientations and are more concerned with financial matters than division managers. They also tend to work in less formalized units. This differentiation between corporate and division managers seems to be necessary for each to perform their own tasks effectively, but it also contributes to the problems of achieving corporate-divisional integration.

Effective corporate-divisional integration is also important in these conglomerate firms if they are to generate effective decisions around the issues of planning, budgeting, and resource allocation for the total corporation. Related to this point, corporate-divisional integration is also necessary to gain commitment among division managers to long-term corporate goals. As we have seen, these requirements for integration call for joint decision making between the headquarters unit and its divisions.

Achieving integration at the corporate-divisional interface is complicated not only by the amount of differentiation between the corporate headquarters and each division but also by the extent to which each division poses an economic risk for corporate whole. Greater differentiation means that managers on each side of the interface are more likely to focus on different facets of a problem and to hold divergent views about desirable courses of action. This tends to lead to conflicts between the headquarters and divisional units. When a division, through declining performance and/or heavy funding requirements, poses an economic risk for the corporate whole, headquarters management tends to focus more attention on the problem child and this increases the complexity of the integrative task. In effect, greater differentiation and/or higher economic risk tend to raise the potential for conflict between the two units; and this complicates the task of achieving integration.

However, we have seen that if a division is performing poorly, it is less likely to be highly differentiated from the headquarters. This seems to be a direct result of the increased corporate management interest in a low performing division. Corporate management devotes more integrative effort to such a division, which can place pressure on divisional management to do it "the corporate way," thus resulting in lower differentiation. Under some environmental conditions this may be perfectly appropriate. But under other conditions lower differentiation can make it more difficult for the division to meet the demands of its particular environment and may result in even lower divisional performance. All of this is another way of restating the cyclical effect described in Chapter III, which can make it difficult for a low performing division receiving a great deal of corporate attention to improve its performance level.

But in the high performing organizations low performing corporate-divisional relationships in particular and all corporate-divisional relationships in general were managed so as to achieve both greater differentiation and higher integration with less management effort. In these firms a more effective pattern of decision making helped to make this possible. Information flows, particularly those from the corporate headquarters to the divisions, were more adequately managed in the high performing firms, and the headquarters units in the high performing firms were more prompt in their response to divisional requests for information and help. The performance evaluation procedures in the high performing firms tended to encourage collaboration between corporate and divisional executives rather than accentuating their conflicting views.

Effective decision making was also facilitated in all the firms, except low performing Firm 4, by the fact that division general managers and group vice presidents tended to be intermediate in their outlooks between the extremes of corporate and divisional executives. This facilitated their roles in exchanging information and resolving conflict across the corporate-divisional interface. The high influence of general managers and group executives in the same three firms also enabled these executives to play an effective leadership role in resolving conflict. In addition, in the two high performing firms there was at least a balance of influence between corporate and divisional units and in the case of Firm 1 the divisions actually had greater influence than the headquarters. Both of these indicators of influence distribution suggest that the high performing firms had struck a more appropriate balance in the decision-making process between corporate control and divisional autonomy. Finally, in the high performing firms the confrontation of conflict was more frequently practiced than in the low performing firms.

While each of these factors points to aspects of the decision-making process which were more effective in the high performing firms, it must be emphasized that it was the total pattern of these decision-making variables which discriminated between the effective and less effective situations. This suggests that what may really be crucial in achieving appropriate patterns of differentiation and integration with a minimum of management effort is a climate of trust and confidence between corporate and divisional executives. Taken together, all of these decision-making variables create such a climate. The accurate and timely flow of information means that corporate and division managers have an understanding of why decisions are reached and more confidence in such decisions. Similarly, the resolution of conflict in a manner which emphasizes a balance between corporate control and divisional autonomy and the open exploration of issues reinforces the trust between the two groups. All of this produces a feeling of confidence in the other party and in the decision-making process which can withstand the temporary setbacks of a decision adversely affecting one's own interests. It thus enables corporate and division executives, in spite of their different concerns, to reach decisions which make sense for the total enterprise.

These decision-making variables and the climate of trust they comprise, however, do not just emerge by chance. Instead, for any headquarters-division relationship the climate is partially the product of the amount of potential conflict in the relationship as a result of divisional performance and the degree of differentiation. Even more important for managers, the organizational assumptions held by top management and the integrating mechanisms used to operationalize these assumptions can affect the decision-making climate across an entire firm. For example, we have seen in the case of Firm 4 that heavy reliance was placed on complex formal planning and control procedures which involved a number of corporate executives in approval of division plans. One impact of these mechanisms seems to have been generally to increase the influence of corporate managers relative to division managers. Another result was a reduction in the communication from headquarters to the divisions. Because of such impacts on the decision-making process, these integrative devices seemed to reduce the effectiveness of decision making between corporate and division executives making it more difficult for them to achieve integration.

This entire set of relationships is represented in an expanded version of the flow diagram presented in Chapter III (Figure V-1).

Worthy of particular attention in this diagram is the dotted line from corporate performance to organizational assumptions and integrative devices. This line is intended to emphasize the importance of top management being alert to the implications of feedback about the results the firm achieves for its own assumptions about organization and management. We have made the line dotted to emphasize both the fact that this is our inference drawn from the data and also its importance if management in a low performing firm is to break out of the cycle we have described.

Managing Problematic Divisions

A clearer understanding of some of the ways these factors interact can be gained by examining how a high performing firm and a low performing

FIGURE V-1

Variables Affecting Corporate-Divisional Relationships

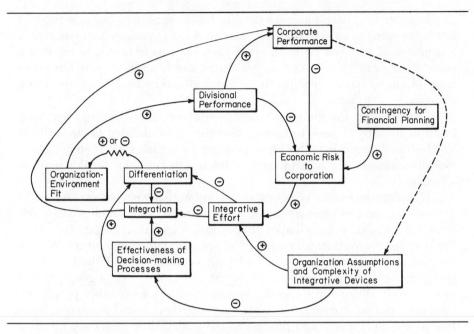

LEGEND: Arrow indicates hypothesized direction of influence.
  Plus (+) indicates positive relationship.
  Minus (−) indicates negative relationship.
  Plus or minus (+ or −) and wavy line indicate contingent relationship.

firm each managed a division which was viewed as posing an economic risk for the corporation.

In Firm 2, which in terms of economic performance and our organizational measures was highly effective, the profits of one of the low performing divisions were under considerable pressure. Current markets were characterized by overcapacity and considerable price cutting, and the division's products were manufactured through a process technology requiring heavy investment in plant and equipment. Also, competition's development of a major new product represented a longer run threat to the division's position.

At the time of our research a new division general manager with considerable experience in the industry had recently been hired. He and his divisional management colleagues felt that large investments would be required over a five-year period to solve the problems the division faced and particularly to introduce a competitive new product. But they were also aware of the need to sell their program to corporate management since this business was very different from those with which most corporate executives were familiar. The division general manager described his view of the situation:

> In order to get the funds we need to build capacity in our new product line we're going to have to present a very convincing package that will return a minimum of 10%. You know, this division is not closely related to any of the other divisions at Firm 2. As a matter of fact, our business is quite foreign to most of the corporate people; it is less well understood than any other division.
>
> The question for the corporation is whether they should go headlong into this industry. I have to assume that they have decided to stay with it for the time being. I base this assumption on the signals I get from my group vice president and the board plus their interest in hiring me for this position a year ago.
>
> If we are to remain competitive, we know that we're going to have to get a lot bigger. Ten years from now this industry will consist of giants which have wide product lines and a lot of backward integration. Despite the heavy funds requirements this will entail, I feel optimistic about the future. We can do part of this through mergers and joint ventures. Also, I think we'll be going through a tight planning exercise each year. We've got a good position to start with. We're already in the business, while a lot of other people are currently starting from scratch. We've got a well-organized marketing function plus a good image and product in the trade. Altogether I see this as a good point from which to jump.

Most corporate managers were more reserved about the division's record and its future potential. The group vice president responsible for the division noted:

> Let's face it, that division was in real trouble last year. At that time we were looking for a new general manager. We found someone who had extensive experience with that manufacturing process. None of us really knows the process well enough. We decided to give him a free rein in marketing and operations and that I would provide the financial overview. Initial results seem to be promising, but we'd like to have a lot more information before we dive into any major expansion programs.

But it is also important to note that corporate management was not getting heavily involved in division operations. They recognized that the business required differentiation and they had enough confidence in divisional management to give them the necessary autonomy. This approach was consistent with top management's organizational assumptions and specifically with the organizational devices used to monitor divisional performance. The comments of the corporate director of financial planning illustrate this point:

As you know, we compute five-year profit-to-volume ratios for all divisions. One measure we look at in this analysis is the "margin of safety." This measure reflects the difference between total sales and the breakeven point; it tells us what proportion of sales are profitable. We tell the divisions to think about hitting a 50% margin of safety. At the current time that division is running at 6.7%, which is a very skinny margin. At that level, if you so much as stub your toe, it's all over. If you have a price decrease in your industry or a strike, you're in the red. . . . This adds up to the fact that that division is still an open question. We're sort of marking time, waiting to see how things go. I'd say the group vice president will be the controlling factor there. If he gets confidence in the division, we'll move.

The group vice president did not just sit by idly. He watched the division's short-term results quite closely and also devoted considerable effort in communicating openly with divisional management about their position relative to investment opportunities in other divisions. The importance of this downward communication is evident from the comments of one of the division's executives.

Our development program is aimed at increasing capacity in our new product line with as little capital as possible. Any justification we have for expansion will have to be supported by significant results on the marketing side. Right now we're not a terribly attractive investment opportunity. If we can get the increased capacity that we need, however, I think we have good future potential. In the long run I believe that everything will pan out, but we have had our setbacks in the market and in timing capacity. As you know, we had capacity coming on last year just when the market was glutted. Hopefully we've taken our "blood-bath" on this decision.

Of course, the corporate goal is to make a profit; and they have to balance the long-run versus the short-run considerations here as well as deciding on the relative emphasis to place on merger versus internal growth. There's a good deal of competition among the divisions for capital, and our new product line will require heavy investments over the next five years. We hope the funds will be available.

There is a broader implication to what I'm saying, and it's simply this. We're a process industry, while most of Firm 2's divisions are hardware manufacturers. Our pattern of investment requirements are quite different. We need big slugs of capital at one time—although we've figured out some ways to space this out. Nevertheless, when you're asking for $10 million in one year and the other divisions are only asking for $2 million . . . well, you've got problems. Our pattern of return is also different: the turnaround time on cash flow tends to be a lot longer.

I am, however, optimistic about getting support from the corporate office. Our short-run goals—e.g., market strategy and cost reduction programs —are aimed at demonstrating positive results by the end of this year. If we accomplish these goals, it will indicate to the corporate people that we're holding up our end of the bargain. They essentially have three alternatives before them. They can either supply us with the funds or they can dispose of the division (a) by peddling it or (b) by running it into the ground. If we can demonstrate results, and make a good case for our new product line, I'm confident we'll get our first increment of investment.

This manager and his colleagues in the division understood the corporate point of view, because the group vice president, as well as other corporate level managers, worked at communicating it. Although the division managers might not always like the corporate frame of reference, they understood it, and they were able to recognize its importance in decisions. It helped them work out tactics to meet corporate requirements without distorting their own differentiated goals.

From all of these comments we can also see confirmation of some of the other aspects of the decision-making process at Firm 2. Clearly, division managers felt they had a major influence over divisional policies and that the general manager in particular was the single most influential person. It also would seem that the flow of information which these comments describe helped both the group vice president and the general manager maintain a more intermediate orientation and begin to develop confidence in each other. Finally, while these comments do not explicitly point to it, we should point out that this relationship was the one in Firm 2 in which the confrontation of conflict was most typical. Because these managers communicated with each other and trusted each other, they were able to sit down and work through their conflicts.

What we see, then, is an effective example of managing a problematic division. The division was allowed sufficient autonomy by corporate management to meet the demands of an environment which was unique in this firm. In fact, this division was one of the most highly differentiated in any of the four firms. In spite of differences in outlook and legitimate concerns about the division's performance, the corporate and division managers achieved effective integration. They did this by maintaining adequate information flows and effectively managing conflict. Particularly important in the decision-making process were the efforts made by the group vice president to allow divisional autonomy while encouraging the division managers through downward communication to recognize corporate goals and requirements. In essence, a degree of corporate control was maintained not through fiat or active intervention but by working in a climate of trust to communicate to division managers the difficulties their division posed for the corporation.

This way of managing a problematic division is in sharp contrast to what we found in the low-performing firms. An example of the approaches used in these two firms is provided by a high-economic risk division in Firm 3. The division in question, which represented the core of the firm's original business, had been a high performer in the company over a period of many years. Recently, however, its profits had declined due to what appeared to be a cyclical downturn in its industry. It also required high levels of fixed investment relative to other divisions at Firm 3. Given this situation, corporate management, as one might expect from our earlier discussion, took a very active interest in this division. This interest manifested itself in the way several integrative devices were applied.

First, top management used its procedures for capital allocation, which were short term and specific as a mechanism for overseeing division operations. The division general manager described his concerns about this practice:

> The capital allocation procedures here are not satisfactory. You submit a project and they cut it or whatever they feel like. The corporate people really take a rather short-term view of things. We get damned few signals concerning their longer-term view of this division. The whole damned thing is based on the wrong measurements. It ends up being based on what money is lying around in the corporate till rather than what the business could stand or what's required.
>
> I think we're the best cash producer in this company, and we've probably done the best job of managing inventory. And yet we have to fight like hell for funds. Don't get me wrong, we've ultimately gotten approval on almost everything we've needed. But it simply takes too long; they want to go over every nitpicking detail with us. I'd like to see division management given a lot more freedom in planning and in capital budgeting. If you don't give people responsibility, then you don't get action.

Later, on a tour of the manufacturing facilities, the general manager gave a more concrete indication of his view of corporate involvement. Pointing to four furnaces he said:

> Now here's a good example of corporate involvement. We were planning four furnaces in this building, and they talked us into two. As you can see, we've now added the other two furnaces and at a considerably higher cost than the first two. By the time we had cut through the red tape the price of the equipment had gone up.

Similarly, he was concerned because he could not get approval for a new office building.

That spot over there is where we'd like to put up our new combined engineering and administrative offices. Our current offices were put up at the turn of the century. We feel that a better working climate would help us to attract and keep the younger engineering talent which we badly need. Unfortunately, a project like this doesn't provide a tangible return to the stockholders. We've been arguing with the corporate office on this one for some time, and you can damned well bet that I'll be an old man before I get this one.

In essence, the complaints of this general manager and his divisional subordinates centered on a lack of divisional autonomy and on being forced into a time orientation which they felt was too short term. Whether the pressures they were feeling had affected their own orientations is difficult to tell from our data. However, it is worth noting that this particular division was the least differentiated of the high performing divisions in any of the companies. One reason for this may have been the fact that its business had historically affected the thinking of corporate managers, but we can speculate that the corporate pressure was also reducing its differentiation from the corporate office.

Corporate involvement in division activity also resulted from the corporate procedures for evaluating divisional performance and also because the corporate staff took a lively interest in divisional operations. The general manager stated his concern with these problems:

You know, the corporate people attempt to control things through their review and approval procedures. This is particularly true in the manufacturing area. It all adds up to too much interference, very little competent help, and a lack of understanding of our operations on their part. Until recently things haven't been all that bad, I suppose. The corporation does manage by exception, and until this year our "go to hell factor" was pretty high. A lot of the corporate staff leaves us alone because they don't feel too comfortable down here.

Even so, we still have trouble with people coming down here trying to tell us what to do. I guess you'd say we're a typical old, successful division that is trying to keep from being taken over by the corporate staff. We're introducing the management innovations that we know are needed, and we'd like to run the business with a minimum of interference.

The division's marketing vice president expressed a similar concern:

One of the major sources of conflict is the feeling on the part of some members of the corporate staff that it's their role to conduct functional audits. This gets them mixed up in second-guessing the guy who's running the show. You know it's pretty easy to go into any division and find some problems.

When you start writing critical reports about them this leads to a lot of friction.

From these comments and the data presented earlier about Firm 3, the impact of these integrative devices and the organizational assumptions upon which they are based is clear. The emphasis on heavy corporate involvement in division affairs, the detailed allocation and evaluation procedures, plus an extremely active staff, created a situation in which corporate executives became heavily involved in the problem division's activities.

Even though they were spending time on division problems, they were not communicating downward effectively and they were also relatively slow in responding to divisional requests. Although there was still an influence balance between this division and the headquarters, it seems apparent that continued corporate pressure might rapidly destroy it. Confronting behavior was also less typical in this corporate-divisional relationship than in most others, especially those in Firms 1 and 2. All of this seemed to add up to a growing climate of mistrust between the units. If the corporate behavior continued unabated, we could expect the climate of mistrust to increase and the decision-making variables to deteriorate even further. In spite of its relatively low differentiation, this division was also achieving relatively low integration with the headquarters even though management was devoting a relatively high amount of effort to integration.

Perhaps the best way to emphasize the contrast between the way problematic divisions were managed in these two firms is to ask the reader himself to speculate about how Firm 3's corporate management might respond to a situation such as that in the example from Firm 2, which was even more threatening to corporate performance. Clearly, more corporate pressure would be placed on the division in question. This would not only distort the decision-making process; it might also reduce differentiation with no benefit in improved integration. As the reader will recall, this is precisely what the data presented in the earlier chapters revealed to be the case in Firm 3 as well as Firm 4 with regard to low performing divisions. But it is in marked contrast to Firm 2 (and also Firm 1), where problematic situations were managed in such a way that appropriate divisional differentiation was maintained and more satisfactory integration was simultaneously achieved. As the example from Firm 2 illustrates, the decision-making process in these firms was handled so that effective information and conflict management were maintained in spite of corporate concern about divisional problems. In this way, the higher performing firms were able to let division managers solve the problems about which they had the most knowledge, while still keeping a check on the total corporate interest.

We should stress, however, that corporate managers in Firm 2 as well as those in Firm 1 did on occasion lose confidence in a divisional management. When this happened, they had a straightforward solution: face up to the issue and replace the manager or managers in question. While this may seem like a harsh solution, it has the important advantage of renewing the climate of trust between headquarters and division so that effective decision making can be resumed. This seems preferable to the deteriorating spiral which often existed in Firms 3 and 4, and in the long run is probably fairer to all concerned.

Improving Corporate-Divisional Relationships

These two examples and the preceding summary are intended to provide a more concise picture of the factors affecting corporate-divisional relations in conglomerate firms. But the reader, especially if he is a practicing administrator, may still be concerned with what implications these findings have for managerial action. One way to answer this question is to examine how the managers in Firms 3 and 4 might have dealt with the major organizational problems they faced.

Looking first at Firm 3, we can recall that it was not so diverse as the other three firms, and that it had achieved a relatively low, but sufficient, degree of differentiation for its divisions to meet the requirements of their respective environments. This firm's problem, however, was in improving corporate-divisional integration. In spite of the relatively low differentiation and a large amount of management time devoted to integrative effort, this firm was not achieving effective integration. Our data, of course, suggest that one cause of this situation was the performance problems the firm faced and the level of conflict this induced. The other factor which contributed to the difficulties in achieving integration, and about which management might take some action, was the decision-making process. The only determinants of effective decision making that this organization met were intermediate position and the influence of general managers and group vice presidents.

The top management at Firm 3, therefore, could give attention to improving the decision-making processes between corporate and division groups. This might require a reassessment of their assumptions about the usefulness of direct corporate involvement in decision making affecting divisional operations. It might also require a redesign of some of the devices used to achieve corporate-divisional integration. The measurement system could be altered to enable divisional management to concentrate more on the goals and time horizons of their particular industrial environments. Similarly, steps might have to be taken to curb the activity of the corporate staff so that it would be less resented by division managers. This might mean reducing the size of the staff, or at least redirecting staff managers' efforts so that they conceived of their role more as providing help when requested and less as directly trying to shape divisional practices. Implicit in any changes in these integrative devices would be the objective of improving communications in both directions between corporate and divisional units and also encouraging more effective conflict resolution.

If we turn to Firm 4, we see a similar but more acute set of problems. Again a great deal of management effort was devoted to achieving integration. However, in this case not only was integration low but there was also insufficient differentiation for the individual divisions to meet the demands of their environments. Here, too, the best hope for improvement seems to rest in altering the integrative devices and the decision-making processes. In fact, Firm 4 scored low on all the decision-making factors. In this firm top management would have to give even more attention to providing sufficient autonomy for its divisions to operate in their diverse environments. Beside those steps suggested for Firm 3, action in Firm 4 would have to include steps enabling the division general managers to achieve more influence over decisions affecting their divisions. This might be accomplished through altering the formal review and evaluation procedures to allow more latitude for division general managers or by altering the role of the corporate staff with regard to divisional matters. It might also be accomplished by getting top corporate managers to change their own behavior patterns so that they are less dominating in their dealings with division executives.

Of course, suggesting that top managers alter their own behavior is often easier said than done. Their ongoing behavior is closely tied to the assumptions they hold about what is the "best" way to organize and manage a company, and both are a result of complex factors in their own personalities. The top managements in Firms 3 and 4 did not make their assumptions about organization because they were unintelligent. Rather they probably made these assumptions because such assumptions made sense to them given their own psychological make-up and their unique view of the world. Since such personality variables are persistent and cannot be altered easily, it is unlikely that we can expect top management of these firms to change their own day-to-day behavior dramatically without altering the climate in which they work.[1] This would require their constant conscious attention to the interaction process with divisional personnel, a difficult approach for anyone to maintain.

This points to a limit in the way the findings of this study can be applied. While our data provide a rational argument for the need for certain changes in organization design and management behavior, we must recognize that there are potent psychological reasons for the behavior of managers in these firms. This does not mean that it is impossible to solve the problems an organization such as Firm 4 was facing. Instead, it means that when top management sees the need for improving corporate-divisional relationships, they should recognize that certain factors are more amenable to change while others are less so.

As was suggested earlier, it is difficult to alter directly the level of division performance. It also seems unrealistic, for the reasons just cited, to expect top managers to alter suddenly and dramatically their day-to-day behavior patterns with division managers. However, it seems more likely that they can use the findings of this study to question their own assumptions about organization and the organizational devices they have used to implement these assumptions. In the process of this reassessment, it will be necessary to recognize and accept the strengths and limits of their own preferred managerial styles. If they can be realistic about their own assumptions and their own individual styles, they can, as we have suggested, make changes in allocation, planning, and evaluation procedures, and in the role of the corporate staff, which can over time have an important impact on their own behavior; on decision-making processes; and ultimately on differentiation, integration, and performance. In essence, they can redefine the rules of the game by which corporate-divisional relations are managed, so that all the players are receiving a set of signals about appropriate behavior which is consistent with the decision-making job to be done. We are not suggesting that individual managers will undergo a sudden personality metamorphosis but that they may learn to play a different game within the limits of their own enduring personal styles.

So far in this discussion we have focused on remedies for the problems faced by the two low performing firms—how to improve integrative devices and decision-making processes so that management effort would result in more satisfactory levels of differentiation and/or integration. There is, however, another organizational issue which all four of these firms might face in the future and for which none had yet found a satisfactory solution. We now want to turn to this issue.

The Matter of Synergy

Among the reasons cited for the increasing emergence of the conglomerate firm as a corporate form, "synergy" is a favorite justification. That is, the results of the whole firm somehow become greater than the sum of its parts operating separately. Both Ansoff [2] and Kitching [3] suggest that synergy can be achieved in numerous ways. It appears that at least three major types of synergy can potentially be achieved in diversified firms. These are:

(1) *Financial synergy*, which may be found in a large conglomerate's enhanced ability to obtain external funding and in its capacity to deploy capital internally to the most promising of a wide range of divisional ventures.

(2) *Managerial synergy*, which entails the ability to develop and effectively apply both managerial talent and techniques to divisions which, if operating on their own, either could not afford or would not be motivated to secure such talent and techniques.

(3) *Operating synergy*, which entails creating links among divisions either in terms of actual market and/or technical interdependence (e.g., the flow of product) or in terms of the cross pollination of marketing and technical skills.

The four firms in this study were heavily engaged in attempting to achieve financial synergy. To a lesser degree they appeared to be engaged in achieving managerial synergy; e.g., through the imposition of planning, budgeting, and funds requests systems and through limited interdivisional transfer of upper level managers. While our conclusions as to how much financial and managerial synergy each firm was achieving must be based on the managers' own evaluation and are therefore speculative, it seems reasonable to conclude from the data presented so far that Firms 1 and 2 were doing a more effective job of managing financial and managerial resources.

At the same time, however, none of the firms appeared to have achieved significant results in terms of operating synergy. Why? The answer is not hard to understand if we recognize that while financial and managerial synergy require only pooled interdependence, operating synergy requires a more complicated pattern of interdependence. To achieve this form of synergy a division not only has to achieve integration with the headquarters but also directly with one or more other divisions. This may either involve managing a sequential interdependence, where one division initiates on another; or in cases where two divisions are jointly processing a total product a reciprocal interdependence may be required.*

Achieving integration around these more complex patterns of interdependence is difficult for two reasons. First, there are simply more relationships involved. As Thompson[4] has suggested, this requires more complex integrative devices. Second, the solutions which even the effective firms (1 and 2) had developed to manage pooled interdependence seem to make it difficult to achieve cross-divisional collaboration. As we have seen, the concept of product divisions implies that each will be accountable

---

* The reader will recall that sequential interdependence is the case where one unit initiates on a second. Reciprocal interdependence is a mutually interdependent situation in which both influence each other.

to the corporation for its own profits. Each division competes at least indirectly with the others for financial and managerial resources to achieve its profit objectives. As long as pooled interdependence is the major type required, such interdivisional competition is not harmful; and it may well be healthy. When divisions are also expected to integrate their efforts, this competition can create additional conflicts which need resolution. Thus, even in firms like 1 and 2, this added dimension would seem to require even more information exchange and conflict management not only between corporate and divisional executives but also among executives in the various divisions.

An example of the difficulties which can be encountered in achieving operating synergy is provided by Firm 3. This company had undertaken a bold effort to get three divisions to collaborate in providing a complex system of products to the government. A central office was set up at the corporate level to integrate this effort. The program immediately ran into the parochial interests of each division. As the director of the corporate coordinating office put it:

> We have stimulated the divisions to look at new products. But the problem is they tend to continue to focus on their existing profit makers. We are all human; and when we get together, while there is little animosity, the immediate divisional problems always take precedence. Each division general manager wants to turn a profit and look good in his own division.
>
> The president has the corporate viewpoint, and he has helped to back the divisional managers time after time. But he can't see why they don't see things from the corporate viewpoint.

Basically, each division manager was more motivated to focus on his own differentiated goals than those of the total corporation. In effect, this is what the control and reward system told him he should do. While the president occasionally gave off signals about the importance of interdivisional collaboration, they were not sufficiently strong; and the division managers continued to focus on existing divisional goals. This example is not presented to be critical of Firm 3's effort. We suspect that if any of the four firms had attempted to nurture a high degree of interdivisional collaboration they would have encountered many of the same problems.

Since we were not able to learn from our data in these four firms how organizations achieve operating synergy among divisions, we decided to examine two other multidivisional companies where efforts to manage more complex types of interdependence were more advanced.

VI

Environmental Demands and Organizational States in Two Vertically Integrated Paper Companies

To find firms achieving operating synergy we turned our attention to another type of multidivisional organization: the large, vertically integrated company.* Our goals in this stage of the research were to get a clearer understanding of how requirements for substantial interdivisional collaboration might affect corporate-divisional relationships and to explore how the patterns of organization we have found to be effective in conglomerate firms might differ from those required in other types of multidivisional companies.

In this chapter we will be concerned with determining what organizational arrangements two vertically integrated paper companies (Firms 5 and 6) had evolved to cope with their particular environments. What sorts of environmental issues did these firms face? What patterns of differentiation, integration, and integrative effort were associated with higher economic performance in this setting? How do processes of joint decision making contribute to the patterns of differentiation and integration? With answers to these questions in hand we will turn in Chapter VII to a com-

---

* By vertically integrated company we mean a firm consisting of several major business units which are involved in the production and sale of a commodity all the way from obtaining the original raw materials to the fabrication and marketing of products (often both end-use and intermediate) derived from that original commodity. The term "integration" used in this context should be distinguished from our use of integration as an organizational state referring to the quality of collaboration among major units in an organization.

parison of the vertically integrated paper companies and the conglomerate firms in our sample.

Background Information

There are a number of domestic industries which are characterized by considerable degrees of vertical integration; e.g., chemicals, petroleum, basic metals, and paper. We focused our research efforts on the paper industry for two reasons. First, it fitted the primary criterion of having multi-divisional firms whose divisions at once manufactured and sold products in different external markets and also sold substantial portions of their output internally to sister divisions. Second, the paper industry was one about which we could gain a suitable understanding during the short period we would be studying two firms.

The two paper firms had achieved vertical integration through both mergers and internal developments. Their operations extended from timber holdings; through pulpmaking; to mills which produced kraft paper, paperboard, white paper, and end-use products such as newsprint and towels; and finally to converting operations which made containers, flexible packaging, envelopes, and the like. Both to keep our study within manageable bounds and to maintain comparability between firms we focused on the interdependence among the mill, container, and packaging segments of each corporation.* Taken together these three segments accounted for approximately 50% of each company's annual sales.

Figure VI-1 shows the organizational units studied in each firm along with their relationships with one another and with their respective market environments. The operating statistics in Table VI-1 provide a more explicit description of what these relationships entailed. In both firms the mills sold a considerable proportion of their total output to external markets in the form of intermediate (e.g., kraft paper, white paper, and linerboard) and end-use products (e.g., newsprint, towels, and tissue). At the same time, however, these mills sold a significant amount of their output in the form of kraft paper, paperboard, and corrugating medium to the container and packaging divisions of their own firms. The significance of these internal transfers becomes clearer if we consider them from the viewpoint of the

---

* This basis for choosing sample divisions is different from the approach we used in studying conglomerate firms. In the conglomerate setting we chose divisions so as to represent the range of different industries encompassed by each firm; in the paper companies we were interested in studying a group of divisions which were highly interdependent. These differing bases of sampling become important when we turn to a comparison of the two types of firms in Chapter VII.

FIGURE VI-1

Organizational Units Studied in Two Paper Companies

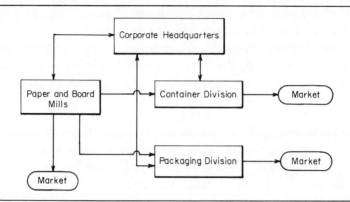

converting divisions. For example, roughly one-third of the total sales of the container divisions in each firm were attributable to the cost of materials obtained from the mills. Internal transfers to the packaging divisions were a good deal smaller; however, the costs of these transfers still amounted to between 8% and 25% of total packaging division sales in Firms 5 and 6. It should also be noted that no significant product transfers occurred between the two converting businesses.

TABLE VI-1

Comparative Operating Statistics for Two Paper Companies:
Net Dollar Sales and Internal Transfers for 1968, Expressed
in Terms of Index Numbers[a]

	External Sales	
Operating Unit	*Firm 5*	*Firm 6*
Paper Mills	302	100
Containers	92	83
Packaging	48	58
	Internal Transfers of Product at Cost	
	Firm 5	*Firm 6*
Paper Mills to Containers	36	29
Paper Mills to Packaging	4	13

[a] Base figure of 100 = external sales of Firm 6's paper mill unit. All other index figures—both costs and sales—are expressed in relation to this base of 100. Index figures have been employed to disguise actual dollar figures.

Table VI-1 also points to some of the broad similarities between Firms 5 and 6. Container and packaging operations had approximately the same annual rate of sales in both firms. Within each firm the largest contribution to total sales was made by the mills, container division, and packaging division, in that order. The major differences between the two companies was that Firm 5 had a considerably larger mill operation.

While the divisions studied in Firm 5 and 6 were fairly similar in terms of size and markets served, the two companies differed somewhat with respect to performance. Two approaches were used to assess relative per-

TABLE VI-2

Performance Statistics for Firms 5 and 6 and Other Comparable Paper Companies

	Sales Growth[a] (compounded)		Profit Growth[a] (compounded)		Average[b] Return on Capital	
	5 yr.	10 yr.	5 yr.	10 yr.	5 yr.	10 yr.
Firm 5	6.8%	5.4%	5.1%	1.9%	7.0%	7.1%
Firm 6	10.0	13.7	4.5	1.6	5.4	6.6
Results for 8 large, integrated paper companies:[c]						
Upper quartile	8.6%	8.0%	10.5%	3.6%	9.3%	9.1%
Median	6.8	7.5	5.8	2.6	7.2	7.5
Lower quartile	6.5	5.6	4.7	1.2	5.7	6.1

[a] Compounded annual rate of growth. Five-year figures are the average of 1960–1962 v. 1967. Ten-year figures are the average of 1955–1957 v. 1967.

[b] Profit after taxes ÷ (total assets − current liabilities). Averages are for 1958–1967 and 1963–1967.

[c] Includes Firms 5 and 6. Firms were included for comparison only if they derived most of their revenues from the manufacture and conversion of paper products and were a major factor in corrugated box and packaging markets. 1967 sales for these firms ranged from $350 million to $1.4 billion. Our reason for employing this comparison group was to get a better fix on what constituted relatively high or low performance among large, integrated paper firms. This approach to comparing performance indices was not employed for conglomerate firms (Chapter II) because they are much more heterogeneous in terms of their product lines.

formance: (a) published figures for overall corporate results and (b) subjective ratings by corporate and divisional managers of results* achieved by each of the three divisions studied.

Table VI-2 contains performance statistics for Firms 5 and 6 and com-

---

* We were not able to secure actual performance statistics by division. Container and packaging divisions were rated on sales, profit, and ROI achieved over the most recent five years. Mills were rated on ROI, cost performance, and ability to meet schedules during the same period.

pares these figures with the range of results for other large, integrated paper companies which operated in similar markets. It is noteworthy that while these eight firms exhibited important differences in return on capital, there were not wide differences in their records of sales and profit growth.* Since all of these companies were serving what were basically commodity markets, these small performance differences do not seem too surprising. However, they do make our comparison of Firms 5 and 6 more difficult.

The data show that for the most recent five years Firm 5 was performing at roughly the median of the comparison group for sales and profit growth and return on capital. This company's profit growth for the most recent five years represents a significant improvement over its ten-year trend. Despite relatively high sales growth, Firm 6 did not record a commensurate improvement in its profitability. Firm 6's higher sales growth reflects considerable merger activity on its part;** however, this company's profit growth and return on capital were both below those of Firm 5 and below the median for the comparison firms. As a matter of fact, Firm 6's return on capital had declined during the most recent five years, while

TABLE VI-3

Subjective Ratings of Division Performance in Two Paper Companies[a]

Division	Firm 5	Firm 6
Mill[b]	9.3	10.2
Container Division[c]	9.8	7.4
Packaging Division[b]	10.5	9.5

[a] Higher numbers indicate higher performance. Scores are subjective ratings by corporate and division managers of sales, profit, and ROI over the past five years for container and packaging. Mills are rated on ROI, cost performance, and ability to meet delivery schedules.

[b] Differences between Firms 5 and 6 are not significant.

[c] Difference is significant at .01 level (analysis of variance).

return on capital for Firm 5 and the comparison group had remained roughly the same.

Managers' subjective ratings of the results achieved by the divisions upon which we were focusing provide further evidence of performance differences between Firms 5 and 6. From Table VI-3 we can see that there were

---

* This provides a marked contrast to the wide differences in all these performance indices we found between higher and lower performing conglomerate companies in Chapter II (see Table II-1).

** Between 1955 and 1967 Firm 6 had acquired some thirty small-to-medium-sized companies in the paper business. By way of contrast, Firm 5 had acquired only two medium-sized converting operations during the same period.

significant differences in ratings of container division performance at the two firms. Managers at Firm 6 rated the container division as a lower performance situation; and this lower rating was supported by our interviews with these executives. On the other hand, managers did not indicate that there were any important differences between the two firms with respect to performance of mill or packaging operations.

Thus, the two pieces of data which were available on relative performance suggest that even though there was not a wide range of difference in the performance of large, integrated paper companies, Firm 5 was a slightly higher performance situation than Firm 6. Furthermore, Firm 6's container division was an important source of the difference between the two companies.

Environmental Diversity

So far in our discussion we have been concerned with the size, product interrelationships, and performance of the divisions studied in Firms 5 and 6. The next task is to examine the diversity of environmental demands faced by these divisions.

The mill operations of each firm consisted of approximately a dozen large paper-making facilities which were located near major U.S. and Canadian supplies of timber. Their organizations consisted of manufacturing, engineering, and product development functions. External sale of mill output was the responsibility of a separate marketing division in each firm.* Company executives indicated that cost and delivery were the single most important selling points for mill output. These executives cited product quality as another important factor; however, given the relatively stable nature of paper technology and the basic commodity nature of mill output, quality was seen more as a necessary condition rather than a source of competitive advantage.

The basic environmental issues faced by the mill organizations were mainly a matter of managing the technology of paper making. This technology is a continuous process in which a solution of pulp and fibers is fed under the press rolls and through the tiered, heated rollers of a large paper machine. Finished paper flows off the "dry" end of the machine in continuous sheets which are wound on large cylinders. The mill stage of paper making is characterized by a high fixed investment in plant and

---

* While the marketing divisions of Firms 5 and 6 played an important role in total company operations, we have chosen not to study them directly in this research. The mill-marketing interface involved the external sale of mill output by a functional unit, and thus it lay outside our primary interest in relationships among product divisions.

equipment as well as high start-up costs for machines. Mill managers pointed to two critical elements of success in their business. First, in order to remain competitive in the face of high fixed costs they had to maintain machine operating rates of 85% or more. Second, they noted that installation of new machines and rebuilding older machines to increase maximum operating rates was a source of longer run competitive advantage. While quality and delivery were certainly important factors, these managers noted, it was cost and volume that were key.

The container operations faced a somewhat different set of environmental requirements. Container divisions in both firms were self-contained to a considerable degree; they possessed all the functional specialties necessary to develop and sell their products and to convert paper and paperboard into corrugated boxes and other containers. Each container division consisted of approximately 25 facilities that sold products in local market areas. This geographic dispersion of facilities was dictated in part by the economics of shipping containers (executives noted that it was seldom feasible to compete in market areas that were more than 200 miles distant from a box plant). Each local market was also somewhat different as to customer requirements. For instance, rural markets consisted primarily of seasonal fruit and produce growers with fairly standard box requirements, while urban areas were characterized by large industrial customers who used a wider range of nonstandard containers and whose requirements were much less seasonal. All orders in the container business were produced on a job shop or small batch basis to meet customer specifications.

Container executives in Firms 5 and 6 cited pricing and product mix plus scheduling and capacity utilization as the major ingredients of success in their business. These requirements stemmed from the fact that the box plants were characterized by fairly high setup costs but also produced what was basically a commodity product which often had to be manufactured for a wide range of individual customer specifications. Furthermore, these box plants were faced with intense local competition, fairly low profit margins, and customers who did not wish to carry large inventories of boxes. On the marketing side, securing high volume, higher margin business and being able to set realistic prices on bids were seen as the critical skills. On the manufacturing side, effective scheduling both to meet delivery requirements and to minimize the high costs entailed in setting up production runs were the major skills. Since box-making was a rather stable technology, engineering and research skills were seen as somewhat less crucial to maintaining a competitive position.

While the packaging divisions at Firms 5 and 6 were also characterized by considerable self-containment, they faced quite different environmental requirements from those of the container divisions. The packaging divisions were lower volume but highly profitable operations which tended to serve a much smaller group of customers. These divisions produced and usually printed packages using paper and a wide range of other materials (e.g., polyethylene and wax). Sales were usually made on a contract basis to companies such as beverage and cereal marketers, dairies, and bakeries. Package design, product innovation, pricing, and promotion were cited by executives as the critical skills in this business. While manufacturing required moderate investment in plant and equipment as well as skills in working with a wide range of materials, marketing and product development were seen as considerably more influential factors in maintaining a competitive position.

The brief profiles presented above suggest that the divisions in Firms 5 and 6 faced relatively diverse environmental requirements. We can assess this diversity more systematically by examining questionnaire data which were collected about environmental requirements. In order to get a rough measure of the uncertainty associated with each major segment of a di-

TABLE   VI-4

Basic Environmental Requirements Faced by Divisions
of Two Paper Companies[a]

	Clarity of Information[b]	Time Span of Environmental Feedback[c]	Relative Importance of Subenvironment[d]
MILLS			
Scientific-Engineering	2.4	3.5	2.6
Manufacturing	2.3	2.6	1.4
CONTAINERS			
Scientific-Engineering	2.6	3.3	2.9
Manufacturing	2.2	2.6	1.9
Marketing	2.2	2.6	1.1
PACKAGING			
Scientific-Engineering	2.6	3.6	1.8
Manufacturing	2.6	2.7	2.6
Marketing	3.0	2.7	1.5

[a] Numbers are combined responses for Firms 5 and 6. Higher scores indicate a greater *lack* of clarity of information, a longer time span of feedback, and *less* importance attributed to a subenvironment.

[b] Difference between marketing subenvironments of divisions is significant at .05 level (analysis of variance). Other differences among subenvironments are not significant.

[c] Differences among divisions by subenvironment are not significant.

[d] Differences among divisions by subenvironment are significant at the following levels: Scientific (.001), Manufacturing (.001), and Marketing (.05).

vision's environment we asked managers to rate these subenvironments in terms of two measures—the clarity of information surrounding decisions and the time span of environmental feedback. We also obtained a measure of the dominant segments of each division's environment by asking managers to rate the degree to which efforts in each subenvironment contributed to the overall ability of the division to compete in its particular business.

These data suggest that these three units did not differ significantly with respect to the uncertainty they encountered in their scientific and manufacturing subenvironments (Table VI-4). However, packaging divisions faced a more uncertain marketing environment than containers. At the same time, all three units differed markedly with respect to the dominant segments of their environments. As our profiles have suggested, manufacturing was the critical sector for the mills, while the marketing and then the manufacturing sector were the critical parts of the container environment. For packaging the critical sectors were market and scientific-engineering, in that order.

With this understanding of the environments facing each division we now turn to the organizational arrangements and management orientations that each company had developed in order to manage these divisions. The first step will be to examine the headquarters organizations of the two companies.

Headquarters Organizations

To understand the headquarters organizations, it is first necessary to determine the relevant dimensions of their environments. Corporate managers were asked how they divided their working time among a number of groups in their firms' environments. The external contacts of corporate executives in the two paper companies were heavily centered on groups which lay within their divisions' industry environments; i.e., customers, suppliers, and trade associations (Table VI-5). Less than one-fifth of the executives' external contacts were devoted to the financial subenvironment and merger candidates. We can conclude that the environmental contacts of these corporate managers were heavily rooted in various segments of the paper industry and that these contacts would overlap considerably with the environmental contacts of their division managers.

Earlier in this chapter we noted that Firms 5 and 6 were fairly similar in terms of size and markets served. Given these broad environmental similarities, we expected that the headquarters units of the two companies would tend to develop similar organizational arrangements and managerial orientations. This, in fact, turned out to be the case (Table VI-6). We

TABLE VI-5

Relevant Dimensions of the Corporate Headquarters' Environment
in Two Paper Companies: Percent of Members' Time
Devoted to Various Environmental Sectors[a]

Financial subenvironment	11.6%
Potential acquisitions, divestitures, and joint ventures	6.6
Legal-governmental subenvironment	14.6
Operating subenvironment (trade associations, customers, and suppliers of divisions)	56.9
Other (community relations, professional associations, and consultants)	10.3

[a] Mean ratings by corporate managers in the two paper companies. Numbers are the proportion of total time devoted to all external groups attributable to specific environmental sectors. See Appendix B for questionnaire items used to secure this information.

found no significant differences between the two headquarters with respect to formality of structure and interpersonal, time, and goal orientations. We also obtained measures of each firm's overall goal set by asking corporate executives to rank 21 specific goal items. Again, we found that the two headquarters units were quite similar (differences in rankings of top 10 goal items common to both firms were not significant, Mann-Whitney U test).*

TABLE VI-6

Basic Characteristics of Headquarters Units in Two Paper Companies[a]

	Firm 5	Firm 6
Formality of structure	15	15
Interpersonal orientations[b]	88.4	87.1
Time orientations[b]	3.2	3.1
Goal orientations:		
Financial[b]	1.71	1.59
Marketing[b]	2.01	2.06
Manufacturing[b]	2.28	2.33
Interdivisional[b]	2.40	2.26
R&D/Engineering[b]	2.63	2.55

[a] Higher scores indicate more formality of structure, more socially oriented interpersonal styles, longer time horizons, and *less* emphasis on various goal items.
[b] Differences between firms are not statistically significant.

* The interested reader can find a comparison of these goal sets in Appendix A.

From the foregoing discussion we can conclude that the headquarters units of Firms 5 and 6, faced with basically similar environmental issues, had developed quite similar cognitive orientations and ways of organizing work. The findings also suggest that the vertically integrated nature of these companies affected the pattern of environmental contacts of the headquarters units (heavy emphasis on the division environments). We now turn to a more explicit consideration of the internal organizational requirements posed by vertical integration in the paper industry and the approaches that Firms 5 and 6 had developed to manage these requirements.

Interdependence and Approaches to Integration

Interviews with executives in both firms pointed to three major sets of issues around which the headquarters and its divisions were interdependent. First, there was a need to maintain control of total earnings and funds flows. Much like the conglomerate firms, Firms 5 and 6 managed the processes of planning, budgeting, and resource allocation through a complex set of paper systems along with direct contacts between the corporate office and division top management. This first set of integrative requirements formed a pooled interdependence. Each year the various divisions separately negotiated their long-range plans and operating and capital budgets with the corporate headquarters.

The interdependence which characterized Firms 5 and 6 extended beyond this pooled type, because it was also necessary for the headquarters and divisions to arrive at a number of joint decisions about the planning and scheduling of mill capacity. This second set of integrative issues involved balancing mill capacity with the demands of converting divisions and external markets, both on a short-term and on a long-term basis. Each of the two companies had a corporate planning and scheduling department which was responsible for achieving a balance between these demands and mill output. The following comments by Firm 5's vice president of distribution and corporate planning provide some insight into the nature of this integrative task:

> Our basic objective is to give the desired level of service to our customers in such a way that the company gets the greatest profit it can out of our integrated businesses. My department schedules all paper machines in the mill side of the business. For instance, with respect to the container division's business, we schedule the mill's machines which make paperboard and corrugating medium and we are responsible for controlling inventory at this stage of production. Of course, we do not schedule the actual converting operations for containers or packaging; that is their responsibility.

We must know both on a daily and future basis what the container and packaging people are converting so that we can insure that they don't run out of paper and board. This requires a tremendous amount of close work because we have a wide variety of products and the converting divisions' business can shift drastically over time. There is always a danger that inventory at the mill level will become very high by grade; and our job is to balance the need for a reasonable level of this inventory with the danger of running out of paper.

The basic issue is to keep everything going. The paper machines must run 100% of the time if the mills are to make a reasonable cost showing. If we come in with a lot of shifts in scheduling, then mill costs suffer. We try to be responsive to these cost requirements, but at the same time we have to take care of our market demand. Unanticipated market shifts in one area can also raise hell above and beyond their impact on the mills. Over the last few years we've been fairly tight on mill capacity; we have virtually no unused capacity. Thus, an emergency change in schedules for one converting unit can put another converting unit on the spot.

Because of our intimate involvement in day-to-day planning of product flow we are in a position to play a central role in planning long-range facilities expansions along with the mills. We secure forecasts of future needs on a two-, five-, and ten-year basis and then pull together the capital projects which will be presented to the corporate officers. In this side of the business long-range planning cannot be an "ivory-tower" sort of thing; it is closely tied to our day-to-day planning and scheduling.

From the foregoing comments we can see that production planning and scheduling formed a major integrative task, and these issues entailed considerable interdependence among the mills and converting divisions. It is also important to note that in both firms this interdependence was managed mainly through contacts with the corporate planning and scheduling unit rather than through direct contacts between the divisions in question. Our interviews also indicated that transfer prices for the paper and paperboard which flowed from the mills to the converting divisions were set by corporate officers rather than by direct negotiation between the divisions involved. Finally, we also found that the corporate planning function played an important role in defining the facilities expansion projects of the mills. Executives at both companies indicated that, while the mill organization was heavily involved in determining the nature of future facilities to be built, it was the corporate planning function which had the market information necessary to justify an expansion. By way of contrast, the packaging and container divisions prepared their own expansion plans (although they were obliged to secure some information from the corporate planning unit regarding the potential availability of paper and paperboard).

The third set of integrative issues faced by the two paper companies did require direct interdivisional contacts. These issues involved achieving integration around quality and product development. In both companies technical service managers had been designated at fairly high levels within the mill organizations to insure that mill output met the quality requirements of the converting divisions and to coordinate changes in these requirements which might result from new products or product modifications. One of these technical service managers in Firm 6 described his work as follows:

> Our primary function is to be an integrating factor—to convey to the mills what the converting divisions need. On a routine basis this might involve "riding herd" on a customer complaint or some problems that our converting plants might be having which they believed were caused by the quality of the paper or board they had received. Usually these routine issues involve a deviation from long established standards, and my job is to determine how the problem occurred and to work with the mill people to do something about it. Less routine matters might involve getting agreement about changing specifications on how certain paper should be produced. In this case I work more as a catalyst in getting mill and converting people together to arrive at a decision about how to proceed. In a sense, you might say that I am a sort of product manager for the mills' internal customers.

While quality and product change issues did require a certain amount of direct contact among the mills and converting divisions, these issues were of a sort which often could be handled at a fairly high level within each of the units. Rather than requiring a complex set of relationships among mill and converting plant personnel, these issues could usually be resolved by channeling communications through a single integrative position—the technical service manager. The general manager of Firm 5's container division summed up these integrative requirements in this way:

> We have almost a customer-vendor relationship with the mills. My key subordinates and I deal directly with corporate planning on quantity allocation issues. When issues of quality or changes in product specifications arise, they are settled between my vice president of manufacturing and the technical service manager at the mills. When you get to the next level in our organization—the regional manager—there is seldom any need for direct relationships between our people and the mill organization.

The interdependence in Firms 5 and 6 is a good deal more complex than that which characterized the four conglomerate companies and approximates what Thompson has termed sequential interdependence.[1] At the same time, however, this more complex form of interdependence did not seem to require extensive direct contacts between the mills and con-

verting divisions. Indeed, it seems that a significant proportion of the interdependence in Firms 5 and 6 was managed through contacts between the
corporate headquarters and the divisions. Only around the issues of quality
and product modifications were significant amounts of direct interdivisional
contact required.

TABLE VI-7

**Managers' Perceptions of Frequency of Contact Required Among
Major Units in Two Paper Companies[a]**

	Firm 5	Firm 6
CORPORATE-DIVISIONAL CONTACTS		
Corporate—Mills	3.3	4.5
Corporate—Container Division	3.4	5.1
Corporate—Packaging Division	3.8	5.7
INTERDIVISIONAL CONTACTS[b]		
Container Division—Mills	3.1	5.1
Packaging Division—Mills	4.3	4.9

[a] Numbers are mean ratings by division managers only. Higher scores indicate less
frequent required contact (1 = daily, 8 = annually). Differences between required frequency
of corporate-divisional and interdivisional contacts are not statistically significant in either
firm. Overall differences between Firms 5 and 6 are significant at the .001 level (analysis of
variance).
[b] Combined ratings of managers in both units.

The data in Table VI-7 provide additional perspective on the integrative requirements posed by sequential interdependence in the two paper
companies. Managers in each division were asked to rate how frequently
contact with the corporate headquarters and other divisions should occur
in order to obtain the necessary integration. In both firms executives indicated that direct divisional contacts were required at roughly the same
frequency as headquarters-divisional contacts. By way of contrast, research
by Lawrence and Lorsch indicates that food and plastics firms, which are
characterized by reciprocal interdependence among functional departments, depend very heavily on direct interunit contact at several organizational levels.[2] Of course, our data only measure required *frequency* of
contact and not intensity of contact, which is a function of the number of
managers involved in contacts as well as frequency. Indeed, this may account for why the questionnaire data suggest that corporate-divisional and
interdivisional contact should occur at roughly the same frequency while
our interviews indicated that corporate-divisional contacts tended to play
the major role in achieving integration. At any rate, we can still conclude

from Table VI-7 that much of the interdependence in these paper companies was managed at higher levels in the organization and across the corporate-divisional interface.

The data in Table VI-7 also raise a whole new set of questions about differences between Firms 5 and 6. It appears that managers in Firm 5 perceived a need for more frequent contact—both corporate-divisional and interdivisional—than their counterparts at Firm 6. In view of the basic similarities between the two firms with respect to size, product lines, and integrative requirements these differing managerial perceptions seem a little surprising. Had Firms 5 and 6 chosen to take different approaches to managing the same basic issues of environmental diversity and interdependence? In order to find an answer to this question, let us examine more closely the integrative devices which were employed by each company along with measures of the integrative effort which was devoted to managing interunit relationships.

From Table VI-8 we can see that the major integrative devices employed by Firms 5 and 6 were similar in most respects. Each company used paper systems, integrative positions, and direct managerial contact to

TABLE VI-8

Major Integrative Devices in Two Paper Companies

	Firm 5	Firm 6
PAPER SYSTEMS		
Five-year planning system	X*	X
Annual budgeting system	X*	X*
Monthly budget review	X*	X*
Monthly operating reports	X*	X
Formal goal-setting system	X*	
Approval systems for major capital and expense items	X*	X*
INTEGRATIVE POSITIONS		
Senior vice presidents	X*	X*
Planning and scheduling department	X*	X*
Technical service managers	X*	X*
COMMITTEES, TASK FORCES, AND FORMAL MEETINGS		
Mill supply task force		X*
Trade relations committee		X
Capital expenditures committee		X*
DIRECT MANAGERIAL CONTACT	X*	X*

X—indicates presence of devices in each firm.

*—indicates those devices that managers felt played the most significant role in interunit relations.

SOURCE: Interview data and company records.

achieve the required integration. The companies did differ, however, with respect to the relative emphasis placed on different types of devices. While Firm 6 placed considerable emphasis on the use of task forces and committees at the top three levels of its organization, Firm 5 placed heavier emphasis on paper systems.

TABLE VI-9

Formal Integrative Devices in Two Paper Companies

	Firm 5	Firm 6
ORGANIZATIONAL STRUCTURE		
1. Total management employees at corporate office	479	250
2. Number of major staff units	6	8
3. Number of senior vice presidents	5	5
FORMAL PLANNING AND CONTROL DEVICES		
1. Number of major devices used by corporate management[a]	10	9
2. Character of review of divisional plans, requests, and results	Informal, detailed	Informal, detailed
3. Number of corporate executives involved in approval of plans and requests	7	10
MEASUREMENT SYSTEMS		
1. Criteria	Costs (mills), sales and profits (converting divs.)	"Return on capital employed" (all units)
2. Time span of evaluation	Annual	Annual

[a] Derived from Table VI-8.
SOURCE: Interview data and company records.

Table VI-9 provides a more detailed picture of these formal integrative devices. Both companies had similar organizational structures at the corporate level; however, Firm 5 had a much larger corporate staff. While Firm 5 involved less people in approval procedures, its formal planning and control devices were quite similar in other respects to Firm 6's. In terms of measurement systems, Firm 6 employed a profit center/return-on-capital approach for all units, while Firm 5 treated its mills as cost centers and its converting divisions as profit centers.

At this point in our discussion it is rather difficult to determine whether the differences between Firms 5 and 6 with respect to integrative devices are really significant. If we examine the actual patterns of integrative effort which characterized each company and then attempt to link these patterns with our data in Tables VI-8 and VI-9, we should be able to establish whether Firms 5 and 6 were actually taking significantly different approaches to the management of diversity and interdependence.

TABLE VI-10

Effort Devoted to Achieving Corporate-Divisional and Interdivisional Integration in Two Paper Companies[a]

	Firm 5			Firm 6		
	Corp.	Div.		Corp.	Div.	
CORPORATE-DIVISIONAL EFFORT	Mgt.	Mgt.	Total	Mgt.	Mgt.	Total
Mills	202.0	224.5	426.5	114.2	156.0	270.2
Container Division	75.6	262.0	337.6	95.9	112.0	207.9
Packaging Division	85.9	103.0	188.9	59.2	94.0	153.2
Total	363.5	589.5	953.0	269.3	362.0	631.3
DIRECT INTERDIVISIONAL EFFORT BY:						
Mills			190.5			66.0
Container Division			170.0			32.0
Packaging Division			98.0			35.0
Total			458.5			133.0
OVERALL TOTAL FOR EACH FIRM			1,411.5			764.3

[a] Numbers are a summation of all managers' time devoted to interunit relationships during the most recent year. Higher scores indicate greater integrative effort.

From Table VI-10 we can see that Firm 5 devoted considerably more effort to achieving integration among its various organizational units. This comparatively greater effort was exhibited at the corporate-divisional interface and even more dramatically at the interfaces among divisions.

In order to test the importance of these differences it may be useful to recall some of the basic characteristics of Firms 5 and 6. At the beginning of this chapter (Table VI-1) we noted that Firm 5 had a considerably larger mill operation than Firm 6; thus, higher integrative effort scores for this unit do not necessarily suggest a difference in approaches to integration. Container and packaging divisions, however, were roughly the same size in each company; and Firm 5's higher integrative effort scores for these units does suggest important differences in how the companies managed interunit relationships. For one thing, Firm 5's larger corporate staff was clearly affecting integrative effort. Also, Figure VI-10 indicates that Firm 5 was encouraging considerably more upward communication from its divisions as well as more direct contact between its mills and converting divisions. Finally, it is interesting to note that Firm 5's container division—a relatively high performing unit (see Table VI-3)—was characterized by much higher integrative effort than its counterpart at Firm 6—a lower performer.

Our findings indicate that patterns of corporate-divisional relationships did differ in fairly systematic ways between Firms 5 and 6; and these differences appear to be related in part to differences in their formal integrative devices. First of all, Firm 5's larger headquarters unit devoted more effort to corporate-divisional relations than its counterpart at Firm 6. But division managers in Firm 5 also devoted more effort to achieving integration than did their counterparts in Firm 6. One explanation for this greater divisional involvement may be Firm 5's extensive reliance on paper systems coupled with a less elaborate approval and review system. Dependence on such planning, control, and goal setting systems to manage joint decision making may allow greater divisional participation relative to headquarters involvement. By way of contrast, it seems reasonable to assume that Firm 6's more extensive use of committees for joint decision making is one factor which would tend to require more corporate time relative to divisional time in arriving at joint decisions even though corporate and division managers, in absolute terms, spent less time attempting to achieve integration at Firm 6.

All this is not to say that larger corporate headquarters staffs and heavier dependence on paper systems are by themselves either more or less effective approaches for managing organizations in the paper industry. At this point in our discussion all that we can conclude is that (a) Firms 5 and 6 were taking different approaches to the management of interunit relationships, (b) that these different approaches led to different amounts and patterns of integrative effort, and (c) that patterns of integrative effort seem to be linked to each firm's choice and use of integrative devices (although other factors which we haven't explicitly examined—e.g., the history of the firm or the quality of decision-making and conflict resolution processes—might also be linked to these patterns of integrative effort). The next step is to compare how each approach worked in practice. Did one approach lead to more appropriate differentiation and/or more effective integration and how was this related to corporate performance?

Differentiation, Integration, and Performance

Differentiation* and integration were measured in the same way that we had measured these variables in the conglomerate firms. Table VI-11

---

* With the exception of a lower range of differences in formality of structure, the range of differences in orientations among divisions in the paper companies was quite

TABLE VI-11

Overview of Corporate-Divisional Relations and Performance in Two Paper Companies[a]

	Firm 5	Firm 6
Mean corporate-divisional differentiation	14.3	13.3
Corporate-divisional integration[b]	4.53	4.05
Corporate performance[c]	Higher	Lower

[a] Higher numbers indicate higher differentiation and integration. Scores are mean ratings for the three businesses studied in each firm; i.e., Mills, Containers, and Packaging.

[b] Difference is significant at the .001 level (analysis of variance).

[c] Derived from Tables VI-2 and VI-3.

presents overall scores for Firms 5 and 6 on both of these dimensions as well as suggesting their relationship to corporate performance. Turning first to the measures of differentiation we see that both firms had approximately the same level of differentiation between their headquarters and divisional units. Since both firms were operating in similar businesses, it appears that both had developed levels of corporate-divisional differentiation that were broadly consistent with the environmental diversity with which they were faced.

The important difference between the two companies was in terms of the corporate-divisional integration they were achieving. Firm 5 was achieving a higher quality of collaboration between its headquarters unit and divisions. Firm 5 was also a somewhat higher performer. It is also noteworthy that Firm 5 had been devoting considerably more effort to achieving integration; and it seems that this higher level of effort was paying off in terms of developing both appropriate differentiation and higher integration.*

Table VI-12 provides a breakdown of differentiation, integration, and integrative effort scores by major unit. This breakdown suggests that Firm 5 was more effectively managing its corporate-divisional relations on a unit-by-unit basis as well as on an overall basis. Patterns of corporate-divisional differentiation were similar in each of the companies except in the case of

---

similar to the range found in the conglomerate firms (Table II-8). See Appendix B for range of scores underlying differentiation scores in all settings.

* This relationship between integration and integrative effort is in marked contrast to our findings in conglomerate firms, where higher effort seemed to be associated with lower differentiation and lower integration. We will explore this contrast in greater depth in Chapter VII.

TABLE VI-12

Corporate-Divisional Relationships by Major Unit
in Two Paper Companies[a]

	Differentiation	Integration[b]	Effort Devoted to Integration
FIRM 5			
Mills	18	4.72	426.5
Container Division	10	4.57	337.6
Packaging Division	15	4.28	188.9
FIRM 6			
Mills	17	4.28	270.2
Container Division	13	3.93	207.9
Packaging Division	10	3.94	153.2

[a] Higher numbers indicate greater differentiation, integration, and integrative effort. Scores are combined ratings of headquarters and divisional executives for each corporate-divisional relationship.

[b] Differences between Firms 5 and 6 are significant as follows (analysis of variance): Mills (.05), Containers (.01), Packaging (not statistically significant).

packaging divisions. It appears that Firm 5's packaging unit was permitted a good deal more differentiation than its counterpart at Firm 6. One important reason for this greater differentiation undoubtedly was that Firm 5's packaging unit was much less dependent on the mills for paper than was Firm 6's packaging division (see Table VI-1). Not only was Firm 5's packaging division somewhat smaller in terms of total sales but, more importantly, paper represented a much lower proportion of the value added to its final products.

Corporate-divisional integration for both mills and the container division were significantly higher for Firm 5. At the same time, Firm 5 was achieving roughly the same level of integration with its packaging division that Firm 6 was with its packaging unit; however, Firm 5 was achieving this level of integration in the face of much higher differentiation. In terms of integrative effort we can again see that for each unit Firm 5 tended to devote more executive time and attention to managing the corporate-divisional interface; and in each case this higher effort was related to more effective relationships between the headquarters and the division.

Earlier in this chapter we noted that Firm 5 devoted more effort to direct divisional contacts than did Firm 6. Did this higher integrative effort at the divisional interface also lead to more effective management of these relationships? The data presented in Table VI-13 suggest that Firm

TABLE VI-13

Measures of Interdivisional Relations in Two Paper Companies[a]

	Firm 5	Firm 6
MILLS—CONTAINER DIVISION		
Differentiation	14	9
Integration[b]	3.8	3.4
MILLS—PACKAGING DIVISION		
Differentiation	13	15
Integration[b]	3.7	3.8

[a] Higher scores indicate greater differentiation and integration.
[b] Differences in integration are not statistically significant.

5 was more effectively managing the direct interface between its mills and its container division. Despite the fact that the difference in mill-container integration at Firms 5 and 6 was not statistically significant, Firm 5 was achieving its integration in the face of considerably higher differentiation. Indeed, mill-container differentiation appears to be quite low at Firm 6. One possible explanation of this lower differentiation is that mill goals and orientations may have taken precedence over those of the container division, and this state of affairs would be consistent with the lower container performance we found in Firm 6. In the case of the mill-packaging interface there were no important differences between the two companies.

In this section we have presented data which indicate that Firm 5 was managing interunit relationships more effectively than Firm 6, and these more effective relationships are related to somewhat higher long-run corporate performance and particularly higher performance for Firm 5's container division. Of course, it is important to realize that the differences between the two companies are a matter of degree; and they are not as wide as those which we found among the four conglomerate firms. Firm 6 was achieving a moderate degree of integration and its profit performance was only somewhat below the median for comparable firms; however, Firm 6 was not operating as effectively—either in an economic or in an organizational sense—as Firm 5.

One set of factors which help explain why Firm 6 was less effective is the lower total amount of integrative effort which this company expended on interunit relationships and its higher proportion of corporate involvement in achieving integration. This set of factors does not tell the whole story, however. We also found differences in the decision-making processes which characterized the two firms.

Patterns of Decision Making

In Chapter IV we identified seven aspects of corporate divisional decision-making processes which were associated with achieving appropriate differentiation and high integration in conglomerate firms. We reasoned that the relative presence or absence of these same factors would help explain why Firm 5 had been able to develop more effective interunit relationships than Firm 6. Table VI-14 summarizes our findings with respect

TABLE VI-14

Determinants of Effective Decision Making: An Overview of Corporate-Divisional Relations in Two Paper Companies[a]

	Firm 5	Firm 6
1. Quality of communications	H	L
2. Rapidity in responding to divisional requests	H	L
3. Performance evaluation system	H	L
4. Intermediate position of managers and departments in integrative positions	L	H
5. High influence of integrators	H	H
6. Balance between corporate and divisional influence	H	L
7. Modes of conflict resolution	H	H

[a] This comparative summary is based on the degree to which the sample of three subunits in each firm met each determinant relative to the scores for all six subunits which were studied. H = High and L = Low degree. The statistical comparisons upon which this summary is based may be found in Appendix A.

to the corporate-divisional interface.[*] Firm 5 met six of the seven factors to a high degree, while Firm 6 met only three of these determinants of effective decision making to a high degree.

A closer look at each of the determinants suggests that there were moderate differences between the two companies; and this seems consistent with our conclusion that Firm 6 was achieving a somewhat lower degree of integration and performance. Indeed, both companies had corporate-divisional decision-making processes which were characterized by a high

[*] In the interest of brevity we have not included statistical comparisons for each factor in this chapter. However, the interested reader can find these comparisons in Appendix A.

quality of upward communications, high influence of managers in integrative positions, and a high level of confrontation behavior in resolving conflicts. On the other hand, decision-making processes at Firm 6 appeared to be less effective than those at Firm 5 with respect to four factors:

(1) Division managers rated the quality of *downward* communications from the corporate headquarters as lower (difference significant at .05 level).

(2) Division managers rated the rapidity of the corporate headquarters in responding to their requests as lower (significant at .05 level). This finding is consistent with our previous findings that while Firm 6 had more elaborate formal mechanisms for approval of plans and budgets (see Table VI-9), its corporate personnel devoted less time to achieving integration. This could result in slower decisions.

(3) Firm 6's performance evaluation system seemed to be less flexible and less well understood by division managers. For one thing, there was much less agreement between corporate and division managers in Firm 6 about the relative emphasis which was placed on criteria used in measuring divisional performance. Also, there was less of a balance between short-run and long-run performance criteria in Firm 6's evaluation system.

(4) There was an imbalance in the perceived influence exerted over division policies by the corporate headquarters versus divisional management at Firm 6. In the case of mills and the container division the corporate headquarters was seen as exerting considerably more influence (differences significant at .05 level). For the packaging division considerably more influence was attributed to divisional management relative to the headquarters (differences significant at .05 level). By way of contrast, in Firm 5 there was a parity in the power exercised by the headquarters and the various divisions.

There was only one aspect of Firm 5's decision-making processes which appeared to be less effective than those found in Firm 6; managers in integrative positions tended to be less intermediate between the headquarters and the divisions in their orientations. Nonetheless we can see that overall Firm 5's corporate-divisional decision-making processes were more effective.

The next step in our analysis is to look at the patterns of interdivisional decision making which characterized the two paper companies; i.e., the quality of decision making which was found at the interfaces between the mills and the container division plus mills and the packaging division. In making this assessment we will focus on five factors. Four of these factors— quality of communications, rapidity of responding to one another's requests, modes of conflict resolution, and intermediate positions of integrators— coincide with the measures we have used in assessing corporate-divisional decision-making processes. The fifth factor—the degree to which integrators see their rewards as being based on total corporate performance—was suggested by the previous work of Lawrence and Lorsch.[3]

Given the patterns of interdivisional differentiation and integration which we had found at Firms 5 and 6, we were predicting that patterns of interdivisional decision making would be more effective for the mill-container interface at Firm 5 but that there would be no significant difference in the patterns for the mill-packaging interface. The summary data in Table VI-14 support this prediction. Firm 5 met four of the five determinants for its mill-container interface, while Firm 6 met only two out of five. Decision-making processes at Firm 6's mill-container interface tended to be less effective on the following counts:

(1) Quality of communications between the two units was lower (significant at .01 level).
(2) Confrontation behavior was seen as less common in resolving interdivisional conflicts (significant at .05 level).
(3) Individuals who had major integrative responsibilities saw total corporate performance as relatively less significant in determining the rewards they received from the company (significant at .05 level).

Again, the only determinant which Firm 5 did not meet to a high degree was intermediate position of integrators. Turning to the mill-packaging interface, we see that both companies met four of the five determinants.

We can conclude that Firm 5 met more of the determinants of effective decision making, both at the corporate-divisional and mill-container interfaces. This higher quality of decision-making processes along with the higher effort which Firm 5 devoted to interunit relationships takes us a long way in understanding why this company was at once able to achieve appropriate levels of differentiation, higher integration, and somewhat higher economic performance than Firm 6.

Summary

In this chapter we have examined the environmental requirements and organizational arrangements which characterized two vertically integrated paper companies. We have seen that the basic issues facing these companies were those of managing divisions which operated in moderately diverse environments and which were also sequentially interdependent with one another. As in the case of the four conglomerate companies, we found that appropriate levels of corporate-divisional differentiation and high integration are positively associated with higher long-term corporate performance. Similarly, the presence of several determinants of effective decision making were again found to be associated with a company's ability to achieve appropriate patterns of differentiation and integration.

TABLE VI-15

Determinants of Effective Decision Making: An Overview of Interdivisional Relations in Two Paper Companies[a]

	Firm 5	Firm 6
MILLS—CONTAINER DIVISION		
1. Quality of communications	H	L
2. Rapidity in responding to each other's requests	H	H
3. Modes of conflict resolution	H	L
4. Intermediate position of managers and departments in integrative positions	L	H
5. Degree to which integrators see their rewards based on total corporate performance	H	L
MILLS—PACKAGING DIVISION		
1. Quality of communications	H	H
2. Rapidity of responding to each other's requests	L	H
3. Modes of conflict resolution	H	H
4. Intermediate position of managers and departments in integrative positions	H	H
5. Degree to which integrators see their rewards based on total corporate performance	H	L

[a] This comparative summary is based on the degree to which the divisions in question met each determinant relative to the four interdivisional relationships studied. H = High and L = Low degree. The statistical comparisons upon which this summary is based may be found in Appendix A.

At the same time, however, the vertically integrated firms faced certain unique environmental requirements and had evolved organizational arrangements aimed at coping with these particular issues. The corporate headquarters units in these firms tended to get heavily involved in contracts within the industry environments of their divisions. Also, the need to manage both pooled and sequential interdependence in these firms gave rise to a fairly complex set of integrative devices, and led to a situation where high levels of integrative effort seemed to pay off.

The final step in our research effort will be to contrast more systematically the ways conglomerate and vertically integrated firms were uniquely different from one another. A fuller understanding of these differences can provide several valuable insights. First, such a comparison can provide clues to the sorts of organizational problems that may be indigenous to each of these corporate forms. Second, it can allow us to make predictions about some of the problems conglomerate firms will face if, and/or when they attempt to nurture more interdivisional collaboration. Finally, it can provide us with a fairly broad information base for developing a *contingency approach to corporate organization;* i.e., a systematic way of thinking about organizational decisions (such as the design of organizational units and integrative devices) within the context of the major requirements for diversity and interdependence which arise from a corporation's strategy.

VII

A Comparison of Corporate-Divisional Relationships in Conglomerate and Vertically Integrated Firms

THE evidence presented so far suggests that effective long-run performance of a multidivisional firm is associated with its ability to achieve appropriate differentiation and integration within the context of its overall environment. Having explored how both conglomerate and vertically integrated firms tried to achieve this fit between environmental conditions and organizational states, we are now in a position to raise a broader set of questions. Are the environmental demands faced by these two types of multidivisional firms sufficiently different to require fundamentally unique approaches to organization in each case? Do similar organizational devices and similar behavior on the part of top management tend to produce different effects in each of these settings? Do the organizational approaches which prove effective within each setting seem to have certain inherent strengths and weaknesses? Do the basic environmental characteristics of each setting place limitations on the organizational approaches which top management might wish to pursue?

In seeking answers to such questions, we are not proposing that there is an ideal approach for organizing either type of firm. Indeed, our findings clearly point to the need to design organizations to fit the requirements posed by the complex interplay among the environmental forces and management goals and strategies peculiar to each individual firm. Nevertheless, it is both theoretically and practically important to question whether and for what reasons the range of feasible options for managing and organizing conglomerate firms differs from that available to vertically integrated firms. By identifying broad similarities and differences among our two types of research sites we can begin to clarify what this range of feasible options for organization and management may be and whether it is distinctly different for different types of multidivisional firms.

The four clusters of factors upon which we have focused in this study —environmental demands, organizational choices, organizational states and decision-making processes, and economic performance—provide an efficient way to map and analyze corporate-divisional and interdivisional relationships in any large, complex organization. In the following pages we shall focus on each of these sets of factors as a way of comparing and contrasting the conglomerate and vertically integrated firms in our sample.

Comparison of Environmental Requirements

In comparing and contrasting the environmental requirements faced by each type of firm, we shall be concerned with four factors: (1) the diversity of external demands posed by the products and markets of each firm, (2) the overall degree of uncertainty posed for the firm by these products and markets, (3) the interdependence required among headquarters and divisional units in order to achieve effective performance within each firm's total environment, and (4) the funding requirements faced by each firm. Table VII-1 presents measures of the first two of these factors.

In order to get a rough indication of the relative environmental diversity faced by each firm we counted the number of three-digit Standard Industrial Classification categories which it encompassed.* By and large, the businesses of the conglomerate firms extended across a much wider range of SIC categories, thus presenting them with a considerably higher degree of environmental diversity. Firm 3 provides the one exception to this statement; it had roughly the same lower degree of diversity as the vertically integrated firms.

The earlier work of Lawrence and Lorsch[1] indicated that environmental uncertainty also had an important impact on patterns of organization in single industry settings. We reasoned that if there were consistent differences in the degree of environmental uncertainty facing the conglomerate and vertically integrated firms, these differences might well have an

---

* This same approach was used in Chapter II, and the reader may recall that this measure of overall diversity coincided quite closely with our questionnaire measures of environmental diversity for the sample divisions in the four conglomerate firms. These two measures of diversity were not used in our discussion of vertically integrated firms in Chapter VII both because we had drawn our sample of divisions to reflect interdependence rather than overall diversity and because the nature of mill operations did not permit us to construct a comparable index of diversity from questionnaire data.

important impact on the patterns of organization we sought to understand. In order to gauge the *collective* uncertainty faced by each of the firms, we calculated from questionnaire data uncertainty scores for each major sub-environment of each sample division and then computed an overall mean score for each firm. From Table VII-1 we can see that the conglomerate

TABLE VII-1

Summary Measures of Environmental Diversity and Uncertainty in Six Firms[a]

	Diversity[b] (No. SIC Categories)	Mean Uncertainty[c]
CONGLOMERATE FIRMS		
1	28	10.96
2	17	10.36
3	7	10.74
4	21	10.23
VERTICALLY INTEGRATED FIRMS		
5	11	9.35
6	8	9.28

[a] Higher scores indicate greater diversity and greater uncertainty.

[b] Number of three-digit Standard Industrial Classification categories encompassed by each firm.

[c] Uncertainty was measured by summing scores for clarity of information, certainty of causal relationships, and time span of environmental feedback for each functional area of each sample division. Scores reported above are the overall means for each firm. Difference between conglomerate and vertically integrated firms is significant at the .01 level (analysis of variance).

firms were faced with significantly greater uncertainty in their collective divisional environments than were the vertically integrated paper companies.* These data are consistent with what we already know about the basic businesses of each of the firms. The conglomerates were involved in the defense, capital goods, and consumer durable areas, which are often characterized by fairly uncertain markets and at least moderate technological change. By way of contrast, the paper companies operated in somewhat more certain markets often using long-established technologies.

---

* We can place these scores in further perspective by comparing them with those reported by Lawrence and Lorsch in their studies of three industries. These authors report the following overall uncertainty scores: Plastics (10.4), Food (10.3), and Containers (7.0). (*Organization and Environment*, pp. 90–91.) Thus, the conglomerate firms tended to face at least as much uncertainty *in toto* as the plastics and food companies, whereas our vertically integrated paper companies faced somewhat more uncertainty than the container organizations.

In our treatment of the interdependence which firms must manage we have focused on the overall complexity of interdependence and distinguished three basic patterns: pooled (least complex), sequential (more complex), and reciprocal (most complex). There can be considerable variation within each of these patterns, and at this point we need to get a better fix on the *degree* of interdependence each firm was trying to manage. We have devised two measures to quantify this factor. First, we computed a simple index of required connections among major units. From our interview data we determined where significant connections were required among the divisions in our sample as well as between these units and the headquarters. An index of required connections within each firm was computed by dividing the number of these required connections by the total number of possible connections. Figure VII-1 shows how this measure was

FIGURE VII-1

Measures of Required Connections in Two Firms

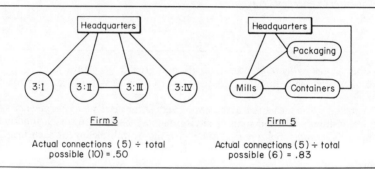

Firm 3

Actual connections (5) ÷ total
possible (10) = .50

Firm 5

Actual connections (5) ÷ total
possible (6) = .83

applied to Firms 3 and 5. While this measure is based only on the divisions sampled, it does provide a rough rank-order measure of the degree of interdependence faced by each firm.

Since connections are obviously required between the headquarters unit and each division in all firms, we hoped to get a more specific reading on the degree of corporate-divisional interdependence by employing a second measure. From questionnaire data we had computed the amount of time that corporate headquarters personnel spent with contacts in their divisions' industry environments (i.e., with trade associations, customers, and suppliers of the divisions). This measure indicates the degree to which headquarters and divisional environments tended to overlap and thus provides one indirect measure of the degree of required interdependence among these units. The greater the environmental overlap, the greater the need to integrate efforts.

TABLE VII-2

Measures of Required Interdependence in Six Firms[a]

	Required Connections Among Major Units	% Headquarters External Contacts Devoted to Divisions' Industry Environments
CONGLOMERATE FIRMS		
1	.50	9%
2	.40	23
3	.50	17
4	.60	22
VERTICALLY INTEGRATED FIRMS		
5	.83	64
6	.83	50

[a] Higher scores indicate higher interdependence.

Table VII-2 indicates that differences in degree of interdependence tended to be quite consistent between the two types of firms. The conglomerate firms were faced with a lower degree of interdependence—both in terms of required connections among all major units and in terms of the overlapping environmental contacts of corporate and division managers. The vertically integrated companies were faced with requirements for more intensive linkages among major organizational units.

In summary, the products and markets encompassed by the conglomerate firms entailed more diverse and uncertain environments *but* less complex requirements for interdependence than did those of the vertically integrated firms. Let us now consider another aspect of these firms' environmental requirements—funding availability and requirements.

In order to compare the funding availability and requirements faced by each type of firm, we used the same five measures which were used in Chapter II to compare the financial positions of the four conglomerates.[*] For this purpose we have limited our comparison to the high performing firms because performance problems have a direct impact on financial position and would thus tend to obscure differences between types of firms. The first two measures in Table VII-3 provide a rough picture of the external funding available to each of the firms. All three companies enjoyed roughly the same price-earnings multiples for their common stock. Although Firm 5 had more dollars of available debt capacity, it also had a much

---

[*] For a detailed definition of these measures see Chapter II, pp. 32–34.

TABLE VII-3

Measures of Financial Position for Three High Performing Firms

	Median P/E of Common Stock[a]	Available Debt Capacity[b] (in millions)	NCF/CE[c]	Std. Dev. NCF[c] x̄ NCF	NCF/GFA[c]
CONGLOMERATE FIRMS					
1	15x	$20.3	1.61	.148	.274
2	13x	27.4	1.52	.206	.096
VERTICALLY INTEGRATED FIRM					
5	15x	74.7	.72	.054	.125

Key: NCF = Net cash flow after dividends
     GFA = Gross fixed assets
     CE = Capital expenditures

[a] Computed on basis of median market value during most recent calendar year.

[b] Based on managers' estimates of maximum debt-equity ratio minus existing debt for most current year.

[c] Ratios are five-year averages, and the standard deviation is based on a five-year, least squares regression line.

larger sales and investment base than either of the conglomerate firms. The important point is that all three firms seemed to have considerable unused debt capacity relative to their current needs.

Turning to our three measures of internal funds patterns, we see some marked differences between the two types of firms. First of all, Firm 5 had much higher capital expenditures relative to its net cash flow; indeed, it was a net importer of capital (ratio of less than 1.0). The conglomerate companies tended to generate a good deal more cash than they invested internally. This greater internal demand for capital funding at Firm 5 undoubtedly posed additional requirements for achieving integration between the headquarters and its major operating units. A second important difference between the two types of firms was that Firm 5 enjoyed a much more stable cash flow than the conglomerate firms. This finding is closely related to our earlier argument (see Table VII-1) that the vertically integrated paper companies tended to face more certain environments. Our third measure of internal funds patterns—the ratio of gross fixed assets to net cash flow—does not indicate any consistent difference between the two types of firms. That is to say, Firm 5 tended to be more capital-intensive than Firm 1 but somewhat less capital-intensive than Firm 2.

While these five measures of financial position represent a simplified view of some rather complex economic interrelationships and depend on a three-firm comparison, they do suggest two noteworthy differences between the two types of firms: (1) that the vertically integrated paper firm tended to expend a larger percentage of its cash flow internally and (2) that it enjoyed more stable patterns of cash flow. These economic factors seem quite consistent with what we already know about the markets and technologies of the vertically integrated paper companies (relatively certain markets; stable, process technology of the mills; and interdependent operations requiring balanced expansion of capacity) versus those of the conglomerate firms (more uncertain markets; changing batch and job shop technologies; and divisional operations which could be expanded independently).

From the foregoing discussion we can see that the two types of firms faced distinctly different sets of environmental requirements. The two conglomerate firms tended to be faced with more diverse and uncertain environments and less complex requirements for interdependence than the vertically integrated firms. At the same time, the conglomerate firms tended to spend less of their funds flow on internal capital investments and were characterized by less stable funds flow patterns. Holding in mind these differences in environmental requirements, let us now examine the formal organizational devices used by each type of firm to deal with these basic facts of life.

Differing Patterns of Organizational Choice

While both types of firms had multidivisional organizations, they did differ in the degree to which their divisions were self-contained. Divisions in each of the conglomerate firms tended to enjoy a high level of self-containment of facilities and personnel. In a few cases these divisions had established enduring relationships with one another; e.g., joint ventures into new markets and customer-vendor, contractor-subcontractor arrangements; however, these cases proved to be the exception rather than the rule and did not account for a large proportion of divisional sales or expenses in the conglomerates. By way of contrast, in the vertically integrated paper companies the container and packaging divisions were characterized by somewhat less and the mill operations by a good deal less self-containment.

The organizational choices leading to divisional self-containment represent only one side of the equation; the other side consists of decisions regarding the role to be played by the corporate headquarters plus the basic integrative devices to be used in managing corporate-divisional relations. There were important differences in the ways that the conglomerate and vertically integrated firms had designed their corporate headquarters units (Table VII-4). First, the size of the corporate units of the conglom-

TABLE VII-4

Basic Characteristics of Corporate Headquarters Units in Six Firms[a]

	Conglomerate Firms				Vertically Integrated Firms	
	1	2	3	4	5	6
A. Size—total number of management and professional employees	17	20	25	230	479	250
B. FUNCTIONS PERFORMED IN REFERENCE TO DIVISIONS						
1. Financial/control	X_P	X_P	X_P	X_P	$X_{O,P}$	$X_{O,P}$
2. Long-range planning	X_P	X_P	X_P	X_P	$X_{O,P}$	$X_{O,P}$
3. Legal	$X_{O,P}$	$X_{O,P}$	$X_{O,P}$	$X_{O,P}$	$X_{O,P}$	$X_{O,P}$
4. Industrial relations	$X_{O,P}$	$X_{O,P}$	$X_{O,P}$	$X_{O,P}$	$X_{O,P}$	$X_{O,P}$
5. Operations research					X_P	
6. Marketing		X_P	X_P	X_O	X_O	X_O
7. Manufacturing/industrial engineering			X_P	X_P		
8. Planning and scheduling of output					X_O	X_O
9. Purchasing					X_O	X_O
10. Engineering (other than industrial)				X_P		
11. Research and development				$X_{O,P}$	X_O	X_O

[a] X indicates that certain functions in specified areas are performed by the headquarters unit for the divisions. P indicates that corporate involvement is of a policy setting nature; i.e., setting policies, advising, providing basic approaches. O indicates an operating responsibility for the headquarters unit; e.g., actually carrying out some purchasing activities for certain divisions.

erate companies tended to be quite small compared with those of the vertically integrated firms. Firm 4 represents the one exception to this statement.

A clearer understanding of why these corporate offices differed in size emerges by examining the functions which they performed with reference to the divisions. In Table VII-4 we have summarized these functions and classified them as entailing policy setting activities, operating activities, or both. By policy setting activities we mean that the headquarters played a somewhat indirect role; e.g., setting broad policies and procedures, recommending basic approaches for planning and control systems, and providing advice or consultation at the divisions' request. By operating activities we mean that the corporate headquarters actually performed an important proportion of a function for one or more of the divisions; e.g., centralized research and development activities.

In three of the four conglomerate firms the corporate offices' involvement with divisions tended to be limited to three broad areas: (1) general management; i.e., a policy role in planning and budgeting; (2) consultation and assistance in limited functional areas; e.g., market research and industrial engineering; and (3) both operating and policy activities in the legal and industrial relations areas. The corporate headquarters in the vertically integrated companies played a much more extensive role. For one thing, the managers who were responsible for control and long-range planning functions in the divisions reported formally to the Corporate Controller. Also, the corporate offices actually performed a significant proportion of activities in the areas of marketing (for the mills), planning and scheduling of output, purchasing, and R&D.

It appears that the conglomerate firms, faced with greater diversity, higher environmental and financial uncertainty, and lower interdependence, tended to develop patterns of organization which we might describe in summary as a federalized organizational system.[2] That is to say, divisions tended to be more self-contained while the headquarters units were small and performed basically general management and a few highly specialized staff functions. In contrast, the vertically integrated companies, faced with less diversity, less uncertainty, and higher interdependence, tended to develop patterns of organization which we might describe as a composite organizational system.[3] Divisions tended to be less self-contained, depending on large headquarters units both for general management functions and for numerous specialized operating activities. The only exception to this contrast is Firm 4. This low performing conglomerate, which faced most of the same broad environmental requirements as the other conglomerates, represents something of an anomaly in terms of its organizational patterns. Despite its large corporate staff, however, Firm 4 did exhibit many of the other characteristics of a federalized organizational system— both divisions with fairly high self-containment and headquarters functions which were mainly of a policy variety.

The final step in comparing patterns of organization in each type of firm is to examine the integrative devices employed by corporate management. In addition to its corporate headquarters and division general managers each of the firms had created group or senior vice president positions to help manage corporate-divisional relationships. The paper companies had also created planning and scheduling departments to manage the flow of product between mills and converting divisions and technical service manager positions to manage the direct relationships required among these operating units. By way of contrast, the lower interdivisional interdependence within the conglomerates did not seem to require these permanent integrating positions. In these firms interdivisional relations were managed on an *ad hoc* basis by the specific managers involved in each division and through the management hierarchy (i.e., division general managers, group vice presidents, and the headquarters).

Although both types of firms employed group or senior vice presidents to perform permanent integrating roles, there were differences between firms with respect to both the number of these positions and the particular integrative roles which they played (Table VII-5).

TABLE VII-5

Number of Group/Senior Vice Presidents in Six Firms

	No. of VPs
CONGLOMERATE FIRMS	
1	5
2	2
3	1
4	9
VERTICALLY INTEGRATED FIRMS	
5	5
6	5

In the conglomerates, there was a close connection between the firm's relative diversity and the number of group vice presidents it employed. Firms 1 and 4, the most diverse in our sample, employed more of these integrative positions than Firms 2 and 3. Group vice president positions seemed to be used mainly to deal with the problems of span of control faced by the corporate headquarters. A group vice president at Firm 2 provided the following description of his role, and this was fairly representative of what was occurring in all four firms:

My goal for the group is to contribute X% more to overall corporate earnings next year. In achieving this goal I work separately with each of the division general managers mainly through discussion of their plans and budgets. These men bear the primary responsibility for their own plans, budgets, and funds requests; however, I oversee them and bring the corporate point of view to bear. Essentially my job entails selecting, motivating, and evaluating eight division general managers—and not on the basis of day-to-day contact. It involves a good deal more counseling than demanding. I tend to spend more time with the corporate people than with the division managers. Most of this time is spent with the president because I am his eyes and ears for these eight divisions.

I have very limited involvement in interdivisional matters, either within this group or between groups. Take the joint venture that is currently being discussed by one of my divisions and a division in another group. I'm kept informed of developments, but the general managers actually handle it. Of course, I eventually have approval power on this project once it reaches the point of going into the budget or requires major funding.

In the vertically integrated companies senior vice presidents played a very different role. Despite the lower diversity of these companies, both employed five of these senior vice presidents; and their roles included both overseeing their own divisions and managing the interdependence among divisions. The senior vice president for converting operations at Firm 5 described his role as follows:

You can really talk about my job on two related levels. First of all, I'm concerned with the individual sales and profitability of our container and packaging divisions. This entails overall budgeting, facilities planning, and longer-range inputs from corporate R&D and engineering. At the same time, however, I'm just as concerned about the integrated profit which the corporation gets from all operations as well as the issues of product flow between the mills and converting divisions. This entails three-way talks between my group, the corporate headquarters, and the mills. The issues involved range from rate of expansion of the converting businesses, internal vs. external supplies of paper and linerboard, transfer pricing, and even major quality and scheduling problems.

Thus, we see that the use of senior vice presidents in the vertically integrated firms was dictated as much by interdependence as by diversity. Also, the lower environmental and financial uncertainty faced by the paper companies probably enabled managers in these high-level integrative positions to take a much more direct and active role in influencing divisional decision making.

We can conclude from these comparisons that the vertically integrated firms had developed more complex organizational arrangements for managing corporate-divisional and interdivisional relationships than had the conglomerates. These firms tended to have larger headquarters units which performed a wider range of function, and they also employed a more complex set of permanent integrative positions. These more complex organizational arrangements seem to be consistent with the higher level of interdependence faced by the vertically integrated paper companies. At the same time, it would seem that the lower environmental diversity and the lower environmental and financial uncertainty faced by these paper companies made their more complex organizational arrangements a feasible response to the interdependence which they sought to manage. By way of contrast, it seems reasonable to assume that the conglomerates would have found these more complex organizational patterns both less congruent with their environmental and financial requirements and less feasible responses to achieving integration. Indeed, we have seen in Chapter III that Firm 4, which was characterized by the most complex organizational arrangements of any of the conglomerates, was encountering difficulties in several areas. The final step in this comparison is to trace the impact that these differing environmental requirements and related patterns of formal organization had on the organizational states and decision-making processes found in each type of firm.

Similarities and Differences in Organizational States and Decision-Making Processes

Basic Patterns of Interunit Relationships

Table VII-6 compares interunit relationships in each type of firm in terms of the three basic measures which lie at the center of this study—differentiation, integration, and integrative effort. Two measures were used to compare corporate-divisional differentiation in each setting. First, mean differentiation scores were computed by dividing the total differentiation scores for our sample divisions by the number of divisions in the sample. Second, an estimate of total corporate-divisional differentiation was arrived at by multiplying these mean scores by the total number of divisions in each firm.

We can see that the mean corporate-divisional differentiation for the conglomerate firms was not consistently higher than that of the vertically integrated firms (Table VII-6). On the other hand, the two types of firms did tend to differ widely with respect to *total* differentiation. This suggests that the difference between the two types of firms did not stem from a tendency of individual divisions in conglomerate firms to be more differentiated from their headquarters units but rather from the fact that the conglomerates had segmented their total environments into a greater number of parts (or more simply, that they consisted of more divisions).[4] These

TABLE VII-6

Comparative Measures of Interunit Relationships in Six Firms[a]

| | Corp.-Div. Differentiation | | | | | |
	Mean Differ- entiation[b]	Total Differ- entiation[c]	Corp.-Div. Integration[d]	Corp.-Div. Integrative Effort[b]	Interdiv. Integrative Effort[b]	Relative Perform- ance
CONGLOMERATE FIRMS						
1	14.0	476	4.86	55.5	39.2	High
2	16.3	272	4.23	66.5	12.5	High
3	9.5	86	3.77	147.9	61.0	Low
4	11.0	231	3.88	114.2	71.0	Low
VERTICALLY INTEGRATED FIRMS						
5	14.3	114	4.68	317.6	152.8	High
6	13.3	106	4.25	210.4	44.3	Moderate

[a] Higher scores indicate greater differentiation, integration, and integrative effort.

[b] Numbers are mean scores based on sample of four divisions in conglomerate and three divisions in vertically integrated firms.

[c] Total differentiation scores were computed by multiplying mean differentiation scores by the number of divisions in each firm.

[d] Numbers are mean ratings by corporate managers for all major divisions, weighted to reflect the size of the respective divisions.

findings suggest an important refinement in our thinking about corporate-divisional differentiation in each type of firm. It seems entirely possible that there is a cognitive, or perceptual, limit beyond which it becomes impossible to effectively manage the relationship between the headquarters and a single division; and it appears that neither type of firm exceeded this maximum level of mean differentiation.* The conglomerates differed from their vertically integrated counterparts more in terms of the *number* of differentiated relationships that they had to manage rather than in terms of the degree of differentiation that they faced in any single corporate-divisional relationship.

Another difference between the two types of firms was the amount of effort they tended to devote to achieving integration. The conglomerates

---

* Indeed, the greater danger probably lies in the other direction; i.e., of achieving differentiation below what environmental diversity requires, as in the case of Firm 4 (see Chapter II, pp. 49–52).

tended to devote considerably less effort to corporate-divisional integration (Table VII-6). This finding fits with our earlier data which indicated that the conglomerates were faced with lower degrees of interdependence and possessed less complex integrative devices. Despite this lower level of integrative effort, the high performing conglomerates were achieving roughly the same level of integration as the vertically integrated companies. In the case of interdivisional integrative effort the pattern was similar but less strong. Clearly Firm 5 was devoting a good deal more effort to achieving interdivisional integration than its conglomerate counterparts. However, Firm 6 was devoting somewhat less effort to interdivisional relationships than either Firm 3 or Firm 4.* By and large, however, Table VII-6 indicates that the higher interdependence and more complex integrative devices of the vertically integrated firms were related to higher integrative effort.

Perhaps the most intriguing finding in Table VII-6 is that different levels of integrative effort seemed to have differing effects on integration in each of the two types of firms. In the conglomerates higher levels of integrative effort were associated with lower corporate-divisional integration, while in the vertically integrated firms higher effort seemed to be connected with higher integration.

Recent work by Driver and Streufert provides one way of explaining how integrative effort had different effects in these different environments and different organizations.[5] These authors have developed an empirically based model of information processing systems which they suggest can be applied to individuals, groups, and organizations. Their basic notion is that for any system there is a curvilinear relationship between the complexity of information inputs received by that system (environmental complexity) and the complexity of the information processing network which it develops to cope with these inputs (internal complexity). This relationship may be represented by a bell-shaped curve with an optimum point. The authors further indicate that while every system tends to develop its own characteristic relationship between environmental and internal complexity, different systems exhibit distinctly different optimal relationships between internal and environmental complexity.

The Driver and Streufert model can be used in the following manner to explain the differing relationships we have found between integrative

---

* One possible explanation for this finding is that Firm 6 was using its relatively high corporate-divisional integrative effort as a means of also managing interdivisional relations. This approach probably worked to some degree, although as we have seen in Chapter VI it also seemed to be associated with less effective integration and somewhat lower performance.

FIGURE VII-2

Hypothetical Relationships Among Interdependence, Integrative Effort, and Integration in Six Multidivisional Firms[a]

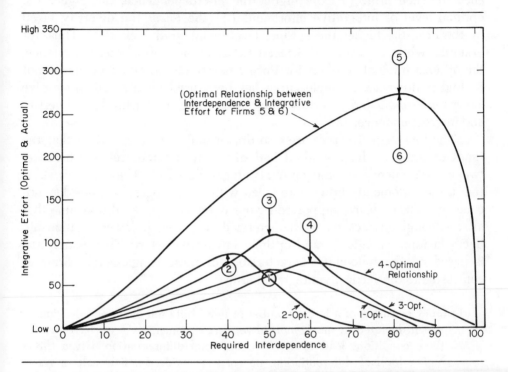

[a] Interdependence scores for each firm are from Table VII-2 and integrative effort scores are from Table VII-7. Optimal relationship curves are hypothetical. The more each firm diverges from its hypothetical curve, the *lower* the corporate-divisional integration found (see Table VII-6 for integration scores).

effort and other organizational states (particularly, corporate-divisional integration) in each type of firm. Figure VII-2 represents interdependence (a measure of the complexity of required information inputs for corporate-divisional relationships) on the horizontal axis and actual and optimal integrative effort (measures of the complexity of optimal and actual corporate-divisional information flows) on the vertical axis. To the degree that there is a fit between the degree of interdependence faced by a firm and its actual integrative effort, we would expect to find that firm achieving higher corporate-divisional integration. What is needed to determine this fit is an assumption about the optimal relationship between integrative effort and interdependence for each firm. Thus, we have superimposed hypothetical curves on Figure VII-2 to represent what our findings suggest these optimal relationships might look like.*

The five bell-shaped curves are drawn to represent two assumptions about the optimal relationship between integrative effort and interdependence for each firm: (1) the higher the interdependence, the higher the optimal level of integrative effort and (2) the *lower* the diversity faced by the firm, the higher the optimal level of integrative effort.** Thus, for example, while Firms 1 and 3 faced the same degree of interdependence, the optimal integrative effort for Firm 1 is assumed to be lower because of its higher diversity. A single curve has been used for optimal integrative effort for Firms 5 and 6 because they faced quite similar levels of diversity and interdependence.

The bell-shaped curves are also drawn under the assumption that the types of firms we have studied had distinctly different relationships between interdependence and optimal integrative effort. These curves show that the conglomerate firms were faced with lower degrees of interdependence, and this is clearly supported by our data. The curves also assume that all the conglomerates were characterized by a much lower relationship between interdependence and optimal integrative effort. This assumption is based on the following characteristics of these conglomerate firms as contrasted to the vertically integrated firms:

(1) They consisted of a larger number of more fully self-contained divisions which operated in much more diverse environments. As we have seen, these conditions lead to much higher total differentiation. Given this higher level of differentiation, no corporate-wide decision-making system could handle all of the information complexity related to divsional activities. Thus, as we have seen, interdependence was limited to major policy issues and mostly to their financial implications. The most complex interdependencies were, of necessity, managed within the various divisions.

(2) With both a higher level of total differentiation and smaller headquarters units the conglomerate firms were faced with a simpler information network; i.e., fewer "channels" over which information might flow between the headquarters and its divisions. Thus, high levels of corporate-divisional integrative effort might lead to both overloading of existing channels of communication and a slowing down of joint decision-making processes.

---

* The precise slope of these curves is relatively unimportant and obviously cannot be supported with data. However, the location of optimal points and the height of the curves do represent key assumption we shall attempt to support.

** This assumption fits with the negative relationship found between differentiation and integrative effort in conglomerate firms.

Having stated the assumptions for the curves shown in Figure VII-2, let us now consider how they help explain our findings. Each of the firms has been located on the diagram at the approximate point where its levels of interdependence and *actual* integrative effort intersect (indicated by circles). The more a firm's actual integrative effort diverges from its optimal (represented by its bell-shaped curve) the lower the corporate-divisional integration we would expect to find. Thus, Firms 3 and 4, even though they were characterized by somewhat higher optimal relationships between interdependence and integrative effort, were still devoting excessive effort to integration and achieving lower corporate-divisional integration than Firms 1 and 2. At the same time, it would appear that Firms 1 and 2 could have profited from devoting slightly more effort to integration.

Given the distinctly different interdependence/optimal integrative effort curve for the two vertically integrated firms, we can begin to understand why a positive relationship between integration and integrative effort would seem to obtain in this setting. While Firms 5 and 6 were faced with the same levels of interdependence and the same relationship between this interdependence and integrative effort, Firm 5 was devoting more effort to integration and in fact achieving higher integration. It would seem that Firm 5 was nearer and perhaps slightly above the optimal relationship between required interdependence and integrative effort. One explanation for Firm 6's lower integration would seem to be that its integrative effort was a good bit below this optimum point.

The basic issue with which we are concerned is the relationship between actual and optimal integrative effort at a given point in time (on the vertical axis of Figure VII-2). It is interesting, however, to consider how a firm could move along its optimal integrative effort curve (i.e., along the horizontal axis) and what this would mean. If the interdependence required by a firm's environment either increased or decreased dramatically but its formal organizational arrangements and its environmental diversity and corporate-divisional differentiation remained unaltered, we would expect to see another form of organization-environment misfit which would lead to less effective patterns of corporate-divisional integration. Unfortunately we would need to collect data over time to trace out such a pattern. Nonetheless, it appears that Firm 3 had encountered just this sort of problem in its abortive attempt to nurture operating synergy within constraints posed by its existing organizational devices and organizational states.*

The foregoing discussion is one means of explaining the differing relationships we have found between integration and integrative effort in the

---

* This issue was discussed in Chapter V, p. 114, and we shall return to it at the end of this chapter.

conglomerate and vertically integrated settings. The important point, however, is that the evidence suggests that there were some important internal
differences between these two types of firms which were related to their
overall environmental requirements and the complex ways these requirements were interrelated with organizational choices and all organizational
states. In other words, the range of feasible options for managing each type
of firm which we studied did differ. In order to further understand the
internal differences between these two types of firms, let us now compare
the corporate-divisional decision-making processes which characterized
each type of firm.

Corporate-Divisional Decision-Making Processes

Earlier we examined several aspects of joint decision-making processes
that tended to be associated with appropriate differentiation and integration. At this point we wish to consider whether these several factors differed in systematic ways between the conglomerate and vertically integrated firms. Our discussion of these decision-making processes will cover
only the high performing, high integration firms (1, 2, and 5) because, as
we have already seen, the lower performing firms tended to have less effective decision-making patterns and thus their inclusion would obscure
the comparison we wish to make.

There were no important differences between the conglomerate and
vertically integrated firms in four of the seven factors.* These basic similarities were as follows:

(1) *Intermediate Orientations and High Influence of Linking Functions*—
Each type of firm had set up certain integrative positions which were responsible for mediating between the goals and concerns of the corporate office and those of the various divisional managements. In both
settings more effective integration was related to these managers having
goal, time, and interpersonal orientations which were intermediate between those of the units they linked. In each type of firm these managers and/or departments also possessed high influence relative to the
two units that they bridged. It would seem that (a) responsiveness to
the needs of both units and (b) the ability to play a significant role in
joint decision making are necessary conditions for playing an effective

---

* For actual measurement of the four aspects of decision making that did not differ
between types of firms see Appendix A.

integrative role regardless of the environmental characteristics faced by a firm.

(2) *Corporate-Divisional Influence Balance*—In both settings we found underlying similarities in the balance which was maintained between influence exerted by the corporate headquarters and by divisional managers over the joint decisions which affected future courses taken by the divisions. The higher performing firms in each setting tended to achieve either a rough balance of influence between corporate and divisional managements or a difference in the direction of slightly more power being exerted by divisional management. One reason that the divisions may have held somewhat more sway in policy decisions is that they probably tended to possess or have access to more of the information required by the decisions.[6] While influence balance among major organizational units does not seem to be linked to differing environmental requirements, we shall see later in this chapter that environmental conditions do seem to affect the relative influence exerted by each hierarchical level.

(3) *Modes of Resolving Conflicts*—The degree to which confrontation, or problem solving, was used to resolve corporate-divisional conflicts also tended to be much the same in both settings.

(4) *Overall Quality of Upward and Downward Information Flows*—There were no consistent differences between the conglomerate and vertically integrated firms with respect to the perceived quality of upward and downward information flows. Initially we were hypothesizing that the conglomerate firms would tend to find it more difficult to maintain high quality communications between their headquarters and far-flung divisions; however, the data did not support this hypothesis. It may well be that the communication difficulties which could have arisen from greater environmental diversity were offset by the lower interdependence faced by these firms. At any rate, the evidence suggests that high performing firms in both settings were able to achieve overall information flows of roughly the same perceived quality.

There were three aspects of corporate-divisional decision making in which we did find important variations between the conglomerate and vertically integrated firms. Table VII-7 indicates that the two conglomerate firms tended to respond more rapidly to requests from their higher performing divisions than did the vertically integrated firm. At the same time, the headquarters of Firms 1 and 2 tended to respond at least as rapidly to their lower performing divisions as Firm 5 responded to any of its divisions. Even though Firms 1 and 2 faced greater environmental uncertainty and diversity than Firm 5, it appears that their lower levels of interdependence and less intensive capital requirements permitted them to move more

TABLE VII-7

Rapidity of Corporate Headquarters in Responding to
Divisional Requests in Three High Performing Firms[a]

CONGLOMERATE FIRMS	
1—higher performing divisions	3.15
—lower performing divisions	2.75
2—higher performing divisions	3.4
—lower performing divisions	2.5
VERTICALLY INTEGRATED FIRM	
5—Mills	2.70
—Containers	2.85
—Packaging	2.42

[a] Higher numbers indicate greater rapidity in responding to requests. Scores are mean ratings by managers in each sample division. Differences between all divisions in Firm 5 and higher performing divisions in Firms 1 and 2 are significant at .01 level (analysis of variance). Differences between Firm 5 and lower performing divisions in Firms 1 and 2 are not statistically significant.

rapidly in responding to divisional requests. By way of contrast, Firm 5's higher interdependence and more intensive capital requirements did not permit it to move as rapidly on divisional requests.

Figure VII-3 indicates that there were also important differences between each type of firm with respect to the distribution of influence over divisional policies. In the two conglomerate firms the division general manager (3 levels down in the hierarchy) was seen as having the highest influence. The next most influential levels tended to be group vice presidents (2 levels down) and the corporate headquarters, respectively. In the vertically integrated firm, however, senior vice presidents (2 levels down) exerted the most influence. The conglomerate firms, faced with a larger number of divisions, lower interdependence, more uncertainty, and less intensive funding requirements, had evolved decision-making patterns in which the division general manager was the organizational level at which most of the required economic, market, production, and scientific information could be drawn together to formulate policies.

By way of contrast, the higher interdependence faced by the vertically integrated firms militated against division general managers having most of the necessary information for formulating policies and plans. For instance, the mills depended on market inputs from sister units and scientific inputs from corporate R&D before they could decide upon future courses of action. The greater interdependence which characterized the vertically integrated

FIGURE VII-3

Influence Over Divisional Policies Attributed to
Four Major Organizational Levels in Three High Performing Firms[a]

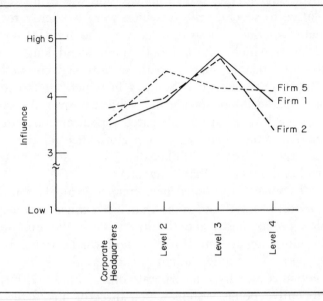

[a] Scores represent overall mean for four divisions in conglomerate firms (1 and 2) and three divisions in vertically integrated firm (5), based on ratings by corporate and division managers for each of the divisions. Differences between Firms 1 and 2 and Firm 5 are significant as follows: Level 2 (.001) and Level 3 (.001). Other differences are not statistically significant.

paper company does not provide a sufficient explanation of why senior vice presidents tended to exert such high influence, however. Use of interdivisional committees might have provided division general managers with the added information they needed, and with these arrangements we might still have found the highest influence at this level. It seems that it was the lower uncertainty faced by Firm 5 combined with higher interdependence that led to the high influence of the senior vice presidents. As suggested in the previous chapter, it was this lower environmental uncertainty that permitted—and seemingly made it more efficient—to manage much of the interunit communication and decision making at somewhat higher organizational levels in the paper companies.

The final aspect of decision-making processes which we wish to explore centers around the performance evaluation systems used by the corporate headquarters to assess and reward the results achieved by divisions. The most striking differences between performance evaluation systems employed by the two types of firms were (1) the explicitness with which criteria were defined, (2) the degree to which results were directly linked to the rewards received by division managers, and (3) the specific criteria which received the most weight in each setting.

In the two conglomerate firms each division was evaluated on its performance relative to several criteria which were explicitly recorded prior to the evaluation period. These criteria took the form of some ten pre-established indices which reflected both annual and longer term trends, and each division's results relative to these criteria were tied directly to rewards in the form of incentive bonuses in which all top level division managers participated. More specifically, subject to overall corporate financial constraints, each division was allocated a pool of bonus funds the size of which was determined mainly by its performance relative to the established criteria. Each division then allocated its bonus pool among management personnel in the manner that it saw fit.

By way of contrast, divisional performance evaluation in Firm 5 proceeded in a more informal and somewhat less explicit manner. Divisional goals for sales, profits, costs, and the like were built into this company's planning and budgeting system. However, no formal divisional performance evaluation system existed independent of the periodic reviews of the budgeted versus actual results by the corporate office. Similarly, Firm 5 did not employ an incentive bonus system which directly linked rewards for division managers to the results which they had achieved.

Another difference which we found between the two types of firms was the relative emphasis they tended to place on specific performance criteria. Table VII-8 indicates that the conglomerate firms tended to place major weight on financial and/or "end result" sorts of criteria; e.g., sales, profits, and ROI. By way of contrast, the vertically integrated firm tended to place considerable weight on both financial/end result criteria and operating/intermediate performance criteria; e.g., market share, rate of new product development, management development, and control over various expense items.

How did these differing approaches to performance evaluation impact on corporate-divisional decision-making processes? Table VII-9 indicates that they seemed to have roughly the same effect. Despite the more informal approach taken by Firm 5, the data suggest that this company was able to communicate its expectations regarding criteria of performance just as effectively as the two conglomerate firms. At the same time, both types of firms were able to achieve a rough balance between long-run and short-run performance criteria, which presumably would allow them to be more sensitive to the diverse time horizons of their several divisions.

Why did these differing approaches to performance evaluation seem

TABLE VII-8

Relative Emphasis Placed on Criteria for Divisional Performance Evaluation in Three High Performing Firms[a]

	Criteria	
	Financial/End Result[b]	Operating/Intermediate[b]
CONGLOMERATE FIRMS		
1	1.67	2.48
2	1.67	2.46
VERTICALLY INTEGRATED FIRM		
5	1.89	2.14

[a] *Lower* scores indicate a greater emphasis on criteria. Scores are combined ratings by managers in each sample division. See Appendix B for a discussion of how these statistics were computed.

[b] Differences between conglomerate firms and Firm 5 are significant at the .05 level (analysis of variance).

to work equally effectively in each type of firm? Again, the explanation seems to lie in the differing environmental requirements faced by the two types of firms. The greater environmental diversity of Firms 1 and 2 seemed to require more explicitly defined and administered evaluation systems. Faced with a wide range of environmental requirements, these firms could not depend solely on top management's implicit understanding of what constituted effective divisional performance. At the same time, the lower

TABLE VII-9

Perceived Characteristics of Corporate Performance Evaluation Systems in Three High Performing Firms[a]

	Conglomerate Firms		Vertically Integrated Firm
Characteristics	1	2	5
(1) Agreement between corporate and divisional executives concerning relative emphasis placed on criteria (Kendall coefficient of concordance)[b]	.78	1.04	.94
(2) Balance between long-run and short-run performance criteria (mean difference score)	.38	.19	.14

[a] Higher scores indicate higher agreement *but* less long-run/short-run balance. See Appendix B for a discussion of how these scores were computed.

[b] Coefficients of concordance are significant as follows: Firms 2 and 5 (.001); Firm 1 (.01).

interdependence faced by the two conglomerate firms made it a good deal easier to isolate and evaluate the performance of individual divisions; thus, use of explicitly defined criteria which were directly linked to monetary rewards became a viable approach in this setting. Finally, both greater environmental diversity and lower interdependence made heavier dependence on financial/end result criteria both a viable and more efficient means of assessing divisional performance. In other words, in firms which were made up of a diverse set of self-contained divisions financial/end result criteria represented a common set of benchmarks over which each divisional management team could exert considerable control.

By way of contrast, the lower diversity, lower uncertainty, and higher interdependence that characterized the vertically integrated paper firm undoubtedly made less formalized approaches, which avoided direct linkages between results and rewards for single divisions, both possible and more desirable. On the one hand, it was possible in this less diverse and more certain setting for corporate management to depend on a more implicit understanding of what constituted effective performance. On the other hand, higher interdependence among divisions and between divisions and the corporate headquarters left divisional management teams with less direct control over their overall results; thus, direct linkages between monetary rewards and results of single divisions became a less desirable approach to performance evaluation. Similarly, Firm 5's lower diversity and higher interdependence made heavier reliance on operating/intermediate results criteria a more useful means of tracking divisional performance.

Conclusions

In designing this study we began with the underlying hypothesis that the approach which a firm takes to managing corporate-divisional relationships is contingent upon the particular constellation of environmental requirements with which it is faced. By systematically comparing conglomerate and vertically integrated firms in this chapter we are now in a position to draw some more specific conclusions regarding how the internal workings of these companies are contingent upon their environmental requirements.

Although we found that each type of firm was characterized by quite different environmental factors and patterns of organizational choice, we also discovered that four aspects of corporate-divisional decision making were quite similar in each setting. Effective firms in both settings were characterized by (1) integrative positions and/or departments which were intermediate in position between the units they sought to link and which also enjoyed high influence relative to these units; (2) the presence of high levels of confrontation in resolving interunit conflicts; (3) a high quality of both upward and downward information flows; and (4) patterns of influence which were either balanced between corporate and divisional management or slightly in the favor of divisional management. It would seem that the presence of these four aspects of decision making are important for achieving appropriate differentiation and integration and effective performance in any setting.[7] Indeed, Lawrence and Lorsch[8] had previously found that the first two of these factors were present in effective organizations in three distinctly different single-industry settings.

At the same time, we found some marked differences between the internal functioning of the conglomerate and vertically integrated firms; and these differences were related to the differing constellations of environmental factors which characterized each setting. Figure VII-4 summarizes these major contingent relationships and shows how they differed in each setting. In essence, the conglomerate firms had developed formal organizational arrangements which were characterized by a high degree of divisional self-containment and less complex devices for managing corporate-divisional integration. Given these organizational arrangements, the conglomerates tended to expend less effort on achieving corporate-divisional integration, to move more rapidly in response to divisional requests, and to be faced with higher total differentiation. Also, these firms exhibited differing patterns of hierarchical influence and differing approaches to performance evaluation. These internal characteristics of the conglomerates were closely related to the pattern of requirements posed by their environments; i.e., higher diversity and uncertainty, lower interdependence, and their particular funding requirements. In other words, these firms seemed to be well adapted to their particular environments.

By way of contrast, the vertically integrated firms had developed formal organizational arrangements which were characterized by less divisional self-containment and more complex devices for managing corporate-divisional and interdivisional integration. Given these organizational arrangements, the vertically integrated firms tended to devote a good deal more effort to achieving corporate-divisional integration, to move less rapidly on divisional requests, and to be faced with lower total differentiation. At the same time, these firms tended to have influence patterns which peaked at a higher organizational level and to employ differing approaches to performance evaluation. Again, this set of internal characteristics seemed to be well adapted to requirements posed by the environments of these vertically integrated firms—higher interdependence, lower uncertainty and diversity, and heavier internal funding requirements.

The differences which we have found between the conglomerate and

FIGURE VII-4

Summary of Major Differences Between Conglomerate and Vertically Integrated Firms Studied

Environmental Requirements	*Patterns of Organizational Choice*	*Organizational States and Decision-Making Processes*
CONGLOMERATE FIRMS		
Greater environmental diversity.	Higher degree of divisional self-containment.	Higher total differentiation.
Higher environmental uncertainty.	Smaller headquarters units focusing mainly on policy issues.	Lower integrative effort.
Less complex required interdependence.	Less complex integrative devices.	Greater rapidity in responding to divisional requests.
Less intensive internal funding requirements.		Influence peaks at a lower (division general manager) level.
More uncertain patterns of funds flow.		Performance evaluation systems with explicitly defined criteria, direct linkage between results and rewards, and heavier emphasis on financial/end-result criteria.
VERTICALLY INTEGRATED FIRMS		
Lower environmental diversity.	Lower degree of divisional self-containment.	Lower total differentiation.
Lower environmental uncertainty.	Larger headquarters units focusing on both policy and operating issues.	Higher integrative effort.
More complex required interdependence.	More complex integrative devices.	Less rapidity in responding to divisional requests.
More intensive internal funding requirements.		Influence peaks at a higher (senior vice president) level.
More certain patterns of funds flow.		Performance evaluation systems which are more informally administered, without direct linkage between results and rewards, and balanced emphasis on financial/end-result and operating intermediate criteria.

vertically integrated firms point to the conclusion that the range of feasible options for managing each type of firm is considerably different. For instance, where conglomerate firms similar to the ones we have studied attempt to build large corporate staffs and to utilize more complex approaches to achieving corporate-divisional integration we would predict adverse effects on differentiation, integration, and ultimately performance. In Chapters III and V we have attempted to trace how these adverse consequences of organizational choice arise both within the total firm and for single corporate-divisional relationships. In essence, two things can occur as the headquarters attempts to move toward more complex organizational arrangements. First, the divisions devote an increasing proportion of their effort to managing corporate-divisional relations and, in the process, can become less sensitive to the requirements posed by their diverse industry environments. Second, increasing levels of conflict seem to arise around both the process and the substance of corporate-divisional decision making. The vertically integrated firms, on the other hand, had already developed a relatively complex set of organizational devices which appeared to be functioning effectively. Indeed, it is doubtful whether these companies could have effectively managed their less diverse and highly interdependent units without such complex organizational arrangements. Where vertically integrated firms similar to the ones we have studied attempt to reduce the size of their corporate staffs and simplify approaches to achieving integration, we would expect to find increasing differentiation, less effective integration, and ultimately lower performance. As a matter of fact, this was roughly what we found to be happening in Firm 6 (the moderate performing paper company).

What we are arguing is simply this: the top management of every firm develops or chooses a set of formal organizational devices to facilitate the overall control and coordination of the total enterprise. Very often there seems to be an unquestioned logic in management circles which assumes that larger corporate headquarters units and more complex integrative devices will result in "better control and coordination." This study suggests that such an assumption is not only an oversimplified view, but in some instances it may lead to extremely unfortunate consequences. In its place we propose a contingent assumption: *Control and coordination of the total enterprise are most effectively facilitated when top management chooses a set of organizational devices which are congruent with the particular constellation of environmental factors faced by the firm.* Thus, the range of options for organizational choice are quite different in the cases of conglomerate and vertically integrated firms.

We should recognize, however, that these broad conclusions have at least two important limitations. First, our comparison of conglomerate and vertically integrated firms is based on a sample of six companies. Thus while the organizational choices of a number of well-known conglomerates —such as Textron,[9] FMC,[10] and Teledyne[11]—seem to fit quite closely with our conclusions, those of ITT [12]—considered by many as a highly successful conglomerate—seem in certain respects to run counter to these findings.

Also, our discussion of vertically integrated firms is based only on an examination of paper companies.[13] Somewhat different patterns of environmental factors and, thus, organizational choices could be expected in other industries; e.g., steel, aluminum, or chemicals. For instance, a vertically integrated chemical company would probably be faced with higher diversity and uncertainty at the same time that it faced relatively high interdependence.[14] Thus, we can only speak broadly about ranges of feasible options for organization and management of different types of multidivisional firms.

The second limitation of our conclusions centers around the fact that we have studied these two types of firms at one point in time. Environmental requirements and top management goals do change. And, as we completed this study, they seemed to be changing quite drastically for the conglomerates. Let us briefly consider what relevance our findings may have for these changing conditions.

Both longer run governmental activities and a number of financial considerations have made mergers a somewhat less attractive means of growth than they were in the 1950s and 1960s. Thus, we can expect the conglomerates to look more and more for unfulfilled potential in their internal operations. In Chapter V we argued that the conglomerate firms we had studied seemed to be achieving appreciable degrees of financial and managerial synergy but little or no operating synergy. Some of the firms saw little immediate payoff in this operating synergy; others had met with little success in attempting to achieve it. Our comparisons of conglomerate and vertically integrated firms in this chapter suggest that the conglomerates may encounter at least three sorts of costs when and if they attempt to nurture such interdivisional collaboration.

First of all, increases in interdivisional collaboration will entail substantial increases in long-run coordinative costs, both interdivisional and corporate-divisional. As in the case of the paper companies in this study, the conglomerates would begin to require direct interdivisional linkages as well as higher levels of corporate-divisional integrative effort to manage the more complex planning, budgeting, and resource allocation decisions which this higher interdependence requires. The conglomerates would also encounter certain shorter term costs in changing their organizational forms so that they could accommodate higher interdependence. We saw in this chapter how increases in integrative effort tended to reduce the quality of integration in conglomerate firms. One explanation for this state of affairs is that changes in integrative effort also entail shifts in power positions, redefinition of roles and attendant role conflicts, as well as certain inconsistencies with the existing organizational devices; e.g., methods of evaluating divisional performance and the danger of overloading key decision makers at the headquarters. Thus, the conglomerates would have to undertake considerable organizational redesign; and changes of this scale are always costly. Finally, by opting for greater interdivisional collaboration the conglomerates would, to some degree, give up one of their current strengths—the capacity to deploy resources rapidly and flexibly among a wide range of divisions. As in the case of the paper companies, we would expect the rapidity of response of the headquarters to decline as interdependence increases. It seems that achieving operating synergy can entail important opportunity costs in the form of reduced financial synergy.

By dwelling on the potential costs of operating synergy, we do not wish to suggest that it is seldom worth pursuing. Rather, we are arguing that operating synergy is not simply an undiscovered "gold mine" hidden in every conglomerate firm; there are both benefits and costs to be considered. The benefits can be reckoned by a careful examination of the environmental and strategic contexts of each individual firm, both actual and potential. At the same time, this study provides a step in the direction of reckoning some of the possible costs of achieving operating synergy.

In this chapter we have attempted to marshal our data about the functioning of two types of firms to test the validity of what we have termed a contingency approach to corporate-divisional relations. In the final two chapters we shall explore the implications of this study for current and future theoretical formulations and for the management of large, multiunit organizations.

VIII

Toward a Contingency Theory of Complex Organizations

IN CHAPTER I we stated the dual objectives of contributing both to management practice and to organizational theory. This chapter summarizes our findings and links them to the current state of organizational theory. The final chapter will build on the managerial implications already discussed in Chapter V to consider the broader issues of decentralization as well as the particular issues of organizing and managing multidivisional enterprises.

We wish to emphasize that by distinguishing between theory and practice in these two chapters we are not attempting to construct a dichotomy. In fact, as indicated in Chapter I, we see the two as having strong common interests. For organizational theory to be worth its salt it must ultimately illuminate the practitioner's problems in a way that is both comprehensible to him and aids him in planning constructive action. Evidence of the common interests of theory and practice will be found in the final chapter, where we shall use the theory summarized here to place the problems of decentralization in a new and, we hope, a more manageable light.

Contingency Theories of Organization

The basic task which we set for ourselves at the inception of this study was to apply the growing body of research findings and theories developed by the behavioral sciences to the organizational problems faced by the top management of multidivisional firms. We saw the most fruitful set of ideas for developing an understanding of these problems as coming from what has been termed a contingency theory of organization. This approach has its roots in very diverse territories.[1] Contributions have come from the experimental studies of group communication nets and human information processing of Leavitt[2] and of Schroder et al.;[3] the field studies of sociologists, such as Woodward[4] and Burns and Stalker;[5] the studies of pre-industrial civilization of Udy;[6] the theoretical statements of Perrow[7] and Thompson;[8] as well as the organizational comparisons of Lawrence and Lorsch.[9] Similar approaches have also been suggested by the experimental work of Fouraker[10] and the historical study of U.S. corporations conducted by Chandler.[11] Finally, credit for many of the ideas which have either directly or indirectly affected this approach can be traced to the work of March and Simon.[12]

The common denominator for all this work is the notion that the internal characteristics of an effective organization are contingent upon the work it must perform in dealing with its environment. At the managerial level in organizations, as we have seen, much of this work can be conceived of as decision making and the related importation, processing, and transmission of information. In fact, most contingency theorists, ourselves included, suggest that the pattern of internal states and processes developed by an effective organization are heavily contingent upon the complexity of information requirements posed by its environment.

Most of the studies cited above have focused on the relative certainty of information as a key environmental factor affecting the pattern of organizational states required to achieve effective performance. However, several other contingent relationships between environmental characteristics and organizational states have also been identified. Lawrence and Lorsch[13] have also examined the impact of key competitive variables on the required orientations of organization members. Thompson[14] has pointed to the type of interdependence (pooled, sequential, or reciprocal) as another factor affecting organizational form.

In this study we have examined contingent relationships between environmental characteristics and internal states at multiple organizational levels. First, we considered the requirements posed for divisional units by the rate of change, time span of feedback, and key competitive variables which characterize their particular industrial environments and sectors within these environments. Similarly, we have explored the relationships between characteristics of the corporate headquarters unit and the salient characteristics of its environment. Finally, we shifted our attention to the fit between patterns of corporate-divisional relationships and the patterns of environmental diversity, interdependence, and funds flows faced by the firm as a whole.

The internal factors upon which we have focused—organizational assumptions, complexity of integrative devices, differentiation, integration, integrative effort, and decision-making processes—are in no way exhaustive of the factors which have been identified by contributors to contingency theory. It is our hope that as contingency theory continues to develop, other important factors will be identified and both compared and contrasted with the factors employed in this and the other studies we have cited. Only through such a process can we hope to develop a theory which is sufficiently insightful and rigorous to effectively map and understand the complexities of modern organizations.

Even with the limited number of variables addressed in this study and the earlier work of Lawrence and Lorsch,[15] the interrelationships among environment, organization, and economic performance become rather complex. Given this complexity, there is a need to summarize concisely the current state of contingency theory—at least, as it is reflected in our work. Toward this end we shall state below the major propositions which can be drawn from this study as well as from *Organization and Environment*.[16] We shall focus primarily on these two studies because, for the most part, they have used common variables. However, we shall also cite other researchers whose findings prove helpful in developing a coherent set of statements.

A note of caution is in order before we consider this set of propositions. On the one hand, we believe that we have an adequate data base both to make these statements and to use them as a working model to aid practitioners in dealing with concrete organizational problems. On the other hand, we do not want other researchers and students of organization to take these generalizations as definitive and final. Rather, we see them as statements about our current knowledge which need to be tested and refined not only in other business situations but also in nonbusiness settings—such as hospitals, educational institutions, and governmental agencies—and in other cultures. Only through further testing of this sort can we be more certain about the uniformities we see emerging in the contingent relationships between environment and organization.

A Contingency Theory of Multi-Unit Organizations

At this point it is necessary to outline briefly several important aspects of the terminology and format which we have employed in framing the propositions. First, these propositions have been stated in terms of the management level [17] of business enterprises because that is the territory we have examined. The reader who wishes to test these generalizations in a nonbusiness setting will find it necessary both to translate certain terms and modify certain concepts to fit his own needs. For example, "divisional unit," which we view as the primary business unit, might be translated as major activity center and/or service unit. Also, the demarcation between organization and environment may prove less clear in a nonbusiness setting.[18]

A second feature of the propositions is that they focus on four basic levels of organization: the headquarters unit, the division, the basic functional units within the division (i.e., marketing, manufacturing, and R&D/engineering), and the corporation as a whole. In choosing this focus we do not intend to preclude the possibility that some of these propositions may also apply to the functioning of other levels of organization; e.g., behavior within parts of functional units or geographic branches. The limited data we have suggest that some of these concepts are useful in this respect.[19]

The propositions also reflect our view of organizations as information processing systems. It is important to emphasize that we are using the term "information" in its broadest context. Information, to us, includes not only verifiable perceptions of external conditions but also the attitudes and feelings of organizational members. We classify the latter as information because they too are important inputs to decision-making processes. Indeed, they are related both to the willingness of managers to share openly more objective information in decision situations and to their commitment to implement decisions ultimately reached. Similarly, when we discuss information flows, we are referring to the transmission of information through formal reports, plans, and memoranda as well as through face-to-face contact and other less formal means.

Finally, a word is in order regarding the basic format which we have used for the propositions. Each proposition states a relationship between one or more independent variables and one or more dependent variables. This approach is used merely for convenience in communicating our findings. As we have argued throughout this book, all of these factors are interrelated in a complex fashion. In every case we have attempted to state each relationship as specifically as we feel the data will permit.

Taken as a whole, the set of propositions is aimed at specifying the ways in which particular organizational characteristics are interrelated with environmental requirements, other organizational characteristics, and performance. While each of the factors contained in the propositions is systemically linked with performance, the specific linkage between environment, organization, and higher performance is not treated directly in each single proposition. In other words, rather than stating, "*More effective divisions will* develop a degree of differentiation among their functional units consistent with the demands posed by their industrial environments," we shall state, "divisions will *tend to* develop a degree of differentiation among their functional units consistent with the demands posed by their industrial environments." By framing propositions in this way we wish to signal a particular view of performance. First, we are assuming that all organizations attempt to achieve a fit between internal states and environmental requirements. We see higher long-term performance resulting from an organization

actually achieving a comparatively higher fit between its internal characteristics and the demands of its environment. Furthermore, we feel that effective performance can only be predicted by understanding the interrelationships among all the variables we have examined. While single variables or
relationships may correlate with higher performance, they cannot be expected to predict it across a range of settings. Finally, we feel that performance must be viewed as both an output of and an input to on-going
organizational processes. In other words, we are trying to describe a dynamic, systemic process—albeit in static, propositional terms.

Environmental Complexity, the Division of Labor,
and Differentiation

The first factor with which we have been concerned is the differentiation among major organizational units with respect to formality of practices
and interpersonal, goal, and time orientations. This differentiation arises
from the division of labor in large-scale enterprises which, as March and
Simon[20] have pointed out, is the result of the limited cognitive capacities
of individual organizational members *vis-à-vis* the demands of a complex
environment. Simply stated, division of labor occurs in large organizations
because no one individual or group of individuals has the training, experience, or computational capacity to handle and reach decisions on all of the
information which must be considered to cope with the organization's total
environment. This leads to our first proposition:

   1.0—Organizations faced with complex, multimarket environments will tend
       to divide their activities among major units (divisions) and functional
       areas within these units so that the individuals and groups within these
       activity centers, given their cognitive limits, can process the relevant in-
       formation from the environment and reach decisions within a time span
       consistent with the requirements of the environment.

In placing emphasis on the cognitive limits of the individual as the con-
straining factor, we are not unaware of the importance of such factors as
product/market diversity, technology, and geography in determining a
proper basis for division of labor.[21] In this discussion, however, we are
simply interested in the *degree* of division of labor which tends to occur.
Also, we are primarily interested in the managerial level of organizations
where these cognitive and information-processing limits represent a more
important constraint.

From this broad statement about the division of labor we can derive a more specific proposition regarding environmental diversity, a variable with which we, Lawrence and Lorsch,[22] and Galbraith[23] have been concerned.

> 1.1—The greater the environmental diversity faced by the organization, the greater the extent of division of activities which tends to occur among major units and functional areas within these units.

Diversity is one aspect of environmental complexity which helps explain how differentiation arises in organizations.

A second aspect of environmental complexity which affects the division of labor and ultimately differentiation is interdependence. As Thompson[24] has suggested and our own data confirm, the interdependence required by the environment is higher (i.e., toward the reciprocal end of Thompson's continuum) among functional units within a division than that required between the divisional and headquarters units or among divisional units. Thus:

> 2.0—Organizations faced with complex, multimarket environments will tend to divide their activities so that the most complex interdependencies are contained within divisional units and less complex interdependencies are managed between the divisions and the headquarters and among divisions.

We should add that implicit in this proposition is the recognition that there may also be substantial degrees of interdependence within the functional units of a given division.

The division of managerial activities within a firm among headquarters, divisional, and functional units means that managers in each of these units will focus their attention on a particular, limited portion of the firm's total environment. To be effective in its environmental transactions each of these units must develop internal characteristics which are consistent with the requirements posed by its particular subenvironment.[25] Starting with the functional units (e.g., marketing, manufacturing, and R&D) we can now specify contingent relationships between environmental requirements and internal states up through each of the three major levels of organization with which we are concerned.

> 3.0—Within a division each of the functional units will tend to develop organizational practices and member orientations which are consistent with the demands of its particular subenvironment.
> 3.1—The greater the certainty of the relevant subenvironment, the more formalized the organizational practices of the functional unit.
> 3.2—Interpersonal orientations of members of a functional unit will tend

to be contingent upon the degree of certainty which characterizes its relevant subenvironment. More socially oriented interpersonal styles will tend to be associated with subenvironments characterized by moderate certainty. More task-oriented interpersonal styles will tend to be associated with subenvironments characterized by either high or low certainty.

3.3—The time orientations of members of a functional unit will tend to be positively related to the time span of feedback from its relevant subenvironment.

3.4—The goal orientations of members of a functional unit will tend to be contingent primarily upon the dominant competitive issues inherent in its relevant subenvironment and secondarily upon the dominant competitive issues faced by the division as a whole.

While each functional unit tends to develop internal states which broadly fit with the requirements posed by its subenvironment, our data and those of Lawrence and Lorsch[26] indicate that a division's long-term performance is positively related to the *degree* to which its functional units are able to achieve this fit.

The tendency of functional units to develop internal states aimed at coping with their particular subenvironments leads to differentiation among these units. Just how much differentiation will occur among functional units within a division is contingent upon both the heterogeneity of its several subenvironments (e.g., the market, scientific, and manufacturing sectors) and the characteristics of its overall industrial environment.

4.0—A division will tend to develop a degree of differentiation among its functional units which is consistent with the demands posed by its industrial environment.

4.1—The greater the diversity of its several subenvironments in terms of their relative uncertainty, time span of feedback, and concern with dominant competitive issues, the higher will tend to be the differentiation within the division.

4.2—The more critical success in one subenvironment is to the overall performance of the division, the lower will tend to be the differentiation within the division.

In this study we have also focused on the divisional unit as a whole containing not only functional units but also a general management unit charged with the planning and control of its overall activities *vis-à-vis* both its industrial environment and the requirements of the corporate whole. While we have not used our data to examine this issue explicitly, it seems reasonable to assume that the internal characteristics of the division as a whole are related to but more than a single additive function of the characteristics of its functional units. Thus, we shall say,

5.0—A divisional unit will tend to develop organizational practices and member orientations which are contingent upon (a) the demands posed by its industrial environment and (b) the integrative requirements posed by the total corporate environment.

The corporate headquarters unit, consisting of a general management group and certain specialist functions (which may vary widely depending on the type of firm), focuses on a limited segment of the environment but is also responsible for the planning and control of the firm's activities vis-à-vis its total environment. Because of the headquarters' particular role and its own unique set of environmental contacts, it tends to develop internal characteristics which are quite distinct from those of its divisions. Hence:

6.0—The headquarters unit of a firm will tend to develop organizational practices and member orientations which are contingent upon (a) the demands posed by its portion of the total environment and (b) the integrative requirements posed by the firm's total environment.

We will consider the issues of interunit integration shortly, but first we wish to explore the issues of corporate-divisional differentiation which can be derived from Propositions 5.0 and 6.0 and which are also supported by our findings. In general we can state that:

7.0—The degree of differentiation which will tend to develop between each division and the corporate headquarters is contingent upon the demands posed by the division's industrial environment, the demands posed by the headquarters' portion of the total environment, and the integrative requirements posed by the total environment.

Our findings point to the following refinements in this general proposition:

7.1—The cognitive limits of individuals and groups within headquarters and divisional units will place upper limits on the degree of differentiation which will tend to develop between these units.

7.2—The degree of diversity between demands posed by the headquarters' portion of the total environment and demands posed by a division's industrial environment will place a lower limit on the degree of differentiation which will tend to develop between these two units.

7.3—The greater the diversity of the firm's total environment, the higher the total corporate-divisional differentiation it will tend to develop.

Our work suggests that it is important to distinguish between corporate-divisional differentiation for single pairs of these units (Propositions 7.1 and 7.2) and total corporate-divisional differentiation (Proposition 7.3). The former aspect of differentiation provides important insights into the functioning of specific corporate-divisional relationships in a firm, while the latter is crucial to understanding the effects of the overall design of the firm's total organization.

Again it is important to note that while each of the firms studied tended to develop a broad fit between environmental diversity and total corporate-divisional differentiation, one lower performing conglomerate (Firm 4) had achieved a significantly lower degree of fit between diversity and differentiation than the other conglomerates.

One final aspect of differentiation is that which develops among divisional units.

> 8.0—The degree of differentiation which will tend to develop among divisions is contingent upon the diversity of demands posed by their respective industrial environments.

Interdivisional differentiation is a matter of importance only when a significant interdependence exists among particular divisions—as in the case of vertically integrated firms or in a few isolated instances within conglomerate firms.

Environmental Requirements and the Issues of Integration

We have argued that organizations faced with complex environments tend to segment these environments into manageable pieces through the division of labor. This segmentation is only one side of the organizational design issue, however. The other side is the issue of achieving the necessary collaboration among the organization's parts. Essentially, the organization segments its environment for its own convenience; but however it may do this, certain parts of the environment still remain interdependent. Just what pattern this interdependence takes will depend on the nature of each particular firm's total environment.

As a starting point in unraveling the organizational issues posed by interdependence, let's consider integration, which we have defined as the quality of collaboration actually achieved between organizational units. Both this study and the work of Lawrence and Lorsch[27] point to the importance of achieving effective integration among units which are required to be interdependent by their relevant environmental sectors. More specifically, we can say,

> 9.0—A division will seek to achieve effective integration among those functional units within its organization which are required to be interdependent by its industrial environment.

10.0—A firm will attempt to achieve effective integration between divisions and the corporate headquarters and among divisions in a pattern consistent with the demands for interdependence posed by its total environment.

While each of the firms in this study were clearly seeking to achieve effective corporate-divisional and interdivisional integration, we found a close correspondence between long-run economic performance and the degree of integration which managers indicated had actually been achieved among these interdependent units. Lawrence and Lorsch report a similar correspondence between higher performance and higher integration among functions in single-business settings.[28]

Interdependence is not the only factor which we must consider in understanding the problems of achieving integration. The internal state of differentiation also has an important impact. In fact, we have seen that differentiation and integration are basically antagonistic organizational states characterizing any interdependent pair of units. One of the hallmarks of an effective organization is its capacity to manage this internal antagonism or tension. Lawrence and Lorsch[29] have documented this inverse relationship between differentiation and integration for functional units. Thus, we can state that:

11.0—Within a division the greater the differentiation between any pair of interdependent functional units, the greater the difficulties of achieving integration between these units.

At the corporate-divisional level we have found that the relationship between differentiation and integration is complicated by the economic risk that any particular division poses for the corporate whole. In other words, declining performance and/or the tendency to present contingencies for corporate financial planning multiply the potential for conflict between the headquarters and divisional units, thus further complicating the task of achieving integration. Similarly, low overall corporate performance, by definition, increases the economic risk posed by any single division to the firm as a whole, again complicating the task of achieving integration. We can generalize from these findings as follows:

12.0—Within a firm the greater the differentiation between any division and the corporate headquarters and the greater the economic risk posed by that division, the greater the difficulties of achieving integration between these two units.

To this point in our discussion we have described the basic means that organizations employ to cope with the issues of environmental complexity.

We have pointed to how these basic approaches lead to a multi-unit organization characterized by differentiated units. We have seen how a basic internal antagonism arises between the need to achieve integration among these differentiated units both at a single organizational level and across several levels. Throughout the discussion we have been concerned with the basic contingent interrelationships through which differing patterns of environmental complexity lead to differing patterns of differentiation and integration. Our next step will be to consider how multi-unit organizations go about effectively managing the relationship between differentiation and integration under differing environmental conditions. Our findings point to three major sets of factors which are related to the effective management of differentiation and integration: * the integrative devices which are employed, the amount of managerial effort devoted to integration, and the nature of interunit decision-making processes.

Integrative Devices

Within single-business units Lawrence and Lorsch report that the complexity of integrative devices tended to be positively related to the complexity of interdependence and the degree of differentiation required by the environment. (By complexity we mean both the number and the differing types of organizational devices used to achieve integration among the units in question.) In our comparison of conglomerate and vertically integrated firms we found that more complex patterns of interdependence were associated with more complex integrative devices. However, in the conglomerates, which were faced with pooled interdependence, our findings suggest that higher diversity (and thus higher required differentiation) was not positively related with the use of more complex integrative devices. Indeed, the higher diversity in these conglomerate settings seemed to lead to diminishing returns from more complex integrative devices. This was particularly evident in the case of Firm 4. Our findings and those of Lawrence and Lorsch converge with respect to the impact of interdependence on complexity of integrative devices. Thus, we can state:

13.0—Both within divisions and at the corporate-divisional level, the more complex the patterns of interdependence among the relevant units, the more complex the integrative devices that will tend to be developed.

---

* In subsequent propositions we shall refer to this as achieving "appropriate" differentiation and integration. By appropriate we mean the achievement of patterns of interunit differentiation which are consistent with patterns of environmental diversity and achievement of relatively high levels of integration among interdependent units.

The two studies diverge, however, with respect to the impact of diversity (and by inference differentiation) on complexity of integrative devices. It seems entirely possible that for some organizations (e.g., conglomerates) the benefits that more complex integrative devices offer in managing interdependence are more than offset by the costs in loss of sensitivity to environmental diversity (i.e., in lower differentiation). Thus, for firms faced with sequential and reciprocal interdependence and lower overall diversity (and, therefore, lower required differentiation) more complex integrative devices pay off. For conglomerates, faced with pooled interdependence and higher diversity and required differentiation, more complex integrative devices may often prove counterproductive. While this seems a plausible explanation for the divergence of our and Lawrence and Lorsch's findings, this topic will require further investigation before we can firmly support a proposition about the interrelationships among interdependence, diversity, and integrative devices. Such study is important because, as we have seen, the patterns of interdependence and diversity among organizational units are not only related to the types of integrative devices required, but also to the amount of integrative effort which can be productively expended.

Integrative Effort

Since Lawrence and Lorsch did not collect data on integrative effort, our discussion of this variable is necessarily limited to the corporate-divisional interface. At this level, we have found that those firms which were characterized by appropriate differentiation and integration tended to apply integrative effort in amounts consistent with the patterns of interdependence and diversity with which they were faced. For example, in the conglomerate firms, which were characterized by higher diversity and less complex patterns of interdependence, we found that the less effective firms appeared to devote too much effort to integration. It appears that this was one reason that lower performing divisions in these firms found it difficult to achieve appropriate differentiation and tended to get caught in the self-defeating spiral described in Chapters III and V. Conversely, in the vertically integrated firms, where diversity was lower and the interdependence more complex, the more effective organization applied more integrative effort and tended to achieve appropriate differentiation and integration. These findings suggest the following propositions:

14.0—The higher the interdependence and the lower the required differentiation between a headquarters unit and its divisions, the greater the integrative effort which can be effectively devoted to managing these interunit relationships.

While our comparison of conglomerate and vertically integrated firms supports this broad relationship between interdependence and integrative effort, integrative effort scores differed considerably among firms within each of these broad types. Furthermore, we hypothesized in Chapter VII that there might well be an optimal relationship between integrative effort and interdependence for each firm. If a firm's level of integrative effort fell outside this optimal relationship, we began to see dysfunctional effects on integration and (in the case of the conglomerates) on differentiation. These findings fit closely with Schroder et al.'s[30] notion of a curvilinear relationship between environmental and internal complexity in human information processing systems. Thus, we can state:

15.0—Either an excess or a deficit of integrative effort relative to the degree of interdependence and of differentiation required at the corporate-divisional interface will tend to lead to less effective relationships among these units.

Since our design permitted comparison of only four conglomerates and two vertically integrated firms, we could only guess at what the optimal relationship between integrative effort and interdependence and required differentiation might be for each firm. Our data do, however, suggest some of the internal effects of falling outside this feasible range. This permits us to refine the above statement as follows:

15.1—Under conditions of less complex (pooled) interdependence and higher diversity an excess of integrative effort will be associated with lower corporate-divisional differentiation and integration.

15.2—Under conditions of more complex (e.g., sequential) interdependence and lower diversity a deficit of integrative effort will be associated with lower integration.

Further field research will be required to adequately establish whether there is indeed a curvilinear relationship between environmental and internal complexity. Our expectation at this point is such that such a relationship would be found. Thus, under conditions of pooled interdependence and higher diversity we would expect a deficit of integrative effort to be associated with both lower integration and higher differentiation. Similarly, under conditions of higher interdependence and lower diversity we would expect to find a point at which higher integrative effort would begin to have a negative effect on integration. Another issue is what effect increasing levels of integrative effort might have on differentiation in these settings characterized by higher interdependence and lower diversity. Our paper company data did not provide any clues on this question. Clearly this whole topic requires further investigation with a large sample of firms. However, our limited data and that of Schroder et al.[31] suggest that the conceptions stated above represent a fruitful avenue for further developing contingency theory.

Decision-Making Processes

The final set of factors which were found to be related to the development of appropriate patterns of differentiation and integration are what we have termed decision-making processes. Both this and the Lawrence and Lorsch study found that certain of these factors tended to be contingent on environmental requirements, while others were necessary for achieving appropriate differentiation and integration in all settings. Thus, we can begin with the proposition:

16.0—Both within divisions and at the corporate-divisional level, organizations which have achieved appropriate patterns of differentiation and integration will tend to be characterized by certain partial determinants of effective decision making, regardless of their particular environmental requirements.

Specifically, we have found that:

16.1—In organizations characterized by appropriate patterns of differentiation and integration persons acting in integrative roles within divisions and at the corporate-divisional level will tend to have cognitive and interpersonal orientations which are balanced among those of the units whose activities they are expected to integrate.

16.2— . . . persons in integrative roles within divisions and at the corporate-divisional level will tend to have high influence relative to members of the units whose activities they are expected to integrate.

These statements hold whether we are talking about group vice presidents and division general managers who work across the corporate-divisional interface or integrators such as project or product managers who work among functions within a single business unit. They also are closely connected with our conception of an organization as an information-processing system. If managers who are directly responsible for facilitating integration have balanced orientations and relatively high influence, they can more effectively understand, translate, and transmit the information provided by the different parties whose activities they are expected to integrate.

As the foregoing discussion suggests, the overall quality of information flows among units was also found to be a critical factor. Thus, we can state that:

16.3—In organizations characterized by appropriate patterns of differentiation and integration there will tend to be a higher quality of information flowing downward from the headquarters to the divisions and upward from the divisions to the headquarters.

This proposition is stated for the corporate-divisional interface because that is the only level for which we have data. While this statement clearly overlaps with several other propositions, we mention it separately because it did discriminate between effective and less effective organizations. Specifically, we found that in less effective situations there was a lower quality of information flowing downward from the corporate headquarters.

The final characteristics of decision-making processes which was common across all environmental conditions and organizational levels relates to the modes through which interunit conflicts were resolved. The data of both this study and the earlier work of Lawrence and Lorsch[32] strongly indicate that:

16.4—In organizations characterized by appropriate patterns of differentiation and integration confrontation, or problem solving, there will tend to be a more typical mode of resolving conflicts both within divisions and at the corporate-divisional level.

By confrontation, or problem solving, we mean a mode of conflict resolution wherein the various parties to the conflict openly present their views and information and work toward a decision which makes sense in terms of the total information available. In this connection it is particularly important to re-emphasize that this information includes both substantive data and the feelings and attitudes of the persons involved. Not taking these feelings and attitudes into account may be just as damaging to the resolution of conflicts as ignoring pertinent objective data.

As noted earlier, both we and Lawrence and Lorsch[33] found that some aspects of decision-making processes tended to differ as a direct function of environmental requirements. Thus, we can state that:

17.0—Organizations which have achieved appropriate patterns of differentiation and integration will tend to be characterized by certain partial determinants of effective decision making which are congruent with the particular requirements posed by their total environments.

The findings of this study point toward three specific relationships between environmental characteristics and internal decision-making processes.

17.1—The lower the interdependence required by the environment, the more rapidly the headquarters will tend to respond to divisional requests.

We found that the headquarters units of conglomerate firms tended to respond more rapidly to divisional requests than their counterparts in vertically integrated firms. In essence, lower interdependence required and permitted more self-containment of divisions, smaller corporate headquarters units, and less complex integrative devices. All this spelled less complex information transmission and processing requirements at the corporate-divisional interface and, thus, the ability to respond more rapidly.

Closely related to this finding were the differing patterns of influence we and Lawrence and Lorsch[34] found in different environmental settings.

17.2—In organizations characterized by appropriate patterns of differentiation and integration, the distribution of influence over decision making, both lateral and hierarchical, will tend to coincide with the location of the relevant information.

We see the location of relevant information as being determined (a) by patterns of environmental complexity (i.e., uncertainty, diversity, and interdependence) faced by an organization, (b) by the organizational devices it uses to process and transmit information (e.g., planning and control systems and integrative positions), and (c) by how well these organizational devices fit the task of importing, processing, and transmitting information posed by the environment. While much more research will be required before we have an adequate understanding of how specific sets of organizational devices affect patterns of influence, we can begin to make some generalizations about the relationship between environmental factors and patterns of influence.

Lawrence and Lorsch's comparisons among organizations in three industries[35] suggest that the pattern formed by environmental uncertainty, diversity, and interdependence and dominant competitive issues was important in understanding how influence was distributed within an effective organization. In high performing plastics and food companies, which were characterized by higher uncertainty, diversity, and interdependence, influence tended to be more evenly distributed by organizational level. In container companies, which faced lower degrees of uncertainty, diversity, and interdependence, influence patterns were more hierarchical. In all three industries the relative influence of functional units tended to coincide with the dominant competitive issues faced by the company as a whole. For example, in the plastics business, where product innovation was the dominant competitive issue, the integrating department had the highest influence.

In our study we did not attempt to replicate these findings within divisions. However, at the corporate-divisional interface we found that influence tended to peak at the division general manager level in conglomerates, while it peaked at the next highest organizational level (senior vice presidents) in the vertically integrated paper firms. In other words, we found that the conglomerates—faced with higher uncertainty and diversity but lower interdependence—tended to permit division general managers higher influence relative to the headquarters or to group vice presidents.

These findings about distribution of influence also fit with our generalizations regarding the relatively high influence of integrative roles and units (Proposition 16.2). Organizations tend to locate these integrative positions at points where critical information must be drawn together for joint decisions. High influence of these positions is necessary for managing interdependence as well as remaining sensitive to environmental diversity.

Before leaving this topic we wish to outline some of the broader implications which seem to be emerging from these findings about influence patterns. While a wide range of executives will usually be involved in decisions because they have important information to contribute, the data suggest that certain individuals and/or units will possess differing amounts of relevant information; and patterns of influence in more effective organizations tend to be more consistent with the value of the information which these persons or units can contribute. Thus, the appropriate patterns of influence for any firm or division will be different, depending on the particular information-processing and decision-making task posed by its environment. While specifying what this task may entail requires an in-depth look at the particular organization in question, one generalization is clear. The traditional belief that influence over decisions should decline in a linear fashion as one moves down the organizational hierarchy is often neither valid nor desirable. For organizations faced with considerable environmental uncertainty and diversity, less hierarchical patterns of influences seem to be more appropriate. Also underlying this view of the distribution of influence is the belief that influence can be treated as an expandable commodity—that it is not necessarily a fixed sum which must be allocated among competing parties.[36] Thus, for organizations faced with high levels of environmental complexity it is both possible and desirable for influence to be widely distributed among units and hierarchical levels.

The final aspect of decision-making processes which was linked to environmental requirements was the characteristics of performance evaluation systems. In general we can state:

> 17.3—Corporations will tend to develop divisional performance eval-
> uation systems which are broadly consistent with the overall
> uncertainty and the patterns of diversity and interdependence
> which characterize their total environments.

As noted in Chapter VII, we found that the conglomerates, faced with higher uncertainty and diversity but lower interdependence, had developed performance evaluation systems which were characterized by explicitly de- fined criteria, a direct linkage between results and monetary rewards, and heavier emphasis on financial/end result criteria. By way of contrast, the vertically integrated firms, faced with lower diversity and uncertainty but higher interdependence, had developed performance evaluation systems which were more informally administered, without a direct linkage between results and monetary rewards, and with an emphasis on both financial/end result and operating/intermediate criteria. It is also noteworthy that both of the more effective conglomerates had performance evaluation systems which employed multiple criteria and were balanced between long-run and short- run considerations. This was one means of designing considerable flexibility into a single system which was to be used in evaluating a large number of diverse divisions.

In concluding our discussion of decision-making processes we wish to restate the point made in Chapters IV and VI, that while each of the above items is important, it is the total pattern of these variables which contributes to effective management of differentiation and integration—both within divisions and within the firm as a whole. It should also be re-emphasized that these decision-making variables are interrelated in such a way that they not only facilitate the more substantive aspects of interunit decision making but also seem to produce an emotional climate of trust which in itself may facilitate decision-making processes.

Environmental Requirements, Organizational States, and Performance

Having set down 17 basic propositions about the interrelationships among environmental requirements and organizational characteristics, we can now make three summary statements which link this set of contingent relationships to the ongoing economic performance of corporate and divi- sional organizations.

18.0—Higher divisional performance will tend to be associated with achieving the antagonistic states of differentiation and integration required by the division's environment through integrative devices, integrative effort, and decision-making processes which are consistent with the information-processing requirements of the division's environment.

19.0—Higher corporate performance will tend to be associated with achieving the states of corporate-divisional and interdivisional differentiation and integration required by the total environment through integrative devices, integrative effort, and decision-making processes which are consistent with the information-processing requirements of the total environment.

By higher performance we mean longer term economic results *vis-à-vis* comparable firms or organizational units. Throughout this discussion we have stated the propositions in such a way as to suggest that all firms behave in such a way as to attempt to achieve a fit between internal characteristics and external requirements. The two propositions above simply state that performance differences can be explained in part by the degree of organization-environment fit which is actually achieved. Clearly this fit is not the sole explanation for performance differences among organizations. A number of technological and economic factors are also at work; e.g., patent positions, experience levels, comparative economic advantage, and barriers to entry in some industries. However, the correlation between organization-environment fit found by us and Lawrence and Lorsch now extends to some 16 corporate and 23 divisional settings. The evidence seems sufficiently strong to state that fit is an important element in achieving effective economic performance. It is also noteworthy that a recent study by Morse and Lorsch[37] presents evidence indicating that organizations which achieve this fit between internal states and environmental requirements tend to have characteristics which meet important psychological needs of their members.

Propositions 18.0 and 19.0 view performance as an outcome of organization-environment fit. As indicated earlier, however, performance can also be viewed as an independent variable related to organizational states. Thus, our final proposition:

20.0—The greater the economic risk posed for the corporation by lower corporate performance or lower performance of individual divisions, the more difficult it will tend to be to achieve the antagonistic states of differentiation and integration required by the division's and/or the corporation's environments through integrative devices, integrative effort, and decision-making processes which are consistent with the information-processing requirements of these environments.

This concluding proposition provides a dynamic quality to our conception. As suggested in Chapters III, V, and VII, perceptions of economic risk tend to trigger integrative efforts which are, in turn, interrelated with all the organizational states we have discussed. The problem is whether changes in these organizational states (i.e., differentiation and integration), which are brought about by changes in integrative effort, are consistent with environmental requirements.

It is also important to re-emphasize that integrative devices and thus integrative effort are also affected by the organization concept (or assumptions) held by top management. We have not framed a proposition about this interrelationship because we don't feel we have sufficiently systematic data to do so. Nonetheless, some brief speculations seem in order. Our clinical data on organization concepts in Chapter III suggest that these concepts of top management differ on at least four dimensions: (1) desire for information frequency, (2) desire for information differentiation (number of distinctive elements), (3) preferences for intensity of review processes, and (4) beliefs regarding degree of direct intervention in divisional decision making. It seems quite possible that the constellation formed by these four factors could be linked to the characteristics which are designed into integrative devices. Similarly, the linkage between integrative devices and integrative effort could be usefully viewed as having fixed and variable aspects. That is to say, the requirements for integrative effort posed by integrative devices might be thought of as fixed under "normal" performance conditions and as increasing in a linear relationship to the economic risk a division poses for the corporation. While these conceptions are certainly consistent with our data, further research is required before they can be stated with confidence.[38]

Current Perspective and Future Lines of Inquiry

While the set of propositions stated in this chapter point to a number of the factors which underlie the interrelationships among environmental requirements and internal characteristics, much more work will be required before we can point to a full-blown contingency theory of complex organizations. As indicated earlier, even the current conceptions require testing in a larger number of business organizations and in a wide range of institutional and cultural settings. Also, despite a concern for both environmental and organizational factors, this as well as the other contingency studies cited has tended to focus more heavily on the issues of internal control and integration than on the boundary spanning activities through which an organization relates to its environment. It is to be hoped that future work, building on the knowledge which already has been accumulated, will devote even more attention to the measurement of environmental factors and boundary spanning activities.

Even though much effort has been focused on internal organizational states and processes, considerably more work is required in establishing just how management assumptions, concepts of organization, and the choice of particular integrative devices affect these internal states. More systematic means of identifying and measuring the crucial aspects of particular planning, control, and performance evaluation devices, as well as their impact as an integrated constellation of management tools, will be required.

Equally important is the need to develop and test methodologies which can better capture the dynamics through which environment and organization interact. Our own work has depended on point-in-time comparisons of organizational units, supplemented by interview data and limited use of historical company records. This methodology has definite limitations for drawing inferences about how organizations adapt to changing environmental requirements. Several methodological approaches show promise for a better understanding of these dynamics. Longitudinal studies using comparative survey and/or "tracer" techniques[39]—while they are currently time-consuming, expensive, and difficult to execute—offer one possibility. Experiments which are designed to replicate on-going, real-world decision processes are another potentially fruitful avenue.[40] Also, model building and simulation with subsequent field validations offer a number of untapped possibilities for understanding the dynamics of organizational and environmental interrelationships.[41] We hope that the application and further refinement of each of these methodologies and/or combinations of them will serve to further enhance our understanding of the functioning of complex organizations.

In concluding this discussion we wish to point out that our focus on contingency theory and the view of organizations as information-processing systems is not intended to suggest that this is the only conceptual model required for unraveling the behavior of human beings in complex organizations. For instance, if one is concerned with the issues of commitment and motivation of individuals in these organizations, other underlying conceptions may prove more useful. Similarly, if the issues under study are career choices and manpower flows in organizations, yet another set of concepts may be more relevant. Our central concern has been that of understanding how organizations cope with their environmental requirements and achieve control and integration among their major managerial units. We feel that such an understanding is considerably enhanced by the contingent approach we have described.

IX

A Practical Perspective

From the perspective of those who are daily concerned with the management of multidivisional organizations, what have we learned? We shall attempt to answer this question by dealing with three themes. First, we want to return to the issue of centralization versus decentralization, which we introduced at the outset. What light do our findings and the contingency approach shed on this persistent management dilemma? Second, we shall consider specific ways that this contingency approach to part-whole relationships can be helpful in guiding managerial thought and action. Finally, we shall consider some of the broader implications which this study holds for the problems and opportunities which may confront complex organizations in the future. Here, particularly, we shall explore its ramifications for both industrial firms and for large public organizations.

Decentralization: A Contingent View

As we suggested in Chapter I, the typical way of approaching the issues we have discussed has been around the notion of decentralization versus centralization. However, there are several problems with the use of these concepts. First, the traditional view of decentralization suggests that the only thing that distinguishes a "decentralized" organization from a "centralized" one is the distribution of authority to make decisions. Even if one accepts this definition, he still must struggle with what patterns of decision-making authority constitute "decentralization" as opposed to "centralization." Another difficulty with these concepts has been the tendency to argue, depending on one's point of view and the evidence available, that either centralization or decentralization is a panacea for the problems of all large organizations. Perhaps the most basic issue is to get a better understanding of the organizational characteristics people are trying to describe when they use the concepts of decentralization and centralization.

A useful way of getting insight into this issue is to consider Peter Drucker's insightful description of "decentralization" at General Motors.[1] Based on his examination of the General Motors organization, Drucker concluded that what the term decentralization really referred to was a whole new social order within that corporation. This "federalism" had two functions: it enabled each division to be more effective, and it welded the divisions together. According to Drucker, the headquarters was differentiated from its divisions not only in terms of power (or authority) but also in terms of time perspective and in terms of their respective functions. The headquarters management controlled and coordinated its divisions through direct contact, through the approval of financial requests, and through the ultimate authority to remove division managers for inadequate performance. Drucker also emphasized the importance of a two-way flow of information in making this social order work. Objective measures of performance and financial incentives based on these measures were also important in explaining how the corporation functioned. Finally, the corporate staff played a vital role in the General Motors organization. It provided advice to the divisions, served as a liaison between them, helped to set long-range policies, and kept upper management advised about divisional progress.

The similarity between the types of variables identified by Drucker and those we have examined in this study is apparent. Both Drucker's work and our study suggest that the real difference between a centralized and decentralized organization is something much more complex than just its patterns of decision-making authority. If these labels are to capture the realities of how complex organizations work, they must refer to systems of organizational variables which include division of work and differentiation; the integration within and among divisions and between divisions and the headquarters; the types of integrative devices used; as well as information flows and decision-making processes operating within the organization.

While Drucker's work is complementary to ours in more accurately defining the meaning of these terms, there is also an important difference between our approaches which can help illuminate other aspects of the decentralization versus centralization dilemma. In his study, Drucker was asking: Is decentralization, as practiced at General Motors, a useful model for other industrial firms? He concludes "decentralization has been proved to be a promising approach which seems capable of solving the institutional problems of the large organization." [2] Thus he, like many other management writers, was seeking a universally applicable approach.

Of course, it is not just management writers who have been seeking a universal solution to these issues. There is considerable evidence that many managers have been quick to follow the organizational and administrative fashion set by a few pace-setting firms. An excellent example of this tendency is provided by Henderson and Dearden in their discussion of financial measurements and controls in divisionalized firms. They note that the examples of General Motors, Du Pont, and General Electric

> were widely emulated. Unfortunately, this concept [return on investment measurement for divisionalized performance] was copied literally without reference to the subtle side effects and by-products or the limitations. The consequences have been similar to those of a miscalibrated speedometer or compass. It either keeps one from performing as well as one can or leads him into serious trouble.[3]

While Henderson and Dearden are referring mainly to control systems, numerous examples can be found of the blanket application by many firms of the organizational approaches pioneered by these same successful giants.

While the desire to emulate success is understandable, it also points to the belief of many practicing managers (as well as many management theorists) that there is one ideal solution to their administrative and organizational problems. Our own approach is quite different. It is to understand how the organizational and administrative characteristics of firms must vary to meet the demands posed by their environments. Thus, we see a number of dangers in generalizing from the experience of a General Motors, a Du Pont, an ITT, or a Textron. What is called decentralization in any one of these firms may be appropriate given the diversity and interdependence required by its total environment, but it may be very inappropriate for firms with more or less diversity and a different pattern of interdivisional and corporate-divisional interdependencies.

In summary, the findings of this study shed new light on the issue of decentralization in two respects. First, they suggest that the label decentralization refers to a much more complex set of organizational variables than has commonly been recognized by either practicing managers or most writers on the subject. Second, the contingent relationship between these organizational characteristics and environmental requirements means that no matter how one defines decentralization it is not a panacea. Recognizing these facts can enable managers to free themselves from the old arguments about decentralization and centralization. In fact, the authors will feel this book has served a useful purpose if it merely encourages managers to drop these oversimplified labels in their discussions of organizational affairs.

Instead of arguing about decentralizing authority or recentralizing it, managers can deal more effectively with the underlying issues if they employ the contingent approach we have outlined in this study. Let's consider some of the ways this approach can be utilized to deal with administrative and organizational issues faced by large multidivisional firms.

Organizational Design and Management Behavior

We shall focus on the concrete ramifications of this study from two perspectives. First, we shall explore its implications for designing large organizations, including their structures and measurement and evaluation procedures. Second, we shall consider its implications for the day-to-day behavior of managers at both the headquarters and divisional levels as they comfortable and the assumptions which underlie them have an important interconnection between organizational design and managerial behavior. On the one hand, the grand design of an organization places constraints on the day-to-day behavior of its managers. On the other hand, the behavioral tactics with which managers (particularly those at higher echelons) are comfortable and the assumptions which underlie them have an important impact on the choices these managers make about organizational design.

This study provides a way of thinking against which managers can test the costs and benefits which may be associated with their own organizational assumptions. While it does not point to any simple prescription about the design of organizations, it does point to two external factors which have an important impact on the organizational choices managers must make. The appropriate design of both the basic skeletal structure of positions and units and of measurement and evaluation procedures depends upon the diversity of the total environment in which the organization operates and the interdependence required by that environment. What follows is a way of thinking about how diversity and interdependence affect the design of these formal organizational variables.

Structural Choices

One important choice which managers face in thinking about the design of an organization is determining the size and scope of divisional activities. This study suggests that divisional activities should be structured so that the most intense interdependencies are contained within the division. For firms such as those in this study, this means building divisions around products or groups of products, so that the various functional specialists involved can achieve the necessary integration within the divisional unit. Using this approach means that the organization will be structured so that most information will not have to be transmitted any further than necessary. In this way, the loss of relevant information and the possibility of unnecessary distortion through long channels of communication can be minimized. At the same time, a structure based on this approach will encourage decision making at the lowest level in the organization at which the information necessary for decisions can be assembled. This is consistent with the point we have stressed in earlier chapters: influence over decisions in effective organizations is concentrated at the point where the information to make such decisions also exists.

The same guideline can also be applied to another question facing many multidivisional firms, as well as nonbusiness organizations. Should the basic unit be developed around a set of products or services, or around the territories in which the organization operates? The answer would seem to lie in determining where the most intense interdependencies reside and in structuring activities so that these interdependencies can be managed by the organizational hierarchy within units. Given the fact that many large organizations are faced with intense interdependencies around both products (or services) and territories, it is very likely that a supplemental mechanism for achieving integration along the dimensions not contained in the basic unit will also have to be devised. In some multinational firms one device used to accomplish this is the position of "area managers" who work to coordinate the activities of various product units in their sectors of the globe. Another similar device which has been used by both the Federal Government and industrial firms is a team of managers from various divisions or agencies who are expected to coordinate the activities of their units in a given territory.

These two examples suggest a second major decision which managers face in thinking about the skeletal structure of an organization—the selection of appropriate integrative devices. At the corporate-divisional level of organization, we have seen that group executives, corporate staffs, and cross-divisional teams are all devices for facilitating integration. How complex these devices should be depends upon both the diversity of the total environment and the patterns of interdependence required. The higher the diversity and the lower the interdependence, the less effective highly complex devices will tend to be. The greater the required interdependence and the lower the diversity, the greater the benefits which more complex integrative devices can provide.

There are several other ways that we can use the findings of this study to think about the design of such integrative devices at the corporate-divisional level. They can help guide decisions about which divisions to place under a group executive. If there is considerable interdependence among a number of divisions, those divisions which are most interdependent should be placed under a common group executive who can use the organizational hierarchy to facilitate integration among them. Where such interdivisional integration is not required, our findings would suggest that divisions should be collected under a group executive so as to minimize diversity within the group. This enables the group executive to work with a set of divisions whose internal functioning and environments he has the greatest likelihood of understanding in depth. Since, to be effective, group executives need to develop intermediate orientations between their divisions and the corporate headquarters, grouping the least diverse units can also simplify their task in this respect.

Another implication of our findings is that there is no magic number of divisions which should be included in such a group. Rather, the appropriate number depends on the diversity and interdependence of the divisions in question. The more diverse the divisions are and/or the more interdependent they are, the more difficult the task of the group executive will be. Thus, diversity and interdependence provide a criterion for thinking about an appropriate span of control, one of the major concerns of the classical management theorists.[4]

Our research also has implications for the definition of the jobs of group executives and division general managers. Clearly the group executive's job should be defined as an integrator between the corporate unit and his divisions and/or among these divisions. But it is equally important to recognize that the division general manager's position is also partially an integrating role. One function of the division general manager is certainly to direct and coordinate activities within his division, but a second is to link his division to the corporate headquarters, usually through a group executive.[5] Therefore, it is important that the division general manager have a balanced orientation between corporate and divisional affairs and that he have a high amount of influence over divisional policies. One way to assure that these conditions exist is to make them an explicit part of position descriptions and also to communicate these expectations during the selection or hiring process. In defining the division general management position and in selecting incumbents, it is also important to be explicit about the need for both business skills and interpersonal competence. The findings of this study suggest that both sets of skills are necessary for division general managers and for group executives; but it particularly highlights the necessity for high levels of interpersonal skills in these positions. These interpersonal skills help to develop a trustful and problem-solving climate at the corporate-divisional interface.

So far the focus of this discussion has been on integrative positions within the management hierarchy. In the conglomerates relatively low levels of interdependence meant that the necessary integration could be achieved mainly through the hierarchy, supplemented by various planning and control systems. In the paper firms, more complex interdependence required additional integrative devices (e.g., planning and scheduling departments, technical service managers, and teams and committees which supplemented the hierarchy). Thus, both diversity and the complexity of interdependence are important factors in determining the need for extra integrative devices.

Another device which can be used to achieve integration at the corporate-divisional level is the corporate staff. Drucker reported that this was one of the important functions of the corporate staff at General Motors.[6] In considering what this study suggests about the size and functions of a corporate staff, we need to be clear about the nature of the work in which such a staff becomes involved. One type of activity is to aid in business planning and resource allocation. This was the major issue around which corporate-divisional interdependence was required in the conglomerates. However, our experience in these firms would suggest that much of this activity can be carried out directly between divisional managers and the corporate officers. Thus, the staff role is mainly a supporting and consulting one. As our data from the effective conglomerates suggest, such a role can be executed by a relatively small staff.

Another activity in which the corporate staff may become involved is providing technical and managerial assistance to divisions and coordinating and/or standardizing procedures and practices among divisions. This can involve transferring managerial, marketing, and technical ideas among divisions to help them achieve managerial and operating synergy. A corporate staff may also become involved in planning and coordinating the flow of materials and/or products among divisions, again to help achieve operational synergy. These latter types of activities are more typical of what we found in the vertically integrated firms. As we saw, these firms had larger staffs than the conglomerates, and they worked effectively on these issues.

Describing possible staff activities in this way suggests that the size and role of a corporate staff should depend upon the diversity and interdependence of the firm's total environment. If the divisions are diverse, operating in different technologies and markets, it is doubtful that a corporate staff can be very effective in many of these activities except supporting the planning and resource allocation process. It will be difficult for the staff to develop the skills necessary to help with the broad range of divisional market, managerial, and technical problems. Because of these limits in deploying technical skills and because divisions need differentiation to meet the demands of their industrial environments, the divisions in a conglomerate are apt to perceive "help" from a large, specialized staff as unwarranted pressure for impractical conformity. However, higher interdependence among divisions along with lower diversity can create a greater opportunity for corporate staff activity. Such interdependence means that divisions will be further processing each other's products or marketing them. This type of activity creates the need for more technical and operating integration, and a corporate staff can reasonably be expected to facilitate this integration and provide expertise in other areas because there is a commonality among the technological and/or market issues the various divisions face.

Another way to summarize the implications of this study for the design and use of a corporate staff is to return to Drucker's conclusion that the General Motors staff was vital in achieving linkage among divisions. This does not indicate that a large corporate staff is always necessary in large "decentralized" organizations. Rather, by recognizing two facts about the General Motors organization this can be turned into a contingent statement. First, there is a great deal of interdependence among General Motors' divisions. Some are major parts suppliers to others, and all of the automobile divisions are expected to focus on particular segments of the consumer market and to avoid across-the-board competition with one another. Second, within the major product lines, automobiles and automotive parts, there is relatively low diversity. Given these two environmental conditions (high interdivisional interdependence and low diversity for major segments of the company), our contingency approach would suggest precisely what Drucker found—that a large corporate staff would be an effective integrating vehicle.

So far in this discussion we have illustrated how an understanding of the corporate environment in terms of diversity and the required patterns of interdependence can provide useful guidelines for managers in thinking about the basic structure of their organizations and some of the integrative mechanisms which are necessary to supplement the hierarchy. Before leaving this topic, two final points need emphasis. First, because of the nature of the total environments which faced the firms in this study (low interdependence and high diversity for the conglomerates; higher interdependence and lower diversity for the vertically integrated firms), we have stated most of our implications in terms of these conditions. Thus, the implications of this study should be relatively clear for the manager whose organization faces either of these sets of conditions. However, if one's organization faces an environment requiring either high diversity and high interdependence or low diversity and low interdependence, the implications have not been stated so clearly. In spite of this, we believe that if the reader in the latter situations will bear in mind that the problems of achieving integration increase as a result of a more complex interdependence and/or more diversity in the environment, he will be able to interpolate the conclusions we have drawn to fit his own situation.

The second point requiring emphasis concerns the issue of integrative effort. We have not dealt with it explicitly in this discussion, because it is our assumption that one way to assure the appropriate amount of such effort is through the design of the basic structure. Of course, there are other factors which affect the amount and effectiveness of effort devoted to integration, including behavioral styles of individual managers. Before we turn to this topic, however, we want to examine how measurement and evaluation practices can be designed not only to facilitate the necessary integration but also to encourage the appropriate degree of differentiation.

The Design of Evaluation and Measurement Practices

We are concerned here with the planning, control, and performance evaluation systems used to forecast and measure divisional performance and the ways in which information from these systems is used. These systems can affect both the differentiation and the integration achieved in the organization and how well they fit the patterns of diversity and interdependence of its total environment.

In conglomerates, where a major issue is the considerable diversity among divisional environments, a principal objective for designing these measurement systems must be to encourage each division's management to focus on those goals and time dimensions which are critical in its industrial environment. In this way, these devices can encourage the differentiation required by the diversity of the total environment. Taken to its logical extreme, this could mean designing a separate measurement and evaluation scheme for each division. Obviously, such an approach would be costly and difficult.

From our look at the more effective conglomerates, we have seen that there are ways to design measurement systems to achieve flexibility without going to this extreme. At the core of an effective approach lies the profit center concept, but measuring divisions on profit performance must be used in combination with careful reviews, and the measurements must be flexibly applied. One way to achieve this flexibility is for top management to require common reporting on broad financial information such as profits, return on investment, and sales, while allowing each division to design its own measures for internal divisional use. This approach permits divisional management to have considerable influence in tailoring planning and control systems to meet its environmental situation.

Flexibility is not only required in designing planning and control systems but also performance evaluation practices. There are at least two ways to accomplish this. One way, used by the effective conglomerates in this study and suggested by Dearden, is to measure on both short-term and long-term criteria.[7] Then corporate management can use the time frame which seems most appropriate for any particular division.

While the design of these measurement systems is important, we also need to be concerned with how these schemes are applied. Corporate management should consider not only the design of the measurement practices but also the expectations they signal to divisional executives about how performance measurement information is to be utilized. The evidence we have gathered suggests that the measurement practices should be used to help isolate problems and opportunities where corporate decisions are required. These measurement tools should not be used as a club, but rather to identify areas where corporate-divisional problem solving is necessary.

It also seems important for corporate management to be open in sharing information about the performance of the firm as a whole and its problems and opportunities with all group and divisional executives. As a result of receiving this information, these executives are most likely to approach joint decision-making situations with not only their differentiated objectives but also with an understanding of the requirements of the total enterprise. Such a perspective would be most likely to lead to the effective resolution of conflict, which is necessary to achieve both the differentiation and the integration required in these conglomerate firms.

Much of what we have said about use of measurement and evaluation tools in conglomerates also seems to apply to vertically integrated firms. However, the design of these measurement and evaluation systems needs to be quite different in these vertically integrated firms. In these firms, the most prominent environmental features are lower diversity and considerable interdependence among various divisions. This complicates the problem of designing measurement and evaluation practices. As in the conglomerates, procedures for measuring divisional performance at a broad level are important to provide data about how well each division is doing. This is necessary for top management's information and also as a source of feedback to motivate divisional managers themselves. But where interdependence is required among divisions, the flow of information through reports must also provide much more detailed information both to corporate and group management and to the various divisions so that there can be an effective coordination of the efforts of the several interdependent divisions. Operating data about schedules, orders, and quality must be shared to facilitate interdivisional collaboration. While face-to-face discussion is necessary to resolve conflicts, the basis of this discussion must be reports which contain sufficiently detailed data to understand the impact of any decision on the ability of each division to perform effectively.

This is only part of the complication. An even more important problem can be caused by the profit center concept which is used for the measurement of divisional performance in many vertically integrated firms. This scheme has been applied also in the conglomerate firms, where the divisions can be encouraged to focus on divisional profits even though this may cause rivalry among them. Such rivalry can be healthy in motivating individual divisional managers and it is not particularly harmful because the integration which is required is mainly with the headquarters. In vertically integrated firms, however, each division in trying to maximize its own profits can make decisions which could adversely affect the profits of other divisions. Under these conditions, instead of leading to a healthy rivalry between divisions, the profit center concept can lead to open competition and hostility among divisions, which, in turn, endangers the quality of the firm's decision-making processes. For example, each division manager can become so concerned with his own profit performance that he rigidly rejects any action which, though it might contribute to corporate-wide profits, will adversely affect his results. The level of conflict can rise and problems of achieving the required integration may be intensified.

The two paper firms we studied used different solutions to this problem. Firm 5 measured its mills not as profit centers but as cost centers with variable costs broken out and transfer prices to the converting divisions based on variable costs and a negotiated portion of fixed costs. Firm 6 treated all of its divisions as profit centers with transfer prices set by the corporate headquarters on the basis of outside market prices. Even though profits were used as a measure of divisional performance in Firm 6, an attempt was made to remove the cost of materials transferred as a bargaining issue, because corporate management set the transfer price and measured divisional performance using a budget which factored out effects of external variations in the transfer price. While top management of each firm was clearly concerned with the conflicts which could arise around transfer prices and interdivisional integration, the higher corporate-divisional and interdivisional integration achieved by Firm 5's container division suggests that its control system seemed to help it deal with these issues more effectively.

Henderson and Dearden have suggested a similar approach to that used by Firm 5.[8] While their language is different from ours, their conclusion is similar: control systems for vertically integrated firms must deal with requirements different from those faced by conglomerate firms. The objectives of such a system should be to:

(1) Provide relevant information to all managers at each point where a decision must be made.
(2) Provide a basis for evaluating management performance.
(3) Motivate each manager in such a way as to optimize total company performance.[9]

To accomplish these objectives in a vertically integrated firm, they suggest an approach based on a managed cost and contribution budget. The basic advantage of such an approach is to reach the three objectives listed above, by eliminating unnecessary conflicts and competition which can result from using a pure profit center concept in vertically integrated firms.

Thus, interdivisional interdependence does complicate the design of measurement devices. Managers who are concerned with the design of organizations with this sort of interdependence must consider how to develop measurement and evaluation schemes and other integrative devices which encourage both divisional performance and integrated, company-wide performance. However, in both the vertically integrated firms and the conglomerates it is not only the design of the organizational devices which affects the organizational characteristics we have identified as important. It is also the day-to-day behavioral tactics managers use.

Managerial Behavior

In Chapter V we discussed the implications of our data for the ongoing behavior of managers in conglomerate firms. We saw that it was necessary for corporate and divisional managers in those firms to confront conflict and to share influence over decisions related to divisional policy. The importance of a two-way flow of information between corporate and divisional units and the need for the corporate headquarters to respond rapidly to divisional requests for information and assistance were all stressed. All of this adds up to a climate of mutual trust on both sides of the corporate-divisional interface. This in turn helps to achieve both the differentiation and integration required by the environment.

Our look at the two paper firms has both supported and expanded our conclusions about these factors. Again, we noted the importance of the confrontation of conflict, the sharing of influence, and a sound two-way flow of information. These factors seem crucial regardless of the environmental forces facing the organizations. However, both the appropriate pattern of influence and the appropriate allocation of managerial effort devoted to integration seem to vary with environmental circumstances. The pattern of influence of various levels must be congruent with the availability of information at each level to contribute to the decision. There must also be a match between the amount of managerial time and effort devoted to integration and the environmental diversity and complexity of the interdependent relationships to be managed. The more complex the interdependence and the lower the diversity, the more integrative effort can be used effectively.

We can concretely illustrate the meaning of these findings for the day-to-day behavior of managers by composing a list of the issues that corporate and divisional managers might usefully consider as they think about their own behavior.

From the corporate executive's perspective:

- Are we allocating our time to achieving integration with or among divisions in a manner which is consistent with the patterns of diversity and interdependence involved?
- Are we encouraging division managers to achieve a reasonable balance in allocating their time between divisional problems and corporate concerns?
- Do we keep divisional managements informed about our current thinking regarding both the status of their operations and corporate plans and objectives?
- Are we prepared to move rapidly on divisional requests once an adequate case has been made?
- Are we encouraging and permitting divisional managers to exert influence over divisional policy to an extent consistent with the knowledge and information they have available?
- Are we confronting and working through the conflicts which arise between ourselves and divisional management as well as those among divisional managers?
- Are we willing to confront a division manager when we feel things are going wrong? Do we put our concerns on the line in a clear and constructive way? Do we give him enough time and power to correct problematic situations?
- Finally, if our confidence in a division manager falters, are we willing to stand up to the tough issue of replacing him?

From the division manager's perspective:

- Given the interdependencies involved, are we spending an appropriate amount of our time relating to the corporate headquarters and other divisions?
- Are we doing all we can to assure that corporate management understands our business and the problems and opportunities we face?
- Are we giving clear signals about which of our requests are most important and why they are important? Are we forthright in calling delays in re-

sponding to these requests to the attention of appropriate corporate managers?

- Are we working to maintain our influence over divisional policies while being realistic about the need for corporate influence to an extent consistent with the information headquarters executives and the staff can contribute?
- Are we working to confront the conflicts which develop between ourselves and corporate management as well as those with other divisions? Connected to this, are we willing to risk a confrontation with corporate management to spell out how a particular decision may be harmful to us and accept decisions which run counter to our desires if they are in the interest of the total company?

If managers on both sides of the corporate-divisional interface can answer affirmatively to these questions, they will be describing a decision-making climate which, according to our findings, should help the organization to meet the demands of its total environment for diversity and interdependence. If they answer negatively to some or many of these questions, then the problem becomes what can they do about it. This depends upon several factors.

First, it depends upon one's position in the organization. As we have suggested in our discussion of organizational design issues, if one is in a position where he can initiate a process of change leading to an alteration in the design of the structure or measurement practices, he may be able to remedy the situation by this means. By changing these design variables, he would, in effect, be altering the ways through which managers make decisions in the hope that this would produce more effective results.

If a manager is not in a position to initiate such major changes, or even if he is, another alternative is to try to alter his own behavior. This is often more easily said than done. Just as a manager's way of thinking about organizational design is affected by his prior experience and personality, so is his day-to-day behavior. Thus, the same attitudes about power and authority which underlie his assumptions about organizational design will affect his responses to many of the questions listed above. This seems particularly true with regard to the questions about the relative influence between corporate and divisional levels. Whether managers will be able to work out an influence pattern consistent with the availability of information will depend to a considerable degree upon their individual attitudes toward authority and power. But it will also be heavily affected by a widely held assumption in the management culture that the amount of influence an individual should have varies directly with his level in the management hierarchy. While the findings of this study indicate that sticking to this assumption may not always lead to the most effective decisions, the extent to which it affects management thinking about organizations and managerial affairs is an important issue.

In spite of such constraints to the application of the findings of a study such as this, we are not pessimistic about their potential value. In the first place, as we have suggested, being aware of the costs and benefits of one's behavior patterns can be a stimulant to rethinking assumptions and to designing new structures and practices which encourage more effective behavior. Second, this same awareness can also encourage managers to search for approaches which achieve a reasonable, working balance between their preferred styles and the requirements of their firm's environment. Finally, as we mentioned earlier, the results of this study can be useful in encouraging top management to seek for the critical group executive and divisional general manager positions those persons who have the mixture of interpersonal skills required by these jobs.

If group executives and division general managers are selected to have a balanced mix of business and interpersonal skills, they should be able to do a great deal in achieving the organizational states and processes which this study suggests are important. In essence, whatever else such top managers manage—money, technology, people—it is clear that they must also be adept at managing joint decision-making processes. If, by designing organizations and through their own behavior, top managers can create an effective decision-making climate, they will have the greatest likelihood of harnessing the diversity of expertise and technology within the organization to meet the goals of the enterprise as a whole. Our view of the future of large organizations, both public and private, suggests that this will become even more important in the years ahead.

A Broader Perspective on Giant Organizations

This belief stems from two sources: first, our observation that the conglomerate firms were achieving remarkably little operating synergy; second, our prediction that achieving something like operating synergy may be increasingly important in the future for both private and public organizations. There are several reasons why the conglomerates found it difficult to achieve operating synergy. One was simply the diversity of divisions in each firm and the lack of many immediate opportunities for combinations among them. But even to start to search for such opportunities, divisional and corporate managers must see the potential for reward in such interdivisional collaboration. Given the structure and measurement practices in firms such as those we have studied, the attention of each division's management is naturally focused on its own business and the profits it can produce.

The issues of achieving the potential benefits of cross-divisional collaboration is not limited to conglomerate firms. There is considerable evidence that the matter of achieving collaboration between major organizational units (divisions in corporations, agencies in the Federal Government, etc.) is intertwined with the difficulties of solving many of the problems which plague the complex industrial societies of the United States, Europe, and Japan.

Throughout the 1950s and early 1960s much of the emphasis of both practitioners and organizational researchers was on developing organizations which were effective in producing technical innovation. Much of this innovation resulted in the development, production, and marketing of new products within what we have been calling divisions or single business units. Such self-contained units provided sufficient expertise and technology to produce new drugs, electronic devices, plastics, and a host of other new products and services. That this emphasis has been productive is apparent from both the rate of technical innovation and our increased understanding of organizational functioning. Yet the technical and social problems and opportunities which confront not only the United States but Japan and most European countries are growing at a rapid pace—pollution, transportation, housing, education, exploration of space—to name just a few. What all of these problems have in common is their tremendous size and complexity. As any business manager or government administrator who has attempted to tackle such problems will attest, their solution will require the delivery of a complex interdependent system of products and/or services.

A visible example of this sort of task is the United States Space Program. The effort to place a man on the moon involved numerous government agencies and private industrial firms woven together into a complex interorganizational network, which delivered the complex technology to accomplish this feat.[10] While this may appear to be a unique example, it makes the point clearly. If we are to tackle the problems which face us as a society, managers are going to have to develop organizations which can deal with such large-scale systemic problems. This is true whether we are talking about the divisions of a multiproduct firm collaborating to deliver a mass transportation system, a group of several firms working together to develop and deliver a pollution control system, or several government agencies that must collaborate to deliver health and welfare services to urban areas.

All of these organizations will have to find methods to deal with environmental diversity on the one hand and increasingly complex interdependence on the other. This is well illustrated by the complex organizational issues facing many government administrators in the United States. Achieving the more complex interdependence which is necessary for the solution of pressing societal issues is difficult under any conditions. But these executives must find ways to achieve this collaboration under increasingly stringent time demands for results. This means that they are not able to trade the ability to manage complexity for more time in reaching decisions and implementing programs. Further, they must be more sensitive to diverse local conditions. A blanket program aimed at all parts of the country does not seem to be adequate to meet many of our pressing societal problems. What these government administrators, as well as industrial managers, must do if they are going to guide their institutions in tackling the complex problems of a twentieth century industrialized society is to develop organizations with the flexibility and differentiation of a conglomerate but with a capacity to achieve integration among major units which compares to or exceeds what we have found in the vertically integrated firms. Measurements systems will have to place more emphasis on combined divisional performance. This is true both in the case of measurement and rewards in the sense we have been using these terms within one firm, and in the case of the planning and control systems used to tie several independent firms together in connection with a program of contracts and subcontracts, as in the example of the United States Space Program. But such measurement techniques alone will not be adequate integrative devices to achieve both the required differentiation and integration. Individual integrative roles, such as the group executives in this study or program managers in the space effort, will be required. Their integrative task will be not only to link the various operating units to the central headquarters but also to integrate the activities of the operating units.

The information flows required by the diversity and interdependence in these environments will probably be sufficiently complex to also warrant the use of some sorts of cross-unit teams. For example, in the case of an industrial firm such teams might consist of the division general managers involved, plus the group executives. As an alternative or as a supplement, it may also be necessary to develop integrative devices across units at lower organizational levels in order to obtain the integration required around operational issues. Whether any or all of these integrative devices, plus others which managers may develop, will actually result in something resembling operating synergy within the private and public sectors can only be answered by future events. However, the findings of this study suggest that in the absence of such structural change in both public and private organizations, it will be highly unlikely that large organizations will live up to their full potential as valuable societal institutions. Even if such structural changes are forthcoming, we should add that the managerial tactics which we discussed above will be even more critical in dealing with the combination of a more complex set of interdependencies and greater differentiation.

In essence, this view of the future possibilities facing large organizations suggests that there are many problems that they alone have the resources and capacities to tackle. If these organizations are to be successful in this endeavor, the central message of this study should be extremely helpful. It is no longer adequate to think about the problems of managing these large institutions as questions of decentralization or centralization of authority, or even as matters of sensitivity and good human relations. Rather, it is essential to recognize that we are dealing with a complex and interdependent system of variables. The desired pattern of these variables depends upon the characteristics of the environment. If managers adopt this view and use it to design and develop their organizations to meet the challenges of the future, there is every reason to hope that these large organizations can play an even more effective societal role.

APPENDIX A

Supplementary Data

THE purpose of this appendix is to provide the interested reader with actual data which were discussed in summary form in Chapters II and VI. The approaches used in computing the statistics contained in this appendix are discussed briefly in those two chapters and more fully in Appendix B. Exhibits A-1, A-2, and A-3 and Tables A-1, A-2, and A-3 provide additional data on the environmental requirements faced by divisions in the conglomerate firms. Tables A-4 through A-16 present data on corporate goal sets and patterns of corporate-divisional and inter-divisional decision making in the vertically integrated firms.

EXHIBIT A-1

Diverse Industrial Environments at Firm 2

DEFENSE (2:I)

Division 2:I was a small but highly profitable division which manufactured and sold a diverse line of highly engineered components used mainly for defense and aerospace applications. Most of its products were built to order and required close tolerances. They ranged in price from $200 to $2,500. Sales in Division 2:I's industry were on a contract basis, and close contact was required between vendors and customers. The single most important selling point in this market was the performance characteristics and weight of the product. Cost tended to be the next most important consideration. The division operated a single manufacturing facility which also housed its engineering and sales functions.

Divisional management noted that product innovation was the major means of achieving market penetration. Approximately 50% of Division 2:I's sales consisted of products that were either new or represented significantly different modifications of items offered five years ago. Over the years, Division 2:I had been able to develop a growing group of products that, because of their superior performance characteristics, gave it a proprietary market position. At the same time, management had been able to maintain tight control over fixed costs. Division 2:I's general manager emphasized that it was this combination of tight cost control and a high product development capability that permitted the division to consistently outperform its competition.

Of the four divisions that were studied at Firm 2, Division 2:I faced the most dynamic and uncertain environments. Much of this division's product development capability depended upon its ability to import information from the rapidly developing body of scientific knowledge which related to its products. Customer requirements were complex, diverse, and also tended to change a good bit from year to year. Since most of the division's products were built to order, there was also considerable uncertainty associated with the manufacturing function.

At the same time, the nature of Division 2:I's business required a high order of integration among all functions. Engineering and marketing worked closely together both to influence customer specifications and to develop bids for major contracts. Engineering and manufacturing had to be in constant contact to develop new products and to manufacture custom items. Marketing was constantly feeding information to manufacturing concerning changes in contract specifications that were often requested by customers.

AUTOMOTIVE PARTS (2:II)

The business requirements faced by Division 2:II provide a marked contrast to those of Division 2:I. This division had been the core of Firm 2's original business. It was a large, two-plant operation which manufactured and sold a line of standardized (component) products to approximately a dozen automobile and truck manufacturers. Division 2:II's manufacturing operations were characterized by a high volume of output produced mainly through medium- to large-batch technologies. Although this division held long-term contracts with its customers, the customers' requirements for output tended to fluctuate a good deal during any given year. Within Division 2:II's industry there was intense competition for customer contracts, and profit margins tended to be very slim. The major selling points in this industry were price and delivery.

Divisional management stated that the critical issues for Division 2:II were maintaining an efficient factory and meeting customers' delivery requirements. Considerable management attention was focused on scheduling, improvement of materials flow in the factory, and reduction of raw materials inventories. The division's general manager noted that because of Division 2:II's high unit volume, small cost savings could have a substantial effect on profits. During recent years Division 2:II's performance had been equal to or above the mean performance of its competitors.

Compared to Division 2:I, Division 2:II faced rather stable environmental conditions. Although changes in technology were potentially disruptive, they occurred at very infrequent intervals. The marketing environment, although very competitive, was quite certain as to the basis of competition. Also, Division 2:II's business required much less integration among functions. Only in the case of marketing and manufacturing was tight coordination needed to meet customer delivery requirements.

INDUSTRIAL AND APPAREL FIBERS AND YARNS (2:III)

The third division studied at Firm 2 presented a yet different range of issues. Division 2:III manufactured a line of uniform products through a continuous, uninterrupted chemical process. This division's technology required a rigid control over temperatures, time, and chemical processes. Manufacturing operations were centered in one large facility. Sale of output was divided among the apparel industry and manufacturers of tires and industrial goods.

Although Division 2:III was one of the larger divisions of Firm 2, it was one of the smaller manufacturers in its industry. Expansion of output in this industry entailed high levels of fixed investment, and even existing facilities required high sales volume to stay above the break-even point. At the same time of our study, Division 2:III was faced with both overcapacity and a weak price structure in its existing lines and with considerable competitive pressure from newly developed products.

Division management had taken two approaches to these industry conditions. In the short run, considerable attention was being devoted to marketing programs for existing product lines. In order to hold the line on prices, Division 2:III was attempting to get increasing brand acceptance for its products and to broaden its customer base by devising new applications for these products. In the longer run, Division 2:III hoped to build capacity in the newer product lines that had recently gained increased customer acceptance. Although Division 2:III's profits had come under heavy pressure in recent years, management believed that its marketing efforts were beginning to pay off. The division's general manager noted that while Division 2:III could never match the funds spent on product innovation by its larger competitors, it did have a unique ability to live with low margin items.

Division 2:III faced the second highest rate of environmental change of the four divisions which we studied. The primary area of uncertainty for this division was the scientific subenvironment, where the knowledge necessary for development of new lines was evolving at a fairly rapid pace. Although the market subenvironment was highly competitive, there was a good deal more certainty concerning customer needs; the issue was to develop new ways of satisfying these needs. In the area of manufacturing, Division 2:III's process technology made for a fairly high order of certainty.

AIR CONDITIONING EQUIPMENT (2:IV)

The fourth division in our sample at Firm 2 manufactured a line of air conditioning equipment for commercial, industrial, and residential use. Division 2:IV's products were sold mainly through independent wholesalers and distributors. The average retail price for items in its line was $200. Although Division 2:IV's equipment was manufactured on a small batch basis, 80% of its line consisted of standard shelf items rather than items that were engineered to specific customer requirements.

Price was the major selling point in Division 2:IV's industry. Division management noted that while few major technological breakthroughs had occurred in its business, refinements in product design were the primary means of securing price advantages over competitive products. At the same time, Division 2:IV's small batch technology permitted considerable flexibility in redesigning product lines to fit a wide range of uses. Approximately 80% of Division 2:IV's line represented products which were new or significantly redesigned in the last five years.

Division 2:IV was a relatively small division with all manufacturing operations contained in a single facility. During recent years its profits had been under
considerable pressure. In 1967 a new general manager had been brought in from
a large consumer products company. His first major program had been to revamp
Division 2:IV's means of distribution in an attempt to secure greater market
penetration. At the same time this general manager underscored the importance
of maintaining the division's existing competence in the area of product engineering.

Although Division 2:IV's environments were not characterized by a particularly high rate of change, management felt that there was a fairly high degree of

---

TABLE A-1

Basic Environmental Requirements Faced by Four Divisions at Firm 2 [a]

	Rate of Change[b]	Environmental Requirements Time Span of Environmental Feedback[c]	Relative Importance of Subenvironment[d]
DEFENSE (2:I)			
Scientific-Engineering	5.5	4.1	1.0
Manufacturing	5.2	2.7	2.8
Marketing	4.9	3.4	2.2
AUTOMOTIVE PARTS (2:II)			
Scientific-Engineering	4.7	3.6	2.2
Manufacturing	3.9	1.8	1.4
Marketing	4.3	2.7	2.4
INDUSTRIAL AND APPAREL FIBERS AND YARNS (2:III)			
Scientific-Engineering	4.9	3.7	2.3
Manufacturing	3.8	2.2	2.0
Marketing	4.4	3.0	1.8
AIR CONDITIONING EQUIPMENT (2:IV)			
Scientific-Engineering	4.0	3.9	1.5
Manufacturing	3.2	2.2	2.6
Marketing	4.7	3.3	1.9

[a] Higher scores indicate a greater rate of environmental change, a longer time span of
feedback, and *less* importance attributed to a subenvironment.

[b] Differences among divisions by subenvironment are significant at the following levels:
Scientific (.05), Manufacturing (.10), and Marketing (not significant) (analysis of variance).

[c] Differences among divisions by subenvironment are not statistically significant.

[d] Differences among divisions by subenvironment are significant at .01 levels for both
Scientific and Manufacturing. Differences for Marketing are significant at .01 level (analysis
of variance).

uncertainty associated with all three major functional areas. A good deal of this uncertainty—particularly in the marketing and manufacturing areas—was attributed to the need to organize activities on a more systematic basis. The general manager believed that once this reorganization was accomplished, Division 2:IV's small size would give it a considerable advantage in controlling fixed costs as volume grew.

EXHIBIT A-2

Diverse Industrial Environments at Firm 3

MACHINERY FOR EXTRACTIVE INDUSTRIES (3:I)

Division 3:I manufactured and sold a line of very specialized, highly engineered equipment used by several extractive industries. Individual items in this division's line ranged in price from $10,000 to $130,000, and each item was custommade to fit customer requirements. Division 3:I sold its products through its own regional distribution and service outlets. The primary selling points in Division 3:I's market were the dependability of the equipment and its ability to perform specialized functions. At the same time, customer assistance and service in the form of consultations, repairs, supplies, and financing of sales were important elements in marketing.

Division 3:I was small but highly profitable, and it was the largest single manufacturer of its line of products. Originally this division had offered a limited equipment line to one major industry. After a significant downturn in this industry, however, Division 3:I had broadened its line considerably and had also sought out a much broader customer base for its equipment.

Divisional management pointed to two major issues posed by its business. First, the specialized nature of its product required a fairly high level of engineering competence as well as close relations with customers around issues of equipment design and servicing. Second, low margins in Division 3:I's industry led to a heavy emphasis on cost control.

Division 3:I's environments were characterized by a fairly low rate of change and were relatively certain. The specialized field requirements faced by the engineering function entailed the greatest degree of uncertainty. Manufacturing and marketing activities tended to be much more certain. At the same time, the specialized nature of Division 3:I's equipment and services required a fairly high level of integration between both marketing and engineering and between marketing and manufacturing.

INDUSTRIAL AND TRANSPORTATION EQUIPMENT (3:II)

By way of contrast, Division 3:II produced a line of standardized but rather complex devices which were sold mainly to a major segment of the transportation industry. These devices ranged in price from $500 to $1,500 and were manufactured in a fairly high volume through a small- and medium-batch technology.

Division 3:II operated one large, highly integrated plant; and its manufacturing activities represented 75% of the value-added of the final product. This division had always been the major factor in its market, but recently it had been faced with increasingly aggressive price competition from other manufacturers. During the time of our study, Division 3:II's customers had been suffering from a short-term decline. These two factors had precipitated a decline in Division 3:II's profits; however, it traditionally had been a high, if somewhat cyclical, performer.

Division management was devoting considerable effort to redesigning products in an attempt to gain some protection against heavy price competition. Approximately 45% of Division 3:II's products were new or significantly modified within the last five years. At the same time, a good deal of money had been invested in plant modernization programs aimed at reducing costs. Thus, product engineering was the major issue at Division 3:II, with plant efficiency running a close second.

This division faced somewhat more uncertain and changing environmental conditions than Division 3:I did. The problems involved in redesigning and modifying products posed the greatest area of uncertainty for Division 3:II. Reduced customer purchases and price competition had also created considerable uncertainty for the marketing function. The complex nature of Division 3:II's integrated manufacturing facilities entailed a moderate rate of uncertainty for this function. At the same time a relatively high degree of coordination was required among all functions at Division 3:II. Engineering worked closely with both marketing and manufacturing in developing new product designs. Also, the large number of operations performed within Division 3:II's plant required that marketing and manufacturing work closely to schedule the flow of product.

INDUSTRIAL CONTROLS, SPECIAL EQUIPMENT, AND COMPONENTS (3:III)

The third division which we studied at Firm 3 designed, sold, and installed complex industrial systems. Although Division 3:III sold its systems, supplies, and services to several major industries, many of them went to the same customers that were served by Division 3:II. Both divisions had been the original businesses of the parent corporation.

Division 3:III's billings consisted of payments for long-range feasibility studies, large systems, smaller equipment, supplies, and field installation activities. Work on larger systems was on a contract basis, and some of the larger systems contracts entailed total billings as high as $2,000,000. Bidding for major contracts was highly competitive, and price was the determining factor. Division 3:III's systems required significant amounts of both design and field engineering. These systems presented unique engineering problems in that they had to be extremely durable and yet were required to function within very fine tolerances.

Division 3:III operated two plants, and 80% of its products were made on a custom shop basis. Manufacturing activities ranged from forging to the assembly of printed circuits.

Division management cited two major issues posed by its businesses. First, a high level of engineering competence was required to design and install its systems. Second, the competitive nature of bidding for contracts required a tight control over the costs of both products and services.

Of the four divisions in our sample at Firm 3, Division 3:III faced the highest rate of environmental change and uncertainty. Engineering was faced with the task of designing and installing systems to fit the unique needs of individual sites. The marketing subenvironment was characterized by heavy competition and fairly unclear customer requirements in many instances. Only in the case of manufacturing were activities fairly certain; once designs had been completed, production of system components was a fairly straightforward matter. Division 3:III's systems business also required a high order of coordination among all functions. Marketing and engineering had to work particularly closely in arriving at bids for contracts. The custom nature of Division 3:III's business also required close contact between manufacturing and both engineering and marketing.

CONSTRUCTION AND MINING EQUIPMENT (3:IV)

The final division in our sample at Firm 3 produced a line of construction and mining equipment which was sold both to industry and to government. Division 3:IV's equipment ranged in price from $15,000 to $250,000. The lower priced items were made according to standardized designs, while the larger ticket items entailed a good deal of modification to meet particular customer requirements. Division 3:IV's equipment was distributed and serviced through an extensive network of independent dealers. The division operated four manufacturing facilities around the country, and production was mainly on a small-batch and custom basis.

Although Division 3:IV was a very large division, it was the smallest major manufacturer in its industry. Divisional management noted that Division 3:IV's relatively small size made it difficult for the division to offer its dealers a sufficiently broad equipment line to compete across-the-board with the larger manufacturers. At the same time, however, price and the performance characteristics of equipment were important selling points; and Division 3:IV had traditionally boasted a strong product development competence. At the time of our study, Division 3:III's market had suffered a considerable downturn. This industry decline along with distribution problems had resulted in a substantial profit decline for the division.

Divisional management cited three major problems that faced Division 3:IV. First, considerable attention was being devoted to widening Division 3:IV's line and upgrading its distribution and servicing network. The division's general manager stated that marketing efforts were becoming an increasingly important part of successful performance. Second, a good deal of effort was required to maintain Division 3:IV's competence in product design. Finally, inventory control was a critical issue for the division. Larger items in the line often required three or four months to complete and could tie up vast amounts of working capital. These general funding requirements combined with an industry downturn had left Division 3:IV with large inventory commitments.

TABLE A-2

Basic Environmental Requirements Faced by Four Divisions at Firm 3 [a]

| | *Environmental Requirements* | | |
	Rate of Change[b]	*Time Span of Environmental Feedback*[c]	*Relative Importance of Subenvironment*[d]
MACHINERY FOR EXTRACTIVE INDUSTRIES (3:I)			
Scientific-Engineering	4.1	3.9	2.0
Manufacturing	3.3	2.8	2.3
Marketing	3.8	2.8	1.7
INDUSTRIAL AND TRANSPORTATION EQUIPMENT (3:II)			
Scientific-Engineering	4.5	5.0	1.4
Manufacturing	4.6	3.3	2.6
Marketing	4.0	4.0	2.1
INDUSTRIAL CONTROLS, SPECIAL EQUIPMENT AND COMPONENTS (3:III)			
Scientific-Engineering	5.1	4.0	1.4
Manufacturing	4.1	3.1	2.7
Marketing	4.6	3.2	1.9
CONSTRUCTION AND MINING EQUIPMENT (3:IV)			
Scientific-Engineering	4.3	4.6	1.3
Manufacturing	3.0	3.3	2.7
Marketing	4.3	3.9	2.0

[a] Higher scores indicate a greater rate of environmental change, a longer time span of feedback, and *less* importance attributed to a subenvironment.

[b] Differences among divisions by subenvironment are significant at the following levels: Scientific (.10), Manufacturing (.01), and Marketing (.10) (analysis of variance).

[c] Differences among divisions by subenvironment are significant at the following levels: Scientific (.05), Manufacturing (not significant), and Marketing (.05) (analysis of variance).

[d] Differences among divisions by subenvironment are not statistically significant.

Although Division 3:IV's environments were not characterized by a particularly high rate of change, it did face considerable uncertainty in all three subenvironments. The engineering function faced a good deal of uncertainty in designing larger equipment to fit unique customer needs. Also, changes in engineering knowledge relevant to Division 3:IV's four-plant manufacturing setup entailed a moderate amount of uncertainty around issues of scheduling product flow and controlling inventories.

EXHIBIT A-3

Diverse Industrial Environments at Firm 4

INDUSTRIAL EQUIPMENT (4:I)

This division produced a diverse line of heavy capital equipment which it sold to the oil, gas, chemical, transportation, construction, and defense industries. Its product lines included packaged compressors, liquefied petroleum gas tanks, gas turbine silencers, cryogenic vessels for storage of liquefied gases at supercold temperatures, fractionating towers, pressure vessels for storage of chlorine, cement kilns, and sundry heavy, machined metal products. Most of these products were made to order on the basis of firm customer contracts.

Manufacturing was characterized by job-shop technologies entailing the fabrication, machining, and welding of enormous metal vessels. Division management stated that the key success factors in its business were timely delivery, control over manufacturing costs, and the ability to make accurate estimates of costs and effective bids.

DEFENSE (4:II)

Division 4:II was a large, moderately profitable, operation which had diverse skills in precision metal fabrication and made thousands of different metal products. This division was heavily dependent upon government ordnance contracts (80% of 1968 sales). At any one time Division 4:II's large, single location facility was working on approximately 300 different contracts for 100 different government and industrial customers. Most contracts were let on a cost-plus-incentive basis.

Manufacturing, which was carried out on a small- to medium-batch basis, was viewed by divisional management as Division 4:II's critical skill. The ability to control costs tightly and to meet customer delivery schedules were of prime importance. Marketing was cited as the second most important factor in the division's success. In the short run, the ability to discover and bid on a wide range of ordnance contracts and industrial jobs in a highly competitive market was important if the company was to effectively utilize its large plant capacity. In the longer run division management was seeking more stable, commercial sales both to reduce its vulnerability to defense spending cycles and to provide more predictability for factory operations.

LEISURE PRODUCTS (4:III)

This division manufactured a line of sporting equipment which it sold along with accessories and related services. In recent years the market for Division 4:III's equipment had grown mature, placing considerable profit pressures on the division. Division management cited marketing as the critical skill for Division 4:III as it attempted to obtain replacement sales of its equipment as well as sales of related accessories and services. At the time of our study Division 4:III manufactured only moderate quantities of its equipment line. This equipment was rather sophisticated, however, which placed certain difficult demands on its small engineering and manufacturing functions.

CONSUMER DURABLES (4:IV)

Division 4:IV manufactured and sold a line of durable equipment for home use in a highly competitive and seasonal market. Marketing was seen as the division's critical skill; and effective distribution, product quality, and competitive pricing were cited as the key elements of the marketing mix.

Manufacturing was characterized by medium- to large-batch technologies

---

TABLE A-3

Basic Environmental Requirements Faced by Four Divisions at Firm 4 [a]

| | Environmental Requirements | | |
	Rate of Change[b]	Time Span of Environmental Feedback[c]	Relative Importance of Subenvironment[d]
INDUSTRIAL EQUIPMENT (4:I)			
Scientific-Engineering	4.7	3.3	2.8
Manufacturing	4.5	2.0	1.7
Marketing	4.8	2.2	1.6
DEFENSE (4:II)			
Scientific-Engineering	4.7	4.1	2.9
Manufacturing	5.4	2.7	1.1
Marketing	4.4	3.3	2.0
LEISURE PRODUCTS (4:III)			
Scientific-Engineering	3.4	4.2	2.0
Manufacturing	3.0	3.1	2.4
Marketing	3.6	2.9	1.6
CONSUMER DURABLES (4:IV)			
Scientific-Engineering	3.1	4.4	2.1
Manufacturing	4.0	2.1	2.4
Marketing	4.8	3.3	1.6

[a] Higher scores indicate a greater rate of environmental change, a longer time span of feedback, and *less* importance attributed to a subenvironment.

[b] Differences among divisions by subenvironment are significant at the following levels: Scientific (.01), Manufacturing (.01), and Marketing (.05) (analysis of variance).

[c] Differences among divisions by subenvironment are significant at the following levels: Scientific (.10), Manufacturing (.05), and Marketing (.01) (analysis of variance).

[d] Differences among divisions by subenvironment are significant at the following levels: Scientific (.001), Manufacturing (.05), and Marketing (not significant) (analysis of variance).

and was essentially a matter of stamping light metals and assembling a large number of parts. New product development was viewed as moderately important, and it centered around issues of redesigning existing products to be more attractive to consumers and the ability to get such new products into mass production.

TABLE A-4

Overall Goal Sets of Corporate Headquarters Units in Two Paper Companies[a]

	Firm 5	*Firm 6*
OVERALL FINANCIAL GOALS		
Return on investment	1	1
% growth—profits	6	2
% growth—sales	10	5
Profit margin on sales	5	9.5
Absolute level of profits	3	6
Desired profit mix among product lines	7	15
Sales volume	9	3.5
OVERALL PRODUCT-MARKET GOALS		
Product diversification into related areas	15.5	11
Rate of new product introduction	20.5	19.5
Product diversification into unrelated areas	19	9.5
Geographic expansion of product sales	20.5	21
MAJOR OPERATING GOALS		
Market share	14	12
Customer relations	11	17
Product improvement	3	13.5
Cost reduction	2	3.5
Inventory control	15.5	13.5
Level of fixed costs	18	16
Plant expansion	13	19.5
OTHER GOALS		
Development and motivation of personnel	4	8
Corporate image	12	7
Maintenance of unique corporate skills	17	18

[a] Ranking of 21 goal items by corporate headquarters executives. Lower number indicates more important goal item. Differences in rankings of top ten goal items common to both firms are not significant (Mann-Whitney U test). For a more comprehensive listing of these goal items and how they were analyzed, see Appendix B.

TABLE A-5

Overall Quality of Information Received by Corporate and Divisional Management Units in Two Paper Companies[a]

	Quality and Quantity of Information Received	
	Upward Flow (from Division)[b]	Downward Flow (from Corporate)[c]
FIRM 5		
Mills	2.6	2.7
Containers	2.6	3.2
Packaging	2.4	2.6
FIRM 6		
Mills	2.8	2.5
Containers	2.3	2.4
Packaging	2.3	2.5

[a] Higher numbers indicate higher quality of information. Upward flows are mean ratings by corporate managers of the quality of information received from each division; downward flows are mean ratings by managers in each division.

[b] Difference between Firms 5 and 6 is not statistically significant.

[c] Difference between Firms 5 and 6 is significant at the .05 level (analysis of variance).

TABLE A-6

Rapidity of Headquarters in Responding to Divisional Requests in Two Paper Companies[a]

Division	Firm 5	Firm 6
Mills	2.7	2.7
Containers	2.9	1.9
Packaging	2.4	2.5

[a] Higher numbers indicate greater rapidity in responding to requests. Scores are mean ratings by managers in each division. Difference between Firms 5 and 6 is significant at .05 level (analysis of variance).

TABLE A-7

Perceived Characteristics of Corporate Performance Evaluation System in Two Paper Companies[a]

Characteristic	Firm 5	Firm 6
(1) Agreement between corporate and divisional executives concerning relative emphasis placed on criteria (Kendall coefficient of concordance)[b]	.94	.48
(2) Balance between long-run and short-run performance criteria (raw difference score)	.56	1.43

[a] Higher scores indicate higher agreement *but* less long-run/short-run balance. See Appendix B for a discussion of how these statistics were computed.

[b] Coefficients of concordance are significant at .001 level for Firm 5 and .05 level for Firm 6.

TABLE A-8

Balanced Orientation of Integrating Positions in Two Paper Companies[a]

	No. of Integrating Positions Which Were Intermediate on 2 or More Dimensions
Firm 5	4 out of 8
Firm 6	6 out of 6

[a] Since each firm differed in the number of executives who occupied integrating positions, scores indicate the number of executives who had achieved intermediate positions relative to the total number of integrating positions. See Appendix B for a description of how intermediate orientations were determined.

TABLE A-9

Influence Over Divisional Policies Attributed to Four Major Organizational Levels in Two Paper Companies[a]

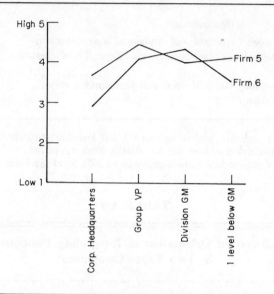

[a] Scores represent overall mean for three divisions in each firm, based on ratings by corporate and divisional managers for each of the divisions. Differences among levels in each firm are significant at .01 level (analysis of variance). Differences between Firms 5 and 6 are significant at .01 level for top management, senior VP, and 1 level below general manager. See Appendix B for questionnaire item and how scores were computed.

TABLE A-10

Influence Over Divisional Policies Attributed to Corporate and Divisional Management Units in Two Paper Companies[a]

	Corporate Management	*Divisional Management*	*Difference*[b]
FIRM 5			
Mills	4.03	4.40	+.37[c]
Containers	4.39	4.43	+.04[c]
Packaging	3.53	4.25	+.72[c]
FIRM 6			
Mills	4.22	3.37	−.85[d]
Containers	3.95	3.88	−.07[c]
Packaging	3.72	4.27	+.55[d]

[a] Numbers are mean ratings by divisional managers only; higher scores indicate higher perceived influence. Corporate management scores include group executives; divisional management scores are division general managers and executives one level below general managers. See Appendix B for detailed description of how scores were computed.

[b] Plus (+) indicates more divisional influence; minus (−) indicates more corporate influence.

[c] Differences are not statistically significant.

[d] Differences are significant at the .05 level (two-tailed t test).

TABLE A-11

Modes of Conflict Resolution in Two Paper Companies[a]

	Factor		
	Confrontation[b]	*Forcing*[b]	*Smoothing*[b]
FIRM 5			
Mills	12.0	7.5	9.0
Containers	11.5	5.7	6.8
Packaging	11.5	7.3	6.9
FIRM 6			
Mills	12.1	7.6	8.0
Containers	10.5	8.3	6.9
Packaging	10.8	6.5	6.4

[a] Scores are based on responses of divisional managers; higher scores indicate more typical behavior. See Appendix B for a description of questionnaire items and approach for computing scores.

[b] Differences between Firms 5 and 6 are not statistically significant.

TABLE A-12

Quality of Information Exchange Between Divisions in Two Paper Companies[a]

Relationship	Firm 5	Firm 6
Mills—Containers[b]	2.5	1.7
Mills—Packaging[c]	2.2	2.5

[a] Higher numbers indicate higher quality of information. Scores are mean ratings by managers on both sides of the relationship.

[b] Difference between Firms 5 and 6 is significant at .01 level (analysis of variance).

[c] Difference between Firms 5 and 6 is not significant.

TABLE A-13

Rapidity of Divisions in Responding to One Another's Requests in Two Paper Companies[a]

Relationship	Firm 5	Firm 6
Mills—Containers[b]	2.6	2.2
Mills—Packaging[c]	1.7	2.6

[a] Higher numbers indicate greater rapidity in responding to requests. Scores are mean ratings by managers on both sides of the relationship.

[b] Difference between Firms 5 and 6 is not statistically significant.

[c] Difference between Firms 5 and 6 is significant at the .01 level (analysis of variance).

TABLE A-14

Modes of Conflict Resolution Between Divisions in Two Paper Companies[a]

	Factor		
	Confrontation	Forcing	Smoothing
FIRM 5			
Mills	11.4	6.9	7.6
Containers	10.3[b]	5.9[b]	5.8
Packaging	10.2	6.9	6.3
FIRM 6			
Mills	11.3	7.1	7.0
Containers	9.2[b]	6.7[b]	5.7
Packaging	9.9	6.0	7.0

[a] Scores are based on responses of managers in each division; higher scores indicate more typical behavior.

[b] Differences between Firms 5 and 6 are significant at the .05 level (analysis of variance). All other differences are not statistically significant.

TABLE A-15

Balanced Orientation of Interdivisional Integrating Roles/Departments in Two Paper Companies

	No. of Major Integrating Roles/Departments Which Were Intermediate on Two or More Dimensions	
Relationship	Firm 5	Firm 6
Mills—Containers	1 out of 3	2 out of 3
Mills—Packaging	3 out of 3	3 out of 3

TABLE A-16

Degree to Which Integrators See Their Rewards Based on Total
Corporate Performance in Two Paper Companies[a]

	Influence of Corporate Performance on Rewards
Firm 5	4.0
Firm 6	3.3

[a] Based on responses of managers in integrative positions and within integrative departments; higher score indicates higher influence. Since many of the respondents were responsible for both mill-container and mill-packaging integration, a breakdown of the data by relationship was not feasible. Difference between Firms 5 and 6 is significant at .05 level (analysis of variance).

APPENDIX B

Research Methodology

THE purpose of this appendix is to give the interested reader a description of the interview and questionnaire techniques employed in this research. Data collected from company records are described *seriatim* in the text. Interview and questionnaire formats are presented separately. The questionnaire material is organized according to the major variables which we sought to measure. Descriptions of the more complicated analytical procedures are included. Also included are cross-references between each major set of variables and the tables in the text in which these variables have been presented. In some instances, questionnaire scales have been reversed in the text for purposes of simplifying our discussion.

A number of the questionnaire items had been developed by Lawrence and Lorsch to study interdepartmental relationships. These items were modified to fit the particular conditions which characterized corporate-divisional relationships. The reader who is interested in the initial development of these measures may wish to refer to the following sources:

Paul R. Lawrence and Jay W. Lorsch, *Organization and Environment: Managing Differentiation and Integration* (Boston: Division of Research, Harvard Business School, 1967).
Stephen A. Allen III, "Managing Organizational Diversity: A Comparative Study of Corporate-Divisional Relations" (unpublished doctoral dissertation, Harvard Business School, 1968).

Interview Formats

Somewhat different sets of questions were used to structure interviews with each of the major organizational levels which were involved in corporate-divisional relationships. Interview formats for each of the four major levels are presented below. The precise wording of these questions differed somewhat for the conglomerate and vertically integrated firms.

Major Corporate Executives

1. Perhaps we can begin with some background on your firm's approach to diversification. What were the goals of your diversification program, and what led you into the areas you are in today? Is there a unifying concept which describes your approach to diversification?
2. Could you describe the corporate organization for us?
   2.1—Role played by
        —corporate staff—basis of involvement with divisions
        —group executives
        —division general managers
3. What organizational devices do you use for achieving coordination between the corporate office and the divisions? Around what issues is coordination required?
4. What sorts of contacts are required between divisions? Do you feel that there is any untapped potential in this area?
5. How do you judge your divisional managers' performance?
   5.1—What information do you use?
        —nature
        —source
6. How are division managers compensated? How does the compensation system relate to their performance?
7. How would you express the corporation's overall goals? What objectives is it seeking to accomplish in the long-run/short-run?
8. How do you test the consistency between division managers' actions and corporate goals? Are there instances where the two diverge or come into conflict?
9. How is capital allocated among the divisions?
10. What are the major areas of expansion currently?
    10.1—In terms of
         —existing sales
         —product line extensions
         —new products
    10.2—Which are the most promising areas?

Corporate Staff

1. I'd like to begin by getting some idea of what's involved in your job.
   Areas of concern.
   1.1—(Publics) What people do you have the most contact with?

	Nature of contact	Frequency
(A) Inside company		1—daily; 2—weekly;
(B) Outside		3—monthly; 4—less than monthly.

2. In evaluating division plans (and specific project proposals) what elements of information do you consider most important? What informational items do you have to "nail down" before you're confident of the ability of the division to make the plan?
3. From where you stand in the organization, what are the overall goals of the corporation? What objectives does it seek to accomplish in the long run and the short run?
4. How do you test the consistency between division managers' actions and corporate goals?

4.1—Are there instances where the two diverge or come into conflict?

4.2—What organizational devices does the corporation use to coordinate its divisions (e.g., committees, coordinators, policies, etc.)? How effective are they?

5. What sorts of contacts are required among divisions? Do you feel there is any untapped potential here?

6. Beyond the contacts you have with the divisions, what other contacts do they have with the corporate headquarters?

7. Are there any areas where you would like to see more corporate involvement? Less?

8. Returning to your own job:

8.1—How long in position, what other jobs?

8.2—On what basis is your performance judged? Do you participate in the bonus plan? If so, what factors do you see as affecting the size of your bonus/(controllability)?

Division Management

A. *Division characteristics*

1. I'd like to begin by getting a feel for the nature of the business your division is engaged in. What are your major products, markets, and their relative importance to divisional sales/profitability?

2. What are the critical elements of success in this business? What tasks, activities must be performed particularly well? What activities receive the most attention?

3. What are the major issues/problems requiring attention at this time in the division?

3.1—During the past 5 years, have any changes occurred in the market or technical conditions in your industry which have proven particularly significant to your organization?

3.2—What percent of your sales is accounted for by products which are either new within the last 5 years or significant modifications of existing products?

3.3—Within the organization, what functional areas have to be most closely coordinated in order to achieve overall division performance? Are certain functional interfaces more critical than others?

4. What are the overall goals of this division? What general objectives does it seek to accomplish in the long run and in the short run?

5. How long has your division been a part of _____ corporation? Has merger with _____ resulted in any changes in your organization, operating procedures, way of doing business?

B. *Structural characteristics*

6. How frequently do you review the results achieved in your functional area?
   —Less often than monthly
   —Monthly
   —Weekly
   —Daily

6.1—Similarly, review by general manager?

7. Could you describe the nature of this review?
   —oral vs. written
   —statistics—yes or no
        —general vs. detailed

8. Could you describe the process through which you review the job performance of the individuals reporting to you?
   —formal evaluation?
   —if yes, fixed criteria?
   —if fixed criteria, less than 5 or more than 5?

9. How important are formal rules in your functional area?
   —for routine procedures
   —operations

C. *Nature of individual jobs*

   10. How long have you been in your current position? What jobs have you held previously?

   11. In your present position, what people do you have the most contact with? (face-to-face, telephone, written)

	Frequency
11.1—Within your division (4 or 5)	1. Daily
11.2—At the corporate level	2. Weekly
11.3—At group level	3. Monthly
11.4—In other divisions	4. Less than monthly

D. *Plans, budgets, and funds requests* (managers other than division general managers):

   12. Could you describe the one-year and five-year planning process?
       12.1—Steps
       12.2—Presentation, contact with corporate management
       12.3—Feedback from corporate
       12.4—Review procedures

   13. Details of capital project development process?
       13.1—Definition, locus of information
       13.2—Nature of projects—cost reduction, sales expansion, replacement, new products
       13.3—Approval mechanisms
            —corporate and divisional roles
            —hurdle rate
            —modifications
            —reviews
            —relation to plans and budgets

   °14. In putting together your annual and five-year plan (and specific project proposals), what elements of information do you consider most important? What informational items do you have to "nail down" before you're confident of the ability of the division to make the plan?

   °15. Similarly, what items do you feel you should emphasize in selling corporate and/or group officers on the plan (or project)?

   °16. Now let's focus on the issues of getting major budget items and capital expenditure projects approved.
       16.1—Whom do you have to influence?
       16.2—Do you feel that the corporation is more favorably disposed toward some types of projects than others? (e.g., new products, cost savings, or replacement/short-lived vs. long/high return-high risk vs. lower risk and return/large outlay vs. small). What kinds of projects do you feel stand the best chances of acceptance?
       16.3—Do you have any projects on the burner that you feel are in the division's interest but that stand little chance of approval? Also, have you ever had a project or major budget item either rejected, shelved, or greatly reduced in the corporate review process? If so, elaborate.

   °17. Do you feel that some divisions have more favorable positions than others—in terms of securing funds or corporate attention? If so, rank them. Why do they?

E. *Other*

   18. From where you stand in the organization, what are the overall goals of the

---

° Division general managers only.

corporation? What objectives does it seek to accomplish in the long-run and the short-run?

19. On what basis is your performance judged? How important is—
    19.1—Performance rel. to other divisions
    19.2—Performance rel. to your competitors
    19.3—Improvement over your own previous performance
    19.4—Short-run vs. long-run sales/profits
    19.5—Development of managerial talent in your division
    19.6—Cooperation with other divisions on joint projects

20. What factors have significant impact on the size of your bonus?
    20.1—Total company performance
    20.2—Your division's performance, etc.
    20.3—How clear are you on this? And what factors can you control/not control?

*21. On what basis do you distribute bonus funds to the members of your own management team?

22. Beyond the matters we have already discussed, what other involvement does (a) corporate and (b) group management have in divisional affairs?

23. Are there any areas where you feel it would be useful to have greater corporate concern or involvement? Less?

24. Are there any areas where you find yourself in competition with other divisions? Do you feel there are any areas where collaboration might prove beneficial?

Questionnaire Items

Task Environment of the Corporate Office

1. We are interested in learning how your working time is divided among the several activities listed below. Using the past year as a point of reference, please indicate what percentage of your working time (0% through 100%) is spent in contacts with or work generated by contacts with each of the following groups. "Contacts" is broadly defined to include meetings, face-to-face conversations, telephone conversations, written requests, formally required reports—i.e., any form of interface with these groups which place demands on your working time. Remember that the sum of the individual percentages should equal 100%.

Activities	Percentage of time
A. Contacts with or work generated by contacts with the *board of directors.*	_____
B. Contacts with or work generated by contacts with people at *corporate headquarters* (including group vice presidents).	_____
C. Contacts with or work generated by contacts with *managers in the various divisions.*	_____
D. Contacts with or work generated by contacts with *people in your company's environment* (e.g., stockholders, financial analysts, governmental agencies, consultants, merger candidates, customers, suppliers, etc.).	_____

* Division general managers only.

E. Other (Please specify additional activities if they represent a significant portion of your time. Examples might be "Time spent working on projects of my own" or "Alone time.")

_____	_____
_____	_____
_____	_____
Total	100%

2. Now we would like to focus just on that proportion of your working time during the past year which was spent in contacts with the divisions (Item C in the previous question). Of the total time you spent working on divisional matters, what percentage (0% through 100%) was devoted to *each of the divisions* listed below? Again, the sum of the individual percentages should equal 100%.

Division	*Percentage of time*
3:II	_____
3:V	_____
3:VII	_____
3:III	_____
3:I	_____
3:VI	_____
3:VIII	_____
3:IV	_____
The Rest of the Divisions	_____
Total	100%

3. Finally, we would like to get a rough idea of the types of contacts which you have with people in your company's environment (Item D in the first question). Below is a list of several "external" groups or organizations with which you might have contact. Of the total time during the past year which you spent working with "outsiders," what percentage (0% through 100%) was devoted to contacts with or work generated by contacts with each of the groups or organizations listed below?

"External" Groups	*Percentage of time*
A. Stockholders	_____
B. Members of the financial community (e.g., commercial banks, financial analysts, finders, etc.)	_____
C. Agencies of the federal government (e.g., IRS, SEC, NLRB)	_____
D. Courts and law firms	_____
E. Agencies of state and local governments	_____
F. Trade associations	_____
G. Consultants	_____
H. Firms which were potential acquisitions, potential customers for divestitures, or potential partners in joint ventures	_____
I. Customers of your divisions	_____
J. Suppliers of your divisions	_____
K. Other groups or organizations (Please specify	

these groups if they account for a significant percentage)

_____		_____
_____		_____
_____		_____
	Total	100%

4. How frequently do you feel contact *should* ideally occur between your corporate function and personnel in the divisions and operating units so that the necessary coordination exists for planning, control, and capital expenditures?

Daily	Weekly	Bi-weekly	Monthly	Bimonthly	Quarterly	Semiannually	Annually

Questions 1, 2, and 3 were asked as an integral package. Responses were used both to determine the relevant dimensions of the corporate office's task environment and to determine the amount of managerial effort which was devoted to achieving integration. Integrative effort scores will be discussed later in this appendix. Question 3 was used to determine the relevant dimensions of the corporate task environment. Managers' responses to Items 3A–K were combined into five major areas of environmental contact: financial subenvironment (3A and B); potential acquisitions, divestitures, joint ventures (3H); legal-governmental subenvironment (3C, D, and E); operating subenvironment (3F, I, and J); and "other" (3G and K). A mean was computed for each of these four external groups for each firm and an overall mean was computed for each type of firm (conglomerate vs. vertically integrated).

REFERENCE: Tables II-2, VI-5, and VII-2.

Question 4 was used as one measure of patterns of required interdependence among headquarters and divisional units. A corresponding question was asked of divisional executives. This question was employed only in later research in vertically integrated firms.

REFERENCE: Table VI-7.

Division Environments

5. Due to rates of change in an industry, or the state of development in the technology used by the industry, or vast differences in customer requirements, etc., division executives often have varying degrees of certainty concerning what their departmental job requirements are and the kinds of activities their departments *must* engage

in to achieve these requirements. The following series of questions is an effort to obtain data concerning this aspect of the industry in which you operate.

a. Please circle the number on the scale provided which most nearly describes the degree to which present job requirements in each functional department are clearly stated or known in your division for the:

Engineering (Research) Department

| Job requirements are very clear in most instances | 1 2 3 4 5 6 7 | Job requirements are *not* at all clear in most instances |

Manufacturing Department

| Job requirements are *not* at all clear in most instances | 7 6 5 4 3 2 1 | Job requirements are very clear in most instances |

Sales (Marketing) Department

| Job requirements are very clear in most instances | 1 2 3 4 5 6 7 | Job requirements are *not* at all clear in most instances |

b. Please circle the number on the scale provided which most nearly describes the degree of difficulty each functional department has in accomplishing its assigned job, given the limitations of the technical and economic resources which are available to it.

Degree of difficulty in:

Developing

A product which can be manufactured and sold profitably

1 2 3 4 5 6 7

| Little | Extremely |
| Difficulty | Difficult |

Manufacturing

Economically a product which can be designed and sold

7 6 5 4 3 2 1

| Extremely | Little |
| Difficult | Difficulty |

Selling

A product which can be developed and manufactured economically

1 2 3 4 5 6 7

| Little | Extremely |
| Difficulty | Difficult |

c. Please check the alternative which most nearly describes the typical length of time involved before feedback is available to each functional area concerning the success of its job performance. For example: the sales department manager may be able to determine at the end of each day how successful the selling effort was by examining the total sales reported by his salesman for that day. In contrast, the production manager may not know whether production meets required specifications until the results of several performance tests are available, often a period of several days from the time his department completes its processing.

Engineering (Research) Department

    _____ (1) one day
    _____ (2) one week
    _____ (3) one month
    _____ (4) six months
    _____ (5) one year
    _____ (6) three years or more

Manufacturing Department

    _____ (1) one day
    _____ (2) one week
    _____ (3) one month
    _____ (4) six months
    _____ (5) one year
    _____ (6) three years or more

Sales (Marketing) Department

    _____ (1) one day
    _____ (2) one week
    _____ (3) one month
    _____ (4) six months
    _____ (5) one year
    _____ (6) three years or more

6. Below is a list of the major functional specializations involved in your division. While an adequate performance by each of these departments is certainly necessary for the division's survival, a high level of competence in one or two of these departments may be more critical to your success than they would be in other divisions. We would like you to rank the departments listed below in terms of the importance of each in contributing to your division's ability to compete successfully in its particular industry.

    Place a *1* beside the department you feel to be most critical

    Place a *2* beside the department you feel to be next most critical

    _____ Engineering (Research)
    _____ Sales (Marketing)
    _____ Manufacturing

7. We would like to get a rough feel for how much change is going on in various segments of your division's environment. Using the past five years as a point of reference, please rate each of the following items according to the rate of change you think has been occurring in it. (Circle appropriate number for each item.)

	Highly stable (infrequent change)			*Highly volatile* (constant change)		
a. Buying patterns and requirements of customers	1	2	3	4	5	6	7
b. Distributors' attitudes	1	2	3	4	5	6	7
c. Industry pricing patterns	1	2	3	4	5	6	7
d. Competitors' strategies	1	2	3	4	5	6	7
e. Technical developments relevant to this division's business	1	2	3	4	5	6	7
f. Changes in production processes	1	2	3	4	5	6	7

Questions 5, 6, and 7 were used as common descriptive measures of environmental requirements faced by divisions in each of the firms. These measures were employed along with interview data to present basic descriptions of divisional environmental requirements. They were also used along with measures of actual managerial orientations to measure degree of organization-environment fit (to be discussed below).

REFERENCE: Tables II-6, VI-4, A-1, A-2, and A-3.

Summary Measures of Uncertainty

A measure of the overall uncertainty posed by each firm's operating environments was devised as follows. First, a summary measure of uncertainty for each functional subenvironment in each division (i.e., Scientific, Manufacturing, and Market), was arrived at by summing mean responses to items 5a, b, and c. These scores were then summed, and an overall mean for each firm was computed.

REFERENCE: Table VII-1.

Computation of Environmental Diversity Index

This index was constructed to reflect the range of differences in environmental requirements faced by the product divisions in each conglomerate firm. Employing questions 5c, 6, and 7 above, it was computed in such a way as to reflect the degree to which the three major subenvironments of each division (i.e., Scientific, Manufacturing, Market) differed from comparable subenvironments of other divisions in its company. First, mean ratings for each subenvironment of each division were computed for the following variables: rate of environmental change (7) [for this measure a combined mean for items 7a, b, c, and d was used for market change]; time span of environmental feedback (5c); and relative importance of subenvironments (6). Second, a midpoint was determined for the range of scores for each subenvironment for each of these variables. Third, the scores for each division's subenvironments were subtracted from this midpoint. Fourth, these differences were summed to arrive at total differences for each division. Table B-1 shows how steps three and four were carried out on one variable (rate of change) for two divisions at Firm 1.

Fifth, the total differences on each variable for each of the divisions at the four conglomerate firms were ranked on a scale ranging from 1 (least difference) to 5 (greatest difference). Table B-2 shows the range of scores on each variable and the ranks which were assigned to them.

Next, these ranks for each variable were summed to arrive at an overall difference score for each division. Summation of the final divisional scores in each firm gave the index of environmental diversity. Table B-3 shows the computations involved in these last two steps for Firm 1.

TABLE B-1

Rate of Environmental Change at Two Divisions in Firm 1

Subenvironment	Midpoint of Range for All Divisions at Firm 1	Division 1:I Score	Diff.	Division 1:II Score	Diff.
Scientific	4.52	5.90	1.38	5.44	.92
Manufacturing	4.02	4.90	.88	3.88	−.14
Marketing	4.74	5.13	.39	4.20	−.54
Total difference from midpoint[a]			2.65		1.60

[a] Signs of the differences are ignored in summing them.

TABLE B-2

Ranking Convention

	Ranks				
Variable	1	2	3	4	5
Rate of change	.65–1.10	1.11–1.55	1.56–2.0	2.01–2.45	2.46–2.90
Time span of feedback	.20– .50	.51– .80	.81–1.10	1.11–1.40	1.41–1.72
Importance of subenvironments	.50– .80	.81–1.10	1.11–1.40	1.41–1.70	1.71–2.0

TABLE B-3

Index of Environmental Diversity for Firm 1

	Divisions			
Variable	I	II	III	IV
Rate of change	5	3	5	2
Time span of feedback	5	3	1	3
Importance of subenvironments	5	4	3	4
Divisional totals	15	10	9	9
Total for Firm 1				43

REFERENCE: Table II-10.

Managerial Orientations

The orientations of corporate and divisional management units were measured in terms of the five attributes detailed below. Questions posed to corporate and divisional managers were the same except for minor variations in the introductory statements preceding them. The questionnaire items included below are in the form used for divisional managers.

TABLE B-4

Ranking Convention: Formality of Structure

	Lower 1	2	3	Higher 4
A. Average span of control	7.01 or more	6.01–7.0	5.01–6.0	5.0 or less
B. Average number of levels to a shared supervision	4.0 or less	4.01–5.0	5.01–6.0	6.01 or more
C. Average time span of review of subsystem performance	2.0 or less	2.01–2.5	2.51–3.0	3.01 or more
D. Specificity of review of subsystem performance (average)	1.0	1.01–2.5	2.51–3.99	4.0
E. Importance of formal rules (average)	0–30%	31–50%	51–70%	71–100%
F. Specificity of criteria for evaluation of role occupants (average)	1.0	1.01–2.5	2.5–3.99	4.0
G. Formality of overall goal structure	4 or less	5–8	9–12	13 or more

8. Formality of Structure

This attribute was measured along seven dimensions. Table B-4 specifies these dimensions along with a four-point scale which was developed for ranking each dimension. Items A–F were based on approaches previously reported by Lawrence and Lorsch, *Organization and Environment*, pp. 255–256. Items A–E were based on data gathered through examination of company records (e.g., organization charts, manning tables, and procedure manuals) and through interviews with managers. Item G was determined by counting the number of goals in question 12a(1) which were rated as "A" by 50% or more of the managers in each unit. The ranges indicated in Table B-4 for items C–F are averages for the chief executive and each of his key subordinates (e.g., in divisions the general manager, marketing manager, R&D manager, and production manager). These averages were based on scores of 1–4 which were assigned to each major subunit using the same scoring system that Lawrence and Lorsch applied to functional departments. A structural score was computed for each headquarters unit and division by summing the ranks on all seven dimensions.

Item E in Table B-4 was derived from the following question:

Most large organizations have numerous standard operating procedures ranging from written rules prescribing steps to be taken in accomplishing a task to standard methods for organizing and transmitting information. For example, a credit manager may follow a well-defined sequence of "tests" in passing on a new account. On the other hand, a man in basic research may be faced with a number of unique problems for which there are no established procedures. Please circle the number on the scale below which best indicates the *relative proportion of the work in your job* for which detailed, comprehensive rules are important.

Few established rules				*Detailed and comprehensive*	
and procedures				*rules and procedures*	
0%	20%	40%	60%	80%	100%

REFERENCE: Tables II-4, II-7, and VI-6.

9. *Time Orientation*

The following question measured time orientation:

Persons working on different activities are concerned to differing degrees with current and future problems. We are interested in learning how your time is divided between activities which will have an immediate effect on company profits and those which are of a longer-range nature. Indicate below what percent of your time is devoted to working on matters which will show up in the corporation's profit and loss statement within each of the periods indicated. Your answers should total 100%.

a. 1 month or less   _____
b. 1 month to 1 quarter   _____
c. 1 quarter to 1 year   _____
d. 1 year to 5 years   _____
                       Total   100%

Responses were weighted by factors ranging from 1 (for 1 month or less) to 4 (for 1 year to 5 years) and then divided by 100 to arrive at a single score for each respondent. Based on these scores, means were computed for each major organizational unit.

REFERENCE: Tables II-4, II-7, and VI-6.

10. *Interpersonal Orientation*

"The Least Preferred Coworker" instrument developed by Fred E. Fiedler was used to measure this dimension. For a description of this instrument see his recent book, *A Theory of Leadership Effectiveness* (New York: McGraw-Hill, 1967). Another description may be found in Lorsch, *Product Innovation and Organization*, pp. 170–173.

REFERENCE: Tables II-4, II-7, and VI-6.

11. *Goal Orientations*

In evaluating and considering the potentialities of a new idea (e.g., development of a new product or expansion of operations for existing products), there are many considerations about which persons in different parts of the organization must be concerned. We recognize, while all of these concerns are important, that certain concerns will be most important to you in your own position. In order to learn which are most important in your job, we would like you to rank the 25 criteria listed below as follows:

a. Place a "1" by the *seven criteria* which are of most concern to you in your position.
b. Place a "2" by the *next seven criteria* which are of *second* most concern to you in your position.

Criteria:

_____ (1) The manufacturing costs associated with products resulting from the proposed idea.

_____ (2) Competition's response to products resulting from the proposed idea.

_____ (3) The return on investment which might result from the new idea.

_____ (4) The technical processing problems which might result from the proposed idea.

_____ (5) The degree to which products resulting from the proposed idea will require continuing research and engineering efforts.

_____ (6) The cost of obtaining the range of technical skills required to develop products from the proposed idea.

_____ (7) The effect that committing funds to the proposed idea might ultimately have on the market price of the corporation's stock.

_____ (8) The capability of the sales organization to sell a product resulting from the proposed idea.

_____ (9) The technical capability of the research staff to conduct research on the proposed idea.

_____ (10) The amount of capital required to develop and/or commercialize the new idea.

_____ (11) The effect of products resulting from the proposed idea on the sales of existing division products.

_____ (12) The effect of products resulting from the proposed idea on the sales of products of other divisions.

_____ (13) The nature of plant facilities which would be required for implementing the proposed idea.

_____ (14) The problems of meeting delivery schedules on products resulting from the proposed idea.

_____ (15) The effect of the proposed idea on divisional sales growth.

_____ (16) The technical difficulty of developing a product resulting from the proposed idea.

_____ (17) The market channels through which the product resulting from the proposed idea would be distributed.

_____ (18) The difficulty of obtaining sufficient funds to bring the proposed idea to fruition.

_____ (19) The problems of scaling up a process for a product resulting from the proposed idea.

_____ (20) The price and volume at which a product coming from the proposed idea could be sold.

_____ (21) The difficulty of maintaining quality specifications on products stemming from the proposed idea.

_____ (22) The degree to which particular customer needs may be satisfied or altered by products resulting from the proposed idea.

_____ (23) The difficulty of economically securing materials required to manufacture products resulting from the proposed idea.

_____ (24) The amount of working capital required to support receivables and inventories associated with products resulting from the proposed idea.

_____ (25) The amount of engineering time required by particular applications which might result from the proposed idea.

The 25 items in this question were sorted into five major content categories, as indicated in Table B-5. Means were then computed for each major content category.

TABLE B-5

Goal Content Categories

Financial	Marketing	Production	Research/ Engineering	Interdivisional
3	2	1	4	12
7	8	13	5	
10	11	14	6	
15	20	19	9	
18	22	21	16	
24	20	23	25	

REFERENCE: Tables II-4, II-7, and VI-6.

12. *Overall Goal Set*

Divisions operating in different markets and under different conditions may set different goals for themselves. In order to learn more about the goals of your division, we would like you to answer two sets of questions about the following list of goals, which might be typical of any business unit.

a. In Column I please indicate the relevance of each goal to your division as follows:
  (1) Place an "A" opposite those items which currently represent important goals for your division and which have either been *stated in measurable terms* and/or *formally communicated to divisional management personnel* (i.e., through written goal statements or in verbal presentations by top management of the division).
  (2) Place a "B" opposite those items which, while they have not been formally stated as divisional goals, are generally viewed as *implicit, broad objectives* which guide divisional management actions.
  (3) Place a "C" opposite those items which are relatively unimportant as broad guidelines for divisional action.

b. Now look at the goal items that you have indicated are important guides to divisional action in Column I—those you have rated as "A" or "B." In Column II rank them according to the *relative importance assigned to each goal by the division as a whole at this time*. Place a "1" opposite the most important goal, a "2" opposite the next most important goal, a "3" opposite the third most important goal, etc., until all the "A" and "B" rated goals have been ranked.

Goal items concerning:	I Relevance to Division	II Relative Importance
(1) Return on invested funds	____	____
(2) Product diversification into related areas	____	____
(3) Profit mix desired among existing or potential product lines	____	____
(4) Rate of new product introduction	____	____
(5) Market share for various products	____	____

(6) Product improvement   _____   _____
(7) Cost reduction   _____   _____
(8) Inventory control   _____   _____
(9) Sales volume   _____   _____
(10) % growth in sales   _____   _____
(11) Absolute level of profits   _____   _____
(12) % profit growth   _____   _____
(13) Profit margin on sales   _____   _____
(14) Product diversification into nonrelated areas   _____   _____
(15) Geographic expansion of product sales   _____   _____
(16) Maintenance of particular customer relation-
     ships   _____   _____
(17) Development and motivation of personnel   _____   _____
(18) Image projected by division to customers and
     general public   _____   _____
(19) Expansion of plant   _____   _____
(20) Maintenance of unique divisional skills   _____   _____
(21) Level of fixed costs   _____   _____

Ranks reported by each respondent for each of the 21 items (Column II) were assigned scores ranging from 1 (most important) to 5 (least important). Goals that were rated as "C" in Column I were ranked as 6. Mean scores were then computed for each goal item on the basis of these ranks. The goal items were then re-ranked to arrive at a profile of the overall set for each major organizational unit.

REFERENCE: Tables II-5, II-8, and A-4.

Corporate-Divisional and Interdivisional Differentiation

To determine the degree of differentiation between the corporate head-quarters and individual divisions, between pairs of divisions, and the degree of total corporate-divisional differentiation which characterized each firm it was necessary to develop a comparable differentiation score for all five attributes, i.e., structure; interpersonal, time, and goal orientations; and overall goal sets. This was done as follows. First, differences between the headquarters unit and each division in each company were computed for each of the five attributes. Differences between pairs of divisions were computed only for the vertically integrated firms. For structure and interpersonal orientations this entailed subtracting single overall scores. Time orientations were broken down into short-range (9a and b), medium-range (9c), and long-range (9d) concerns; and then differences were computed. These differences were then summed. Similarly, differences in goal orientations were determined by major content category, and these differences were then summed. For overall goal sets differences between ranks were computed for each of the 21 items, the differences were squared to deal with differences in signs, and then the squared differences were summed.

Having determined the differences between headquarters and divisions in each firm on each of the five attributes, the differences found in all six firms were

divided into five classes. Each class was then assigned a differentiation score ranging from 1 (least differentiated) to 5 (most differentiated). Table B-6 shows how

TABLE B-6

Scoring Key for Differentiation

	1	2	3	4	5
Structure	0, 1, 2	3, 4	5, 6	7, 8	9 or more
Time	20–35	36–40	41–55	56–70	71–85
Interpersonal	0, 1, 2	2.01–4	4.01–6	6.01–8	8.01–11
Goal orientations	.70–1.10	1.11–1.50	1.51–1.90	1.91–2.30	2.31–2.70
Overall goal set	100–280	281–460	461–640	641–820	821–1,000

the scores were assigned. These five point units of differentiation scores for each
attribute made it possible to arrive at a rough measure of the relative total differentiation between divisional and corporate management systems in each firm.
The individual corporate-divisional differentiation scores were summed to arrive
at a total differentiation score for each firm.

Three sorts of differentiation scores are reported in the text:

(1) *Differentiation between two organizational units*—either between a headquarters
unit and a single division or between two divisions.

REFERENCE: Tables III-3, VI-12, and VI-13.

(2) *Average corporate-divisional differentiation for each firm*—single corporate-divisional differentiation scores were summed for all relationships which were studied
in each firm and then divided by the number of these relationships which were
studied (4 in the conglomerates and 3 in the vertically integrated firms).

REFERENCE: Tables II-10, III-7, VI-11, and VII-6.

(3) *Estimate of overall corporate-divisional differentiation*—average corporate-divisional differentiation scores multiplied by the total number of divisions encompassed by each firm. This score represents an approximation since we did not
actually study all the divisions in each firm.

REFERENCE: Tables III-7, and VII-6.

Measure of Organization—Environment Fit at the Division Level

Along lines suggested by the previous work of Lawrence and Lorsch (*Organization and Environment,* pp. 252, 253) comparisons were made between
required and actual departmental attributes for the primary functions (R&D/
Engineering, Manufacturing, and Sales) in eight divisions of two conglomerates
(Firms 1 and 4). Required departmental attributes were based on ratings of
environmental requirements by division top management as follows:

(1) *Required structure.* Norms were based on division top management's ratings of the rate of change experienced by each subenvironment of its division (Item 7 above) relative to the other subenvironments of that division. For this required attribute intradivisional comparisons were used rather than interdivisional comparisons because it was found that size of a division (as measured in sales $) also had a considerable impact on formality of structure $(r_s = .744, p < .05)$. Thus, the norms were as follows:

Required formality of structure	Relative rate of change (intradivisional)
Lowest	Highest
Middle	Middle
Highest	Lowest

(2) *Required interpersonal orientations.* Norms were based on interdivisional comparisons of perceived rate of subenvironment change (Item 7 above) as follows:

Required inter-personal orientations	Rate of change
Task	5.9–5.0 (High)
Social	4.9–4.0 (Medium)
Task	3.9–3.0 (Low)

(3) *Required time orientations.* Norms were based on interdivisional comparison of responses to questionnaire item on time span of environmental feedback (5c above) as follows:

Required time orientation	Time span of environmental feedback
Short	2.0 –3.0 (Short)
Medium	3.01–4.0 (Medium)
Long	4.01–5.0 (Long)

(4) *Required goal orientations.* Norms were based on relative importance of subenvironment scores (Item 6 above) for each division. Each functional department, except Engineering, was expected to be primarily concerned with its own subenvironment. Engineering norms depended on (1) the strength of the divisions' primary subenvironment and (2) whether engineering activities involved considerable new product development or more mundane functions.

Actual departmental attributes were based on questionnaire responses by managers several levels down in each division. These actual attributes were treated as follows:

(1) *Actual formality of structure.* Scores for Item 8 above were determined for each functional department. The department with the highest, middle, and lowest structural score in each division was determined. This score was compared to the required structure score above.

(2) *Actual interpersonal orientation.* Scores (on Item 10 above) for each department were rated as either more task-oriented (76–100) or more socially oriented (101–125). Comparison was then made with required interpersonal orientation.

(3) *Actual time orientation* was defined as the modal departmental response to Item 9 above (short, medium, or long). Comparison was then made with required time orientation.

(4) *Actual goal orientations.* The relative importance placed on Engineering/R&D, Sales, and Manufacturing goals (from Item 11 above) by each department was compared to required goal orientations.

The total number of positive comparisons between required and actual orientations was then determined for each division. Total possible positive comparisons was 12 (4 attributes × 3 functional departments).

REFERENCE: Table II-9.

13. *Corporate-Divisional and Interdivisional Integration*

The question below was used to secure divisional managers' assessment of the degree of integration which actually had been achieved between their unit and the corporate headquarters. A similar question was asked for interdivisional integration in the vertically integrated firms. Corporate managers were asked to rate integration on the same scale for all major divisions in their firm. Corporate-divisional and interdivisional integration scores for the divisions in our sample were computed on the basis of responses of both parties to a relationship.

Overall corporate-divisional integration scores for all major divisions in each firm were based on corporate headquarters responses only. These responses were weighted to reflect the relative size of the divisions. For instance, we collected integration scores for the eight major divisions at Firm 3. The largest (in terms of 1967 sales) division's integration score was multiplied by 8, while the smallest division's score was multiplied by 1. The sum of the weighted scores was then divided by the sum of the weights. This procedure was employed because it was felt that low integration was more serious in a relatively large division than in a relatively small division.

We would like to know about the relationships between the corporate headquarters and your division. The next four questions are aimed at obtaining your evaluation of these relationships. Whether you do or do not have direct involvement with corporate officers and staff personnel, you probably have impressions about the state of these relationships. Therefore, we would like you to fill out each question.

1. Listed below are seven descriptive statements. Each of these might be thought of as describing the general state of the relationships between corporate headquarters and your division. Please check the *one statement* which you feel best describes these relationships.

_____ (1) Excellent—full cooperation and mutual understanding is achieved. Each group fulfills the expectations that the other has for it.
_____ (2) Almost full cooperation and mutual understanding is achieved.
_____ (3) Somewhat better than average relations.
_____ (4) Average—sound enough to get by, even though there are some problems of achieving cooperation and understanding.
_____ (5) Somewhat less than average relations.
_____ (6) Only a limited amount of cooperation and mutual understanding exists.
_____ (7) Couldn't be worse—poor relations—serious problems exist which are not being solved.

REFERENCE: Tables III-3, III-7, VI-11, VI-12, VI-13, and VII-6.

14. *Effort Devoted to Achieving Integration*

The amount of managerial effort devoted to achieving integration was determined by asking both corporate and divisional executives to indicate the percentage of their working time during the most recent year which had been devoted to corporate-divisional relations. Item A of the question below was used to determine integrative effort for division managers. Corporate scores were derived from questions 1C and 2 of this appendix. The corporate scores were computed by multiplying individuals' ratings for each division in question 2 by their responses to question 1C. The resulting scores were summed to arrive at integrative effort scores for the headquarters. For sample divisions' overall integrative effort scores were computed by summing corporate and divisional scores. An approximation of total integrative effort in each of the four conglomerate firms was obtained by computing the average corporate ratings for all divisions. Comparison between conglomerate and vertically integrated firms was made by computing the average integrative effort devoted to the sampled corporate-divisional relationships in each setting.

We are interested in learning how your working time is divided among the several activities listed below. Using the past year as a point of reference, please indicate what percentage of your working time (0% through 100%) is spent in contacts with or work generated by contacts with each of the following groups. "Contacts" is broadly defined to include meetings, face-to-face conversations, telephone conversations, written requests, formally required reports; i.e., any form of interface with these groups which places demands on your working time. Remember that the sum of the individual percentages should equal 100%.

Activities	*Percentage of Time*
A. Contacts with or work generated by contacts with *corporate headquarters*	_____
B. Contacts with or work generated by contacts with *other divisions*	_____
C. Contacts with or work generated by contacts with members of *your own division*	_____
D. Contacts with or work generated by contacts with *people in your division's environment* (e.g., customers, suppliers, government agencies, consultants, etc.)	_____
E. Other (Please specify additional activities if they represent a significant portion of your time. Examples might be "Time spent working on projects of my own" or "Alone time.")	_____
_____	_____
_____	_____
_____	
Total	100%

REFERENCE: Tables III-3, III-6, III-7, VI-10, VI-12, VII-6.

15. *Division Performance*

Performance scores for each sample division were based on combined ratings by both corporate and divisional executives. The question below was used for division managers. Corporate managers were asked to rate each of the four sample divisions in their firm along the same dimensions. Slightly different performance indices were used for mill divisions in the vertically integrated firms. Percentage figures were transformed into scores of 1 (lowest) to 5 (highest performance). Next, the mean of corporate and divisional ratings was computed for items a, b, and c separately. Overall divisional performance scores were arrived at by summing the means for items a, b, and c only.

If you consider ideal performance for your division as 100%, what percentage value would you assign to your actual performance over the last five years on each of the following dimensions? (Circle the appropriate number for each category.)

a. Return on investment	20%	40%	60%	80%	100%
b. Sales	20%	40%	60%	80%	100%
c. Profit	20%	40%	60%	80%	100%
d. Market share	20%	40%	60%	80%	100%
e. Management development	20%	40%	60%	80%	100%

Firm 2 had provided actual performance data for each of its divisions over the past five years. Rankings based on combined scores for actual growth in sales and profit plus average return on investment correlated perfectly with the rankings based on the questionnaire performance estimates.

REFERENCE: Tables III-3 and VI-3.

Patterns of Decision Making

16. *Quality of Upward and Downward Information Flows*

Division managers were asked the following question to secure their rating of the information they received from headquarters. Corporate managers were asked to rate information they received from each of the major divisions in their firm.

If 100% represents the *ideal quantity and quality* of information that your division's management would like to receive from corporate headquarters, how would you rate headquarters in terms of what you now receive from them? (Circle appropriate percentage.)

20%   40%   60%   80%   100%

REFERENCE: Tables VI-1, A-5, and A-12.

17. *Rapidity of Headquarters in Responding to Divisional Requests*

This measure was based on division managers' responses to the following question:

In general, *how prompt* is the corporate headquarters in reacting to requests from your division, e.g., for capital projects, information, or services? (Circle one item.)

Always very prompt   *Seldom prompt*

         1   2   3   4   5

REFERENCE: Tables IV-2, A-6, and A-13.

18. *Perceived Characteristics of Performance Evaluation Systems*

The question below was used to survey division managers' perceptions of how their units were evaluated by the headquarters. The headquarters was also asked to rate the relative importance it placed on the same criteria in evaluating all divisions.

Please rate each of the twelve criteria listed below in terms of the *degree to which corporate headquarters uses it in evaluating your division's performance*. Place a "1" opposite the *four most important criteria*. Place a "2" opposite the *four criteria which are next most important*.

_____ (a) Capacity to control costs during the current year.
_____ (b) Market share achieved during the current year.
_____ (c) Development of management talent.
_____ (d) Profit improvement over a 3–5 year period.
_____ (e) Ability to control working capital during the current year.
_____ (f) Return on investment over a 3–5 year period.
_____ (g) Sales improvement over a 3–5 year period.
_____ (h) Longer-run trend in market share.
_____ (i) Sales improvement over the previous year.
_____ (j) Profit improvement over the previous year.
_____ (k) Return on investment for the current year.
_____ (l) Rate of development of new products over a 3–5 year period.

The data collected were used in three ways:

(1) Agreement scores were computed between corporate and divisional perceptions on each criterion (using a Kendall coefficient of concordance).

REFERENCE: Tables IV-3, VII-10, and A-7.

(2) The criteria were sorted into longer term (c, d, f, g, h, and l) and shorter term (a, b, e, i, j, and k) concerns. A raw difference score was computed from corporate responses only to measure the degree to which a balance existed between longer-run and shorter-run considerations.

REFERENCE: Tables IV-3, VII-10, and A-7.

(3) The criteria were sorted into financial/end result (d, e, f, g, i, j, k) and operating/ intermediate (a, b, c, h, l) measures. Mean scores were computed from corporate responses so that comparisons could be made between conglomerates and vertically integrated firms.

REFERENCE: Table VII-9.

19. *Perceived Basis of Reward for Integrators*

In the vertically integrated firms we used the following question about basis of rewards. Responses by persons in integrative positions were compared on Item (a).

Please rate each of the following items in terms of the *degree to which it influences the overall level of organization rewards* which you typically receive in your job. Circle the appropriate number. NOTE: In certain instances, Items (b) and (d) will not apply. If this is the case, merely leave them blank.

	Little or no influence				*A great deal of influence*
(a) Overall corporate performance	1	2	3	4	5
(b) Overall performance of the group of which your division is a part	1	2	3	4	5
(c) Overall operating unit performance	1	2	3	4	5
(d) Performance of your own particular subunit	1	2	3	4	5

REFERENCE: Table A-16.

20. *Intermediate Position of Division General Managers, Group Executives, and Other Integrating Roles*

The methods used for measuring overall goal sets and goal, time, and interpersonal orientations (Items 9, 10, 11, and 12 above) were also used for this analysis. Structure scores were not used because most executives reporting to key integrative positions did not, themselves, have direct responsibility for achieving integration. The integrative roles involved were division general managers, group executives, and integrative departments and lateral linking roles (the latter refer mainly to scheduling and internal product management positions in the vertically integrated firms).

Intermediate position of each integrative role and/or department was determined as follows. First, the midpoint between headquarters and each division of the range of scores for each attribute was computed. Second, the difference between the scores for integrative roles and this midpoint was then computed to determine how closely each of these integrating roles approached an intermediate position. For interpersonal orientations, where there was only a single mean score for each unit, this procedure was straightforward. In the case of overall goal sets and goal and time orientations, however, differences were computed according to major components. Thus, for overall goal sets difference from midpoint was determined for each of the 21 items; and these differences were summed without regard to sign to determine the overall degree of difference. Differences for time orientations were computed on the basis of short-term, medium-term, and long-term concerns and then summed. Similarly, differences for goal orientations were computed by major content category and then summed.

The third step was to determine dichotomously whether a given integrative role was or was not intermediate in its position. This determination was made on the basis of both the range and the distribution of the differences from midpoint (step 2 above) found in our sample. Table B-7 shows the norms developed for all integrative positions.

TABLE B-7

Norms for Dichotomizing Intermediate Position

Variable	Range of Differences from Midpoint	Cutoff Score for Intermediate Positions
Interpersonal orientations	1.87–31.0	13.0
Time orientations	9–97	34
Goal orientations	0.8–3.1	1.75
Overall goal set	16.1–30.1	23.6

Because each of the six firms differed somewhat in terms of number of integrative positions, a final step was required. Based on step 3 above, we counted the number of positions which were intermediate on two or more of three variables: (1) interpersonal, (2) time, and (3) a combined assessment of goal orientations and overall goal set. This combined assessment of goal related variables was necessitated because a few integrators had incorrectly completed one or the other of the relevant questionnaire items. While these errors in responding only involved three or four responses in our total sample, they did create potential problems for assessing intermediate position.

REFERENCE: Tables IV-4, A-8, and A-15.

21. *Measures of Influence*

Influence by organizational level was measured via the question below. Division managers were asked to rate influence over policy decisions in their own unit, while corporate executives rated influence over policy decisions in each of the sample divisions. Influence scores for the top three levels (corporate, group, and general managers) were means of both headquarters and divisional responses. Scores for lower levels were computed from divisional ratings only. Managers were also asked to rate the relative influence exerted by the various levels over daily operating decisions; however, these ratings were not reported.

Influence of the corporate office versus divisional management units was determined by combining ratings for the corporate and group levels versus division general manager and persons one level below him. These measures of influence balance were based on divisional responses only.

We are interested in how much influence you feel is exerted by each of the following levels on the *broad policy decisions* made in your division. (Circle the appropriate number.)

		Little or no influence				A great deal of influence
(a)	Corporate executives and their staff	1	2	3	4	5
(b)	Your group vice presi- dent (if applicable)	1	2	3	4	5
(c)	The division general manager	1	2	3	4	5
(d)	Persons 1 level below the general manager	1	2	3	4	5
(e)	Persons 2 levels below the general manager	1	2	3	4	5
(f)	Persons 3 levels below the general manager	1	2	3	4	5

REFERENCE: Figure IV-1, Tables IV-6, VII-8, A-9, and A-10.

22. Modes of Conflict Resolution

The question below was used to determine the modes of conflict resolution which characterized each corporate-divisional and interdivisional relationship. The question was repeated and phrased in two ways: first asking about the *ideal* way conflict should be handled, and then the *actual* way it was handled. Only divisional responses for actual modes of conflict resolution have been reported for corporate-divisional relations. Interdivisional modes of conflict resolution are based on responses of division managers to a similar question.

There is an old proverb that says, "It may be true what some men say; it must be true what all men say." The problem in applying this to the way people work together in organizations is that all men do not say the same thing. Persons in any organization have different ways of dealing with their work associates in other units. The proverbs listed below can be thought of as descriptions of some of the different possibilities for resolving disagreements, as they have been stated in literature and in traditional wisdom.

1. You are asked to indicate *how desirable in your opinion* each of the proverbs listed below are as a way of resolving disagreements which arise between corporate head-quarters and your division. Please use the following scores in evaluating the *desirability* of each proverb:

   1—Very desirable
   2—Desirable
   3—Neither desirable nor undesirable
   4—Undesirable
   5—Completely undesirable

Indicate your evaluation in the spaces below:

_____ 1. You scratch my back, I'll scratch yours.
_____ 2. When two quarrel, he who keeps silence first is the most praiseworthy.
_____ 3. Soft words win hard hearts.
_____ 4. A man who will not flee will make his foe flee.
_____ 5. Come now and let us reason together.
_____ 6. It is easier to refrain than to retreat from a quarrel.
_____ 7. Better half a loaf than no bread.

_____ 8. A question must be decided by knowledge and not by numbers if it is to have a right decision.

_____ 9. When one hits you with a stone, hit him with a piece of cotton.

_____ 10. The arguments of the strongest have always the most weight.

_____ 11. By digging and digging, the truth is discovered.

_____ 12. Smooth words make smooth ways.

_____ 13. If you cannot make a man think as you do, make him do as you think.

_____ 14. He who fights and runs away lives to run another day.

_____ 15. A fair exchange brings no quarrel.

_____ 16. Might overcomes right.

_____ 17. Tit for tat is fair play.

_____ 18. Kind words are worth much and cost little.

_____ 19. Seek till you find, and you'll not lose your labor.

_____ 20. He loses least in a quarrel who keeps his tongue in cheek.

_____ 21. Kill your enemies with kindness.

_____ 22. Try and trust will move mountains.

_____ 23. Put your foot down where you mean to stand.

_____ 24. One gift for another makes good friends.

_____ 25. Don't stir up a hornet's nest.

2. In answering this question, you are asked to shift from *what is desirable* to *what actually happens* in resolving differences between corporate headquarters and your division. As you read the proverbs below, please indicate, using the following scale, to what extent these proverbs describe behavior which actually occurs.

1. Describes very typical behavior which usually occurs.
2. Describes typical behavior which occurs frequently.
3. Describes behavior which occurs sometimes.
4. Describes untypical behavior which seldom occurs.
5. Describes behavior which never occurs.

[The list of 25 aphorisms was repeated]

Based on a previous factor analysis by Lawrence and Lorsch, 12 questionnaire items were sorted into three categories as indicated in Table B-8. Mean ratings for each item were summed to arrive at a score for each of the three modes (confrontation, forcing, and smoothing).

TABLE B-8

Modes of Conflict Resolution

Confrontation	Forcing	Smoothing
5	10	3
8	13	9
11	14	12
19	16	21

REFERENCE: Tables IV-7, A-11, and A-14.

Footnotes

CHAPTER I

[1] Sloan, *My Years with General Motors,* p. 53.

[2] Chandler, *Strategy and Structure,* pp. 50–62 and 449–469.

[3] For data on merger trends in mining and manufacturing, see Federal Trade Commission, *Current Trends in Merger Activity 1970,* and testimony of Dr. Willard Mueller in U.S. Senate, *Hearings, Economic Concentration,* Part 2, pp. 501–520.

[4] Wrigley, "Divisional Autonomy and Diversification."

[5] These include Ansoff and Weston, "Merger Objectives and Organizational Structure"; Berg, "What's Different About Conglomerate Management?"; Bower, *Managing the Resource Allocation Process;* Chandler, op. cit.; and Williamson, *Corporate Control and Business Behavior.*

[6] Funk and Wagnall, *Standard Universal Dictionary.*

[7] Chandler, op. cit.

[8] See, for example, "Some Glitter Is Gone at Gulf and Western," *Business Week,* July 5, 1969; "Litton Down to Earth," *Fortune,* April 1968; and "Rockwell Trims North American," *Business Week,* January 31, 1970.

[9] These studies are Bjorksten, "Merger Lemons"; Booz, Allen, and Hamilton, "Management of New Products"; and Kitching, "Why Mergers Miscarry."

[10] Simon et al., *Centralization and Decentralization in Organizing the Controller's Department,* p. 1.

[11] See, for example, Fayol, *Industrial and General Administration,* and Gulick and Urwick (eds.), *Papers on the Science of Administration.*

[12] See, for example, Blau and Scott, *Formal Organizations,* and Gouldner, *Patterns of Industrial Bureaucracy.*

[13] See, for example, Ashby, *Design for a Brain;* Buckley, *Sociology and Modern Systems Theory;* and von Bertalanffy, *General Systems Theory.*

[14] Forrester, *Urban Dynamics,* p. 109.

[15] Thompson, *Organizations in Action,* pp. 54–55.

[16] Ibid.

[17] For a discussion of some of the organizational issues facing this company, see Burck, "Union Carbide's Patient Schemers."

[18] See, for example, Burns and Stalker, *The Management of Innovation;* Schroder et al., *Human Information Processing;* and Woodward, *Industrial Organization: Theory and Practice.*

[19] Burns and Stalker, op. cit.

[20] Considerable attention is devoted to this issue in March and Simon, *Organiza-*

tions. These authors note: "When tasks have been allocated to an organizational unit in terms of a subgoal, other subgoals and other aspects of the goals of the larger organization tend to be ignored in the decisions of the subunit. In part, this bias in decision making can be attributed to shifts in the focus of attention. The definition of the situation that the subunit employs is simplified by omitting some criteria and paying particular attention to some others" (p. 152).

Other researchers who have measured cognitive differences which are related either to differing professional or differing organizational identifications include Dearborn and Simon, "Selective Perception: A Note on the Departmental Identifications of Executives"; Triandis, "Differential Perception of Certain Jobs and People by Managers, Clerks, and Workers in Industry"; and Zajonc and Wolfe, "Cognitive Consequences of a Person's Position in a Formal Organization."

Other research on the broader aspects of the behavioral consequences of division of labor includes Rice, *Enterprise and Environment*, and Miller, "Technology, Territory and Time."

[21] See March and Simon, op. cit., pp. 127–129, 159–161. Also Thompson, op. cit., pp. 54–56.

[22] For recent work on organizational conflict see Blake, Shepard, and Mouton, *Managing Intergroup Conflict in Industry*, and Pondy, "Organizational Conflict: Concepts and Models."

[23] Lawrence and Lorsch, *Organization and Environment.*

[24] Lorsch and Lawrence, "Environmental Factors and Organizational Integration."

[25] Thompson, op. cit.

[26] March and Simon, op. cit.

[27] One recent study which presents evidence of different attitudes toward risk at different organizational levels is Swalm, "Utility Theory—Insights Into Risk Taking."

[28] For a discussion of this type of conglomerate, see Lynch, *Financial Performance of Conglomerates.*

CHAPTER II

[1] These measures were originally developed in Ackerman, "Organization and the Investment Process: A Comparative Study," Chapter VII, pp. 36–38.

[2] Lawrence and Lorsch, *Organization and Environment.*

[3] The notion that one of the major roles of accounting is to provide a language for intra-, inter-, and supra-organizational communication is discussed in Chambers, *Accounting, Evaluation, and Economic Behavior*, pp. 295–320.

[4] Lawrence and Lorsch, op. cit., pp. 42–44, 102–106.

[5] Ibid.

CHAPTER III

[1] Lawrence and Lorsch, *Organization and Environment*, pp. 137–140.

[2] This finding is consistent with the theoretical linkage between complexity of interdependence and choice of coordinative devices advanced by Thompson, *Organizations in Action*, pp. 54–55.

[3] Lawrence and Lorsch, op. cit., pp. 47–49.

[4] The notion of deviation-amplifying mutual causal processes has become a matter of considerable interest in the literature of cybernetics and general systems theory. See, for example, Maruyama, "The Second Cybernetics: Deviation-Amplifying Mutual Causal Processes."

CHAPTER IV

[1] For a discussion of this general tendency of managers to seek and maintain autonomy, or discretion, see Williamson, *The Economics of Discretionary Behavior: Managerial Objectives in a Theory of the Firm.*

[2] Lawrence and Lorsch, *Organization and Environment*, pp. 54–83 and 109–132.

³ Ibid.

⁴ See, for example, Walton and Dutton, "The Management of Interdepartmental Conflict: A Model and Review."

⁵ Lawrence and Lorsch, op. cit.

⁶ The importance of looking at the overall pattern of these factors also has been emphasized by Lawrence and Lorsch, pp. 78–83, but the present data offer empirical support for what was originally a clinical conclusion.

CHAPTER V

¹ For a discussion of the psychological theory which underlies this statement, see Levinson, *The Exceptional Executive*, especially Chapter II.

² Ansoff, *Corporate Strategy*, Chapter V.

³ Kitching, "Why Mergers Miscarry."

⁴ Thompson, *Organizations in Action*.

CHAPTER VI

¹ Thompson, *Organizations in Action*, pp. 54–55.

² Lawrence and Lorsch, *Organization and Environment*, pp. 96–99, 137–140.

³ Ibid.

CHAPTER VII

¹ Lawrence and Lorsch, *Organization and Environment*, pp. 90–94.

² The distinction between "federalized" and "composite" organizational structures has been employed in March and Simon, *Organizations*, p. 195.

³ Ibid.

⁴ This finding that *total* rather than *mean* differentiation was the important issue suggests that our use of this concept may fit more closely with the traditional sociological definition of structural differentiation (i.e., number of structural components) than we had anticipated. For a discussion of this topic see Blau, "A Formal Theory of Differentiation in Organizations."

⁵ Driver and Streufert, "Integrative Complexity: An Approach to Individuals and Groups as Information-Processing Systems," and Schroder et al., *Human Information Processing*.

⁶ This finding is also consistent with the Lawrence and Lorsch notion that influence tended to be competence, or information, based in their effective research sites. Op. cit., pp. 71–73, 141–146.

⁷ There is considerable research which points to the general importance of these factors. See, for example, Blake, Shepard, and Mouton, *Managing Intergroup Conflict in Industry*; Pondy, "Organizational Conflict: Concepts and Models"; and Walton and Dutton, "The Management of Interdepartmental Conflict."

⁸ Lawrence and Lorsch, op. cit., pp. 146–151. These authors had not attempted to measure quality of information flows or influence balance.

⁹ See, for example, Brown, "How to Manage a Conglomerate," and "Textron: A Time for Testing," *Dun's Review*, May 1968.

¹⁰ See, for example, "What Makes FMC Run?" *Forbes*, June 15, 1962.

¹¹ See, for example, "Making Big Waves With Small Fish," *Business Week*, December 30, 1967, and "Rocket-Like Pace at Teledyne," *Forbes*, January 15, 1968.

¹² See, for example, "ITT: Can Profits Be Programmed?" *Dun's Review*, November 1965; "Management Must Manage," address by Harold S. Geneen before the Investment Group of Hartford and the Connecticut Investment Bankers Association, February 15, 1968; "They Call it 'Geneen U'," *Forbes*, May 1, 1968; and "The Financial Key at ITT," *Dun's Review*, December 1970.

¹³ Even among paper companies there is a wide range of organizational practices. The interested reader can find a description of the practices of four other paper companies in Ackerman, "Influence of Integration and Diversity on the Investment Process."

[14] See, for example, Bower's description of planning and resource allocation in a large, diversified chemical firm in *Managing the Resource Allocation Process.*

CHAPTER VIII

[1] For a more complete description of these contributions, see Lawrence and Lorsch, *Organization and Environment,* pp. 185–210.

[2] Leavitt, "Unhuman Organizations."

[3] Schroder et al., *Human Information Processing.*

[4] Woodward, *Industrial Organization: Theory and Practice.*

[5] Burns and Stalker, *The Management of Innovation.*

[6] Udy, *Organization of Work: A Comparative Analysis of Production Among Non-Industrial Peoples.*

[7] Perrow, "A Framework for the Comparative Analysis of Organizations."

[8] Thompson, *Organizations in Action.*

[9] Lawrence and Lorsch, op. cit.

[10] Lawrence E. Fouraker (unpublished manuscript).

[11] Chandler, *Strategy and Structure.*

[12] March and Simon, *Organizations.*

[13] Lawrence and Lorsch, op. cit.

[14] Thompson, op. cit.

[15] Lawrence and Lorsch, op. cit.

[16] Ibid.

[17] This focus roughly corresponds to Rice's distinction between the "management system" and the "operating system" in organizations. He defines management system as that which is "external to the operating systems, required to service and control them. It contains management of the total enterprise, of each discrete operating system, and any control and service functions that are differentiated from overall management." The operating systems "perform the primary task of the enterprise (i.e., the dominant import-conversion-export process)." Rice, *The Enterprise and Its Environment,* pp. 18–23.

[18] For a discussion of this issue, see Levine and White, "Exchange as a Conceptual Framework for the Study of Interorganizational Relationships."

[19] See Walker and Lorsch, "Organizational Choice: Product versus Function."

[20] March and Simon, op. cit., pp. 136–171.

[21] For a discussion of this topic see Gulick and Urwick (eds.), *Papers on the Science of Administration.*

[22] Lawrence and Lorsch, op. cit.

[23] Galbraith, "Organization Design: An Information Processing View."

[24] Thompson, op. cit.

[25] Lawrence and Lorsch, op. cit., pp. 30–39.

[26] Ibid., pp. 39–44 and 91–106.

[27] Ibid., p. 103.

[28] Ibid.

[29] Ibid.

[30] Schroder et al., op. cit.

[31] Ibid.

[32] Lawrence and Lorsch, op. cit., pp. 146–151.

[33] Ibid., pp. 141–146.

[34] Ibid.

[35] Ibid.

[36] For further discussion of this view of influence see Lawrence and Lorsch, op. cit., pp. 69–71, and Dalton et al., *The Distribution of Authority in Formal Organizations.*

[37] Morse and Lorsch, "Beyond Theory Y."

[38] Work is currently under way in this area by S. A. Allen and Clyde Rettig, "The

Dynamics of Corporate Control: An Industrial Dynamics Model and Field Evaluation" (project title, 1971).

[39] For examples of this technique see Bower, *Managing the Resource Allocation Process*, and Woodward (ed.), *Industrial Organization: Behavior and Control.*

[40] See, for example, Schroder et al., op. cit.; Birnberg et al., "Effect of Three Voting Rules on Resource Allocation Decisions"; and Baumler, "Defined Criteria of Performance in Organizational Control."

[41] For two different approaches to simulation see Cyert and March, *A Behavioral Theory of the Firm,* and Roberts, *The Dynamics of Research and Development.*

CHAPTER IX

[1] Drucker, *The Concept of the Corporation.*

[2] Ibid.

[3] Henderson and Dearden, "New System for Divisional Control," pp. 144–145.

[4] V. A. Graicunas, "Relationships in Organizations," in Gulick and Urwick (eds.), *Papers on the Science of Administration.*

[5] An interesting example of explicitly defining the general manager's job in this way can be found in "Union Carbide's Patient Schemers," *Fortune,* December 1965.

[6] Drucker, op. cit.

[7] Dearden, "Appraising Profit Center Managers."

[8] Henderson and Dearden, op. cit.

[9] Ibid., p. 145.

[10] See, for example, the articles, "What Made Apollo a Success?" *Astronautics and Aeronautics,* March 1970, and Tom Alexander, "The Unexpected Payoff of Apollo," *Fortune,* July 1969.

Bibliography

Ackerman, Robert W., "Influence of Integration and Diversity on the Investment Process," *Administrative Science Quarterly*, September 1970.

Ackerman, Robert W., "Organization and the Investment Process: A Comparative Study" (unpublished doctoral dissertation, Harvard Business School, 1968).

Alexander, Tom, "The Unexpected Payoff of Apollo," *Fortune*, July 1969.

Ansoff, H. Igor, *Corporate Strategy* (New York: McGraw-Hill, 1965).

Ansoff, H. Igor, and J. Fred Weston, "Merger Objectives and Organizational Structure," *Quarterly Review of Economics and Business*. August 1962.

Ashby, W. R., *Design for a Brain* (New York: Wiley, 1960).

Baumler, John V., "Defined Criteria of Performance in Organizational Control," *Administrative Science Quarterly*, September 1971.

Berg, Norman A., "What's Different About Conglomerate Management?," *Harvard Business Review*. November-December 1969.

von Bertalanffy, L., *General Systems Theory* (New York: George Braziller, 1968).

Birnberg, Jacob G., et al., "Effect of Three Voting Rules on Resource Allocation Decisions," *Management Science*, February 1970.

Bjorksten, J., "Merger Lemons," *Mergers and Acquisitions: The Journal of Corporate Venture*, Fall 1965.

Blake, Robert R., Herbert A. Shepard, and Jane S. Mouton, *Managing Intergroup Conflict in Industry* (Houston: Gulf Publishing Company, 1964).

Blau, Peter M., "A Formal Theory of Differentiation in Organizations," *American Sociological Review*, April 1970.

Blau, Peter M., and W. Scott, *Formal Organizations* (San Francisco: Chandler, 1962).

Booz, Allen, and Hamilton, "Management of New Products," 1960.

Bower, Joseph L., *Managing the Resource Allocation Process* (Boston: Division of Research, Harvard Business School, 1970).

Brown, Stanley H., "How to Manage a Conglomerate," *Fortune*, April 1964.

Buckley, Walter, *Sociology and Modern Systems Theory* (Englewood Cliffs, New Jersey: Prentice-Hall, 1967).

Burck, Gilbert, "Union Carbide's Patient Schemers," *Fortune*, December 1965.

Burns, Tom, and D. M. Stalker, *The Management of Innovation* (London: Tavistock Publications, 1959).

Chambers, Raymond J., *Accounting, Evaluation, and Economic Behavior* (Englewood Cliffs, New Jersey: Prentice-Hall, 1966).

Chandler, Alfred D., Jr., *Strategy and Structure* (Cambridge: The MIT Press, 1962).

Cyert, Richard M., and James G. March, *A Behavioral Theory of the Firm* (Englewood Cliffs, New Jersey: Prentice-Hall, 1963).

Dalton, Gene W., et al., *The Distribution of Authority in Formal Organizations* (Boston: Division of Research, Harvard Business School, 1968).

Dearborn, D. C., and Herbert A. Simon, "Selective Perception: A Note on the Departmental Identifications of Executives," *Sociometry*, 64, 1958.

Dearden, John, "Appraising Profit Center Managers," *Harvard Business Review*, May-June 1968.

Driver, Michael J., and Siegfried Streufert, "Integrative Complexity: An Approach to Individuals and Groups as Information-Processing Systems," *Administrative Science Quarterly*, June 1969.

Drucker, Peter F., *The Concept of the Corporation* (New York: John Day Corporation, 1946).

Fayol, H., *Industrial and General Administration* (Paris: Dunod, 1925).

Federal Trade Commission, *Current Trends in Merger Activity 1970*, Bureau of Economics Publication #6-15-10, March 1971.

Forrester, Jay W., *Urban Dynamics* (Cambridge: The MIT Press, 1969).

Galbraith, Jay R., "Organization Design: An Information Processing View" (Working Paper, MIT, October 1969).

Gouldner, Alvin, *Patterns of Industrial Bureaucracy* (Glencoe, Illinois: Free Press, 1954).

Gulick, Luther, and Lyndall F. Urwick (eds.), *Papers on the Science of Administration*, New York: Institute of Public Administration, Columbia University, 1937.

Henderson, Bruce, and John Dearden, "New System for Divisional Control," *Harvard Business Review*, September-October 1966.

Kitching, John, "Why Mergers Miscarry," *Harvard Business Review*, November-December 1967.

Lawrence, Paul R., and Jay W. Lorsch, *Organization and Environment: Managing Differentiation and Integration* (Boston: Division of Research, Harvard Business School, 1967).

Leavitt, Harold J., "Unhuman Organizations," *Harvard Business Review*, July-August 1962.

Levine, Sol, and Paul E. White, "Exchange as a Conceptual Framework for the Study of Interorganizational Relationships," *Administrative Science Quarterly*, March 1961.

Levinson, Harry, *The Exceptional Executive* (Cambridge: Harvard University Press, 1968).

Lorsch, Jay W., and Paul R. Lawrence, "Environmental Factors and Organizational Integration," paper prepared for 63rd Annual Meeting, American Sociological Association, August 27, 1968.

Lynch, Harry H., *Financial Performance of Conglomerates* (Boston: Division of Research, Harvard Business School, 1971).

March, James G., and Herbert A. Simon, *Organizations* (New York: John Wiley, 1958).

Maruyama, Magoroh, "The Second Cybernetics: Deviation-Amplifying Mutual Causal Processes," *American Scientist*, 51, 1963.

Miller, Eric J., "Technology, Territory and Time," *Human Relations*, Vol. XII, No. 3.

Morse, John J., and Jay W. Lorsch, "Beyond Theory Y," *Harvard Business Review* May-June 1970.

Perrow, Charles, "A Framework for the Comparative Analysis of Organizations," *American Sociological Review*, April 1967.

Pondy, Louis R., "Organizational Conflict: Concepts and Models," *Administrative Science Quarterly*, September 1967.

Rice, A. K., *Enterprise and Environment* (London: Tavistock Publications, 1963).

Roberts, Edward B., *The Dynamics of Research and Development* (New York: Harper & Row, 1964).

Schroder, Harold M., et al., *Human Information Processing* (New York: Holt, Rinehart and Winston, 1967).

Simon, Herbert A., et al., *Centralization and Decentralization in Organizing the Controller's Department* (New York: The Controllership Foundation, 1954).

Sloan, Alfred P., *My Years with General Motors* (New York: Doubleday, 1963).

Swalm, Ralph O., "Utility Theory—Insights Into Risk Taking," *Harvard Business Review*, November-December 1966.

Thompson, James D., *Organizations in Action* (New York: McGraw-Hill, 1967).

Triandis, H. D., "Differential Perception of Certain Jobs and People by Managers, Clerks, and Workers in Industry," *Journal of Applied Psychology*, 43, 1959.

Udy, Stanley, *Organization of Work: A Comparative Analysis of Production Among Non-Industrial Peoples* (New Haven: HRAF Press, 1959).

U.S. Senate, Committee on the Judiciary, *Hearings, Economic Concentration*, Part 2, *Mergers and Other Factors Affecting Industry Concentration*, 89th Cong., 1st Sess., 1965.

Walker, Arthur H., and Jay W. Lorsch, "Organizational Choice: Product versus Function," *Harvard Business Review*, November-December 1968.

Walton, Richard E., and John M. Dutton, "The Management of Interdepartmental Conflict: A Model and Review," *Administrative Science Quarterly*, March 1969.

Williamson, Oliver E., *Corporate Control and Business Behavior* (Englewood Cliffs, New Jersey: Prentice-Hall, 1970).

Williamson, Oliver E., *The Economics of Discretionary Behavior: Managerial Objectives in a Theory of the Firm* (Chicago: Markham Publishing, 1967).

Woodward, Joan, *Industrial Organization: Theory and Practice* (London: Oxford University Press, 1965).

Woodward, Joan (ed.), *Industrial Organization: Behavior and Control* (London: Oxford University Press, 1970).

Wrigley, Leonard, "Divisional Autonomy and Diversification" (unpublished doctoral dissertation, Harvard Business School, 1970).

Zajonc, R. B. and D. M. Wolfe, "Cognitive Consequences of a Person's Position in a Formal Organization," Tech. Rept. No. 23 (Ann Arbor: University of Michigan, Research Center for Group Dynamics, 1963).

Index